WANDERLUST CREAMERY PRESENTS

the world of
ice
cream

This book is dedicated to *my* world:
Sebastian, Philip, and Finley.

WANDERLUST CREAMERY PRESENTS

the world of
ice
cream

Adrienne Borlongan

Abrams, New York

CONTENTS

Introduction 7

Chapter 1: Ice Cream 101 16
The Structure 18
The Stabilizers 23

Chapter 2: Making Ice Cream 26
Ingredients 28
Tools & Equipment 34
Techniques 39

Chapter 3: Ice Cream Bases 46
Blank Base 48
Balanced Base 49
Custard Base 50
Mascarpone Base 51
Rice Cream Base 52
Vegan Base 54

Chapter 4: Custards 56
Pasteis de Nata 58
Salted Egg Tart 60
Salted Kaya Toast 62
Nanaimo Bar 65

Chapter 5: Chocolate 68
Namelaka Chocolate 70
Abuelita Malted Crunch 72
Caramelized Milk Chocolate
    & Plantain Brittle 75
Ruby Chocolate 78
Earl Grey Milk Chocolate 80

Chapter 6: Caramel-y 82
Salty Gula Melaka Caramel 84
Caramelized Honey Hojicha 86
Pretzel and Rúgbrauð 88
Real Dulce de Leche 90
Alfajores 92

Chapter 7: Berries, Citrus
& Tropical Fruit 94
Yuzu Creamsicle 96
Strawberriest Ice Cream 98
Passion Fruit Cacao 101
Chè Thái 102
Lilikoi Li Hing Pineapple 105
Green Mango Sorbet 108
Kalamansi Mignonette Sorbet 110

Chapter 8: Nutty 112
Noyaux & Pink Pralines 115
Kinako & Kyoho Grape Jelly 118
Nougat de Montélimar 121
Brown Butter Halva 124

Chapter 9: Corn 126
Coconut & Corn 128
Honey-Butter Corn Dalgona 130
Chicha Morada 132
Thai Candy Corn 134
Elote Ice Cream Bars 136

Chapter 10: Baker's Rack 140
Amalfi Pear Torte 143
Creole Coffee & Donuts 144
Australian Pavlova 146
Okinawan Mont Blanc 148
Pa Amb Xocolata 150

Chapter 11: Cheese, Dairy & Yogurt 152

Labneh & Pomegranate Rose Jam 155
Knafeh 157
Tea-ramisu 160
Burrata & Crema di Pistachio 162
Koldskål 164

Chapter 12: Rice Creams 166

Sticky Rice & Mango 169
Biko 171
Strawberry Daifuku 175
Risalamande 176
Injeolmi 179

Chapter 13: Flowers 180

Blueberry Elderflower 183
Sakura Crunch 185
Violette Marshmallow 188
Rose & Berry Stracciatella 190
Orange Flower Baklava 192

Chapter 14: Plants, Herbs & Botanicals 194

Basil Lime with Strawberry 196
Nopal Sorbet 198
Coconut Lime & Vietnamese Herbs 200
Fig Leaf & Pistachio 202
Calabrian Sundaes 204

Chapter 15: Boozy 206

Sicilian Negroni 209
Nesselrode Bula 211
Oatmeal & Scotch Honey Caramel 214
Pearl Diver Float 217
Royal Prune Armagnac 218

Chapter 16: Filipino American Childhood 220

Pandan Tres Leches 223
Ube Malted Crunch 225
Tita's Fruit Salad Pies 228
Halo Halo 230
Sapin Sapin 235
Brown Butter Sans Rival 238
Lolo's Philippine Mango (Mangga) 240

Chapter 17: Reinvented Classics 242

Palo Santo Mint Chip 245
Vietnamese Rocky Road 247
Almond Cookies & Lychee Cream 250
Japanese Neapolitan 252
Pink Neapolitan 257

Chapter 18: Asian Icons 258

Ramune Sherbet 261
Oolong Pineapple Cake 263
Jasmine Milk Tea with Boba 266
White Rabbit 268

Chapter 19: Toppings, Sauces & Special Ingredients 270

Malted Crunch 272
Crispy Nut Dacquoise 273
Brown Butter Nut Cake 274
Almond Shortbread 275
Sponge Cake Pieces 276
Namelaka Cubes 278
Chocolate Freckles/Stracciatella 279
Jellies 280
Ice Cream "Boba" 284
Mochi Pieces 286
Honeycomb Candy 287
Cookie Crust 288
"Toasted" Flavor Powders 289
Wanderlust Waffle Cones 290
Marshmallow Crème 292

Acknowledgments 296

Index 298

INTRODUCTION

MY STORY

For as far back as I can remember, I've been obsessed with food. Why? I couldn't tell you. Sure, my family liked to eat just about as much as anyone else's, but they were generally ambivalent about cooking. I remember being of preschool age, going with our mother to neighborhood garage sales. My twin sister would be rummaging through boxes of toys, digging for a doll. But I, unexplainably, was drawn to the book section, where hardcovers with photographs of picnics and wok cooking called to me. At the checkout stand of the grocery, my sister would plead for candy, and I . . . the latest issue of *Food & Wine*, *Bon Appétit*, or *Cook's Illustrated*. Their vivid cover photos announced it was pie season or it was the special "Salads, A to Z" issue. It was a little weird of an obsession for a six-year-old. My family thought so, too.

The first thing I ever cooked at that age was a French onion soup recipe from one of those garage sale cookbooks. I begged my mom to buy beef bones, which she put into a stockpot one morning, directing me to lower the heat once it came to a boil. She left for work and when she later called the house on her lunch break, my brother told her how I had been standing on a chair by the stove, watching over it since she'd left. When the soup was finally done, my family had their critiques. It was underseasoned. "Better and easier to just buy this." Despite this, I didn't care. I never cared. Throughout the years, no matter the outcome of whatever I made, nothing could deter me from my compulsion to make a recipe again. And again. Until it was better. It was the process that thrilled me. In the years to come, I'd go through phases of obsessions—one year it was soups, cookies the next. I was especially drawn to the type of cooking that required technical intricacies, like baking soufflés or macarons, where one tiny misstep would render all your efforts a failure. I lived for these kinds of challenges.

My mom, a working immigrant, emphasized that it was just a hobby and not a career path. You can't make a living chopping onions and rolling dough. "Passion won't pay the rent." And so, like any Filipino American child wanting to give their parents peace of mind, I took the beaten path, the road most traveled and considered safe . . . and decided to become a nurse. Two years of chemistry and science courses later, it was time to apply to nursing school. But on the eve of the application due date, I confessed to my mom that I could not wholeheartedly continue. As a compromise, my two years of nursing prerequisite courses qualified me to enter a food science program at a local state university. I envisioned a career in food manufacturing, introducing non-American flavors into mainstream products like potato chips or yogurt—since the only ones that existed always bored me.

But like many millennials who graduated in the late 2000s, my part-time college job became a full-time career. My mom may have been right—passions don't pay the rent—but neither does a bachelor's degree! I had been working in restaurants while going to school and would continue to do so for a decade after. Although I wasn't in the kitchen where I really wanted to be, I was adjacent, working in the front-of-house and earning more than what my degree or passion could ever pay me. I'd continue on this path, aimless, but subconsciously saving up for my dream of being able to do what I love one day. What exactly that was, I wasn't sure, but I knew it involved food somehow, some way.

Throughout all of this, my boyfriend, JP, was in law school. I was always envious that someone could have an interest in something that actually paid well. But even that, as I would eventually find out, would not be all it promised to be.

In 2014, I was bartending for one of the biggest nightlife and hospitality groups in L.A. In addition to pouring Vodka & Red Bulls for young Hollywood into the wee hours of the morning, I was also tasked by the beverage director to help create cocktail menus for the company's portfolio of nightclubs and hotels. For once, I was doing something I was passionate about *and* making a living.

But back at home, those impractical epicurean obsessions still plagued me. They spiraled into a collection of rare and expired ingredients, piles of dusty cookbooks, and bottles of endless variations of homemade orgeat that would go unused but took up all the space in the fridge. I had gastronomy-mania ADD; I could never focus on just one thing . . . until there was ice cream.

One day, my stoner roommate brought home an ice cream machine to make weed ice cream. I, too, became intrigued by ice cream (sans the weed). At the same time, there was this new wave of "artisanal" ice cream brands from all over the country opening shops in Los Angeles. And while the quality of this new-wave ice cream was inspirational, to me, the flavors were not. Yes, they were different from the standard ice cream fare, but they never strayed far from typical Eurocentric dessert flavors—like "farmers' market" fruit, caramel made fancier with salt, better-quality chocolate, and toffee or brittle in some form or another. The flavors they labeled "nostalgic" played to the tune of a typical American childhood, but not to mine. I wasn't raised on boxed rainbow Funfetti cupcakes, sugary cereals for breakfast, super-saccharine s'mores, or American candy bars. For me, dessert growing up was bread dipped in Mexican hot chocolate, cantaloupe shakes, an iced soup of smashed avocados with condensed milk, chile-bathed lollipops from the ice cream truck in the park, and esoteric Eastern European chocolates and candies from the Armenian mom-and-pop grocers

where my mom would buy meat and produce for a quarter of the price that she could at any chain supermarket. So instead, the ice cream flavors in neighborhood heladerías and in the frozen dessert aisles of Middle Eastern and Korean markets excited me more than the hyped new wave of artisanal ice cream. I found familiarity and comfort in them; they quenched my thirst for travel, and inspired more wanderlust. But I wished they were of artisanal quality—with less air and a creamier texture. So I started making artisanal-style ice cream in explorative flavors at home. And since none of the flavors I wanted to make had yet existed in ice cream form, cookbooks didn't offer much help. Instead, I leaned into my knowledge of food science and sought textbooks on ice cream science instead. I dove right in . . . and have still not surfaced.

When my roommate's ice cream machine couldn't keep up with my latest infatuation, I splurged on a $3,000 Italian gelato machine. Taking up half of my tiny home kitchen, I felt the need to justify such a large purchase to myself, and if anyone asked, I said that I'd planned on opening an ice cream shop, not really meaning it. Little did I know that my biggest cheerleaders, JP and his parents—Horace and Hazel, would hold me to that statement.

Having worked briefly in commercial real estate before law school, JP used his old contacts to find a storefront. My ice cream fascination started in November 2014 and by April 2015, he was making me sign a lease on a shuttered Cold Stone Creamery store. The space came with all the equipment to make and serve ice cream, from the expensive Italian batch freezer to a twenty-four-flavor gelato case and a walk-in freezer, even down to bowls and spatulas. Because it had sat vacant for eight years, the landlord wanted nothing for it except a small deposit and a signature on a short-term lease with affordable rent. It seemed like a deal too good to pass up. I poured my life's savings into the renovation and re-permitting. Horace and Hazel matched my investment and then some.

THE STORY OF WANDERLUST

One evening at dinner, JP's family friends—Alec and Celeste Perez—asked me a fateful question over a spread of ice creams I had made for sampling: "What inspires these flavors?" I shrugged and answered, "I don't know, my wanderlust?" From there, Wanderlust Creamery, an ice cream shop inspired by travel, was born.

During the renovation of the Cold Stone space that summer, I posted photos of my ice cream experiments to Instagram every day, with long captions geeking out about the process and flavor inspiration. Very quickly, an audience grew. We weren't even a physical business yet, but people were as excited about the flavors as I was. And then one day I woke up to find that the James Beard Foundation had reposted a photo of a sundae I had made: black tea ice cream topped with Greek bergamot preserves, olive oil, and sea salt. Up to this point, my apprehension about starting a business had me only half-heartedly confident about what I was doing. Can an ice cream shop survive on making these nonstandard flavors? This turned out to be a glimpse into a hopeful future.

We recruited a handful of people to help us. JP had a newly unemployed cousin, Steven, who knew nothing about cooking, let alone making ice cream. He'd eventually become my right-hand man in the kitchen. A friend offered up her little brother, RJ, to help scoop. JP's Auntie Melva stirred pots of sticky rice ice cream base, his mom baked mix-ins and rolled cones, and mine washed dishes.

On Friday, August 28, 2015, Wanderlust Creamery opened its doors without a plain chocolate or vanilla ice cream in sight. Instead, we served up Sticky Rice & Mango, Palo Santo Mint Chip, Caramelized Honey Hojicha, Abuelita Malted Crunch, Thai Tea, Pretzel & Rúgbrauð, and Sweet Cheese with Strawberry Balsamic Jam. We sold out on opening day. And the next day. And the day after. By Sunday evening, we had no ice cream left to sell. We closed the shop with a sign on the door: "Sold out—closed to make more ice cream. We will reopen Tuesday."

Early the next morning, JP and I said our usual goodbyes at home as he left for a court hearing. He told me he'd meet me at the ice cream shop later that evening after he got off from work at the law firm. But when I arrived at the shop just two hours later, I found him standing in the kitchen in his suit. "I just walked into work and quit," he said, smiling. "I don't know why, I have a gut feeling about this place."

He rolled up his sleeves and spent the entire day with me and Steven, spinning batches of ice cream well into the late evening. That night, we had filled up the walk-in freezer. Incidentally, that freezer would die three days later, melting our entire stock just before our second weekend of business. It seemed like the end of us. But as most business owners can attest, it was just a little introductory taste into the world of entrepreneurship.

While JP worked eighty-hour weeks at the ice cream shop, I still kept my bartending job. I'd make ice cream all day, then clock into the nightclub at 9:00 P.M. and come home at 4:00 A.M. That would continue through our first brutal fall and winter. For a long time, every cent made was spent on ingredients, payroll, fees, or some random bill that would surprise us at the most inopportune time. While our sales were far exceeding initial expectations, so was the work, and the expenses.

On my days off from the nightclub, we'd leave the kitchen around the same time I'd be clocking out behind the bar, our socks wet with mop water, counting coins to see what we could buy in a McDonald's drive-thru. Eating in the car, we'd watch our friends living their best lives on social media without us. They were traveling the world and experiencing that sweet spot at the cusp of thirty years old, where "carefree youth" meets "finally making adult money." We moved out of our rented house into an apartment. Then moved out of that apartment into a smaller apartment. We went down to one car. From the outside, successful businesses look like glowing reviews, press write-ups, large social media followings, and lines out the door; no one ever sees this side of struggle and sacrifice. But like that undeterred feeling I had as a child, I inexplicably couldn't care less. Neither could JP. For us, hours would fly by in the kitchen. We'd blink and suddenly it was 2:00 A.M., but it felt as if we had *just* walked in with our morning coffees in hand. There was nowhere else we'd rather be. We survived through the winter to spring. Then summer came, allowing me to quit my moonlighting gig. And then came Smorgasburg LA.

The talk of the town that summer in 2016 was Smorgasburg—a highly lauded, curated weekly food market concept from Brooklyn—making its anticipated arrival in LA. As a brand-new ice cream business in quite possibly the greatest food city in the country, being selected as a vendor at Smorgasburg seemed highly unlikely. We went through the general application process, and as expected, we heard nothing back. When Smorgasburg LA finally opened its gates with such an impressive and exclusive lineup of food concepts, we understood why. But two weeks later, at another food festival, the manager of Smorgasburg LA, Zach Brooks, approached me. "Hey, wanna vend at Smorgasburg?" I was elated and in utter disbelief, until he continued, "Just for *one* day, for National Ice Cream Day." Beggars can't be choosers, so I eagerly agreed.

On National Ice Cream Day, we were among a roster of the biggest ice cream brands in the city (and country) present at Smorgasburg. The entire Mount Rushmore of artisanal ice cream was there. Accordingly, our expectations for our share of the market-goers that day were modest at best. In the middle of the day, when Zach came to us frantically asking if we needed help, we were puzzled. All the other ice cream vendors had long lines except for us. We stood there confused. Zach pointed to the crowds of people in front of the other booths, "That's not other vendors' lines, that's *your* line." It was so

long that he had to redirect it to have it zigzag across the alley of ice cream vendors to make space for other foot traffic in the market. At the end of the day he returned to our tent, "Hey, wanna come back every week?"

Shortly after, another old Cold Stone Creamery store landed in our lap. And every year after that, more defunct ice cream shops. Our team would grow. The customers brought more zealot customers. What started as a concept of travel-inspired ice cream evolved into one that tugged at people's heart strings. We got emotional messages from people thanking us for highlighting their culture, excited to see childhood flavors specific to their unique upbringings, telling us about how a flavor we made transported them to a place, a time, or an experience that other ice creams never did. My odd perspective of embracing far-off, esoteric flavors—something that made me doubtful of success in the first place—was turning out to be our winning trait. And with every new location that came our way, it was as if the city kept presenting us with old ice cream shops begging to be refitted, reinvented, updated for a modern and diverse audience.

Since then, our journey has had its share of unexpected bumps in the road—even bigger freezer meltdowns, three kids in the span of two years, a global pandemic—but each one only narrows our path further in the right direction. The employee count has grown tenfold, but at the end of the day it's still just us—JP and me against an industry of corporate ice cream brands—mainly because I want my imagination for ice cream flavors to roam free and not be bound by the constraints of "what sells" or have to answer to other interests. We now have eight locations across Los Angeles and beyond. The count keeps growing, and the flavors keep changing. And while the challenges only get bigger, the cause becomes more worthy: We are exploring flavors, embracing cultures, and bringing the world to our customers, one scoop at a time.

ICE CREAM IS IN MY BLOOD

People ask me all the time, "Why ice cream?" After all the different obsessions I had, what made me land on this one? Oftentimes I'll shrug. But now, deep down I know it's destiny.

Growing up, I had a mother, a stepfather, a twin sister, and two older brothers. But no family beyond that. Being of Filipino descent—as I understood it from seeing other Filipino families—meant having at least a dozen cousins, and so many aunts, uncles, and enough extended family to consume an entire lechon (roasted pig) on any given holiday or gathering. And while I did grow up surrounded by "family"—people who, although not blood-related, I considered cousins, aunts, and uncles for all intents and purposes—something always felt missing. My mother is the eldest of fourteen siblings, though I've only ever met one of them. My father, who was infrequently present, passed away when I was eight. He never spoke of any siblings or told me about my grandparents. By the time I was ten years old, I had peacefully resigned to the idea that my twin sister and I might've been the last Borlongans on earth.

That all changed with a bar of "World's Finest" chocolate. I was a fifth grader selling chocolate bars for a school fundraiser, trying to win a grand prize of tickets to a theme park or something of the like. I sold a box of chocolate bars to a lady who took it to work, where her co-worker recognized the name "Borlongan" written on one of the candy bar wrappers. The co-worker tracked me down, and weeks later she appeared at my front door and introduced herself as my father's sister. All this time, she had been living nearby with my grandmother.

For the next decade, I'd see my aunt and grandmother regularly, gradually learning bits of details about my father's family. Surprisingly, my father was the eldest of six siblings. He had a penchant for perfectionism and was obsessive, like me. I learned that my passion and love for food and cooking was genetic. My grandmother, a woman of few words by the time I met her, only ever spoke about food . . . and eating . . . and cooking . . . and what we should have for our next meal, upon finishing the current one. Sundays with her were so often spent driving more than two hours away to the San Gabriel Valley, the only place she'd *ever* consider eating Chinese food. She'd send my sister and me home with an entire roast duck every time. Although from Guangzhou, she spoke with a Malaysian/Singaporean accent, punctuating every sentence with "lah." She and my grandfather (who passed away just after I was born) raised their family in present-day Singapore, where they both worked for San Miguel, a Philippine food conglomerate on the scale of Nestlé, or PepsiCo.

As the years went on, I'd learn more about all the uncles, aunts, and cousins I had around the world—it was the proper Filipino family head count I'd always envisioned. I was

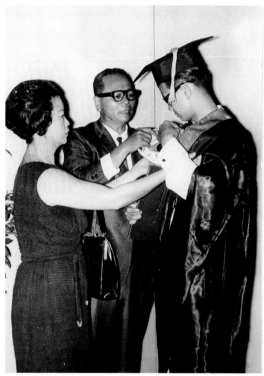

gaining all this inside knowledge of my family as an outsider. On the verge of adulthood, saying my last goodbye to my grandmother in the hospital, I met a half brother I never knew I had for the first time, realizing the circumstances of why my sister and I hadn't known about our father's family for so long and, in turn, why they hadn't known about us. My sister and I were a secret my father took to his grave. A dozen more years would pass before I opened my own ice cream shop and received this congratulatory Facebook message from one of my father's brothers:

"Well I guess your dad being the eldest (and brightest), Lolo Ely wanted him to carry on the ice cream tradition. San Miguel had this policy back then that key employees could have any of their kins work for the company. Unfortunately, your dad decided to take up his MBA instead.

Your Lolo Ely would have been very proud of you and your accomplishments. You're the only one in the family that inherited his "ice cream" ice genes. To think that Lolo Ely wanted your dad to follow in his footsteps (which is why your dad initially graduated in Chemical Engineering), he passed on the baton to you."

It turns out that San Miguel, which I'd always known to be a beer company, has a subsidiary called Magnolia—an iconic Asian ice cream brand. Think: the Häagen-Dazs of Southeast Asia. The ice cream is so renowned that a pirated version using the original decades-old Magnolia logo and branding (San Miguel didn't trademark the brand internationally) can be found at any Asian supermarket in America these days. My grandfather, Eliseo Borlongan, worked as a flavor chemist for the original Magnolia

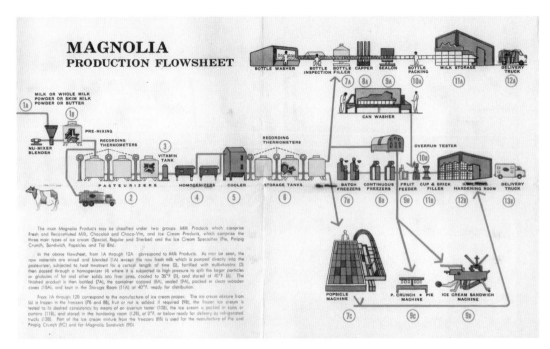

MAGNOLIA
PRODUCTION FLOWSHEET

The main Magnolia Products may be classified under two groups: Milk Products which comprise Fresh and Reconstituted Milk, Chocolate and Choco-Vim, and Ice Cream Products, which comprise the three main types of ice cream (Special, Regular and Sherbet) and the Ice Cream Specialties (Pie, Pinipig Crunch, Sandwich, Popsicles and Tid Bits).

In the above flowsheet, from 1A through 12A correspond to Milk Products. As may be seen, the raw materials are mixed and blended (1A) except the raw fresh milk which is pumped directly into the pasteurizer, subjected to heat treatment for a certain length of time (2), fortified with multivitamins (3) then passed through a homogenizer (4) where it is subjected to high pressure to split the larger particles or globules of fat and other solids into finer ones, cooled to 35°F (5), and stored at 40°F (6). The finished product is then bottled (7A), the container capped (8A), sealed (9A), packed in clean wooden cases (10A), and kept in the Storage Room (11A) at 40°F, ready for distribution.

From 1A through 12B correspond to the manufacture of ice cream proper. The ice cream mixture from (6) is frozen in the freezers (7B and 8B), fruit or nut is added if required (9B), the frozen ice cream is tested to its desired consistency by means of an overrun tester (10B), the ice cream is packed in cans or cartons (11B), and stored in the hardening room (12B), at 0°F, or below ready for delivery by refrigerated trucks (13B). Part of the ice cream mixture from the freezers (8B) is used for the manufacture of Pie and Pinipig Crunch (PC) and for Magnolia Sandwich (9D).

ice cream from the 1930s to the late 1970s. He and the team would work on formulation of the Philippines' most iconic ice cream flavors. Upon opening my own ice cream business, I'd hear stories of his passion for the craft. Older cousins would tell me details of his mad ice cream science laboratory that he built at the back of his house, to which he'd disappear for hours. My aunt, the youngest of the family, credits her childhood figure to being his only taste tester left at home. Even Wanderlust Creamery customers gush about their nostalgia for now discontinued Magnolia products like "Mango Bango," a mango ice cream bar with a crispy mango chocolate shell, or corn-cheese ice cream in the shape of a corn cob, and one that especially haunts me: Barako coffee ice cream swirled with mangosteen jam.

My obsessiveness, my love for dreaming up ice cream flavors, the unexplainable force that kept me in the kitchen late at night (even hours just before birthing my first child) is *that* strong because it runs through my veins . . . it's in my blood.

THE WANDERLUST CREAMERY MISSION

All I ever wanted was to see the flavors I grew up on be equally celebrated alongside peanut butter fudge or cookies 'n' cream.

Ice cream wasn't invented in the West. While its exact origin isn't entirely clear, it is believed that the idea of mixing ice with flavorings to create a frozen dessert dates back to ancient China, around 200 BC, where Chinese royalty enjoyed a frozen mixture of milk and rice flavored with spices and fruit.

The Persians are also credited with developing a frozen dessert in the fifth century, known today as faloodeh, a mixture of vermicelli, rose water, and other flavorings with snow or ice.

In the seventh century, during the Arab expansion, the recipe for a similar dessert spread to the Middle East and North Africa. By the tenth century, ice cream had reached the Mediterranean, and the Moors brought it to Spain. From there, it spread throughout Europe, where it became popular among the nobility.

Overall, the history of ice cream is a long and diverse one, with various cultures contributing to its development over the centuries. So what causes Western ice cream flavors like mint chip, strawberry, and pistachio to be considered the standards, while everything else is deemed weird or odd? This notion is the one Wanderlust Creamery seeks to refute.

I get it. The unfamiliar can be scary. As cliché as this might sound, when I was growing up in the nineties, opening my lunch box of Mom's home cooking at school launched a symphony of "eww," "smells weird," and "gross!" from other kids. You might not always be able to persuade someone to eat a whole plate of a foreign dish, but what about a sample spoon of ice cream? Almost every culture has ice cream. And luckily everyone loves ice cream. It's a medium no one can refuse. Avocado ice cream? Okay,

> " Overall, the history of ice cream is a long and diverse one, with various cultures contributing to its development over the centuries. So what causes Western ice cream flavors like mint chip, strawberry, and pistachio to be considered the standards, while everything else is deemed weird or odd? This notion is the one Wanderlust Creamery seeks to refute. "

"weird" to some. But it's *ice cream*. What's the worst it can be? Don't misconstrue my intent; I'm not trying to make borscht or chicken curry ice cream a thing. While a few of the recipes in this book do dabble in savory twists, for the most part I'm talking about flavors that are categorically considered desserts in other countries.

This book might not be a comprehensive, exhaustive list of ice cream recipes from every corner of the world, but it's a guide, a road map, to looking at ice cream from a broader, more worldly, and adventurous perspective. I hope you'll enjoy making them as much as I did creating them.

ice cr
101

ream

This book isn't just a collection of recipes. It's a guide for exploration and a tool for inspiration. But before you go off on your own ice cream adventure, you need to have a firm grasp on the science and physics of ice cream. Why? Because ice cream is all about balance; it's a dance of water, proteins, fats, sugars, and air suspended in a semi-frozen state. You can add whatever you want to make it your own, but every addition affects that balance. So, now that you're about to take off aboard a flavor flight, allow me to elaborate on the magic that is ice cream science.

THE STRUCTURE

Simply put, ice cream is a structure—a matrix of air bubbles and ice crystals suspended in liquid water and a network of fat and protein. This structure is not only responsible for texture, but taste. How an ice cream's flavor is released on your tongue (known in the world of ice cream as "the meltdown") is the consequence of that structure. To make great ice cream, we need to get all the components of the structure (water/ice, fat droplets, air bubbles) to be as small and uniform as possible and dispersed as evenly as possible within the structure.

ELEMENTS OF THE STRUCTURE

Water

Despite its name, a large portion of ice cream is water. You might be looking at the recipes in this book and thinking, *Where's the water?* The water I'm referring to is in the dairy. Milk is almost 90% water, and cream is just about 50%.

When ice cream is churning in a machine, water in the ice cream base is frozen into ice. As it continues mixing, the ice is broken down into smaller crystals as they form. When the ice cream is finished churning, though, it's not completely frozen—it's soft and pliable. That's because not all the water has frozen. Some of it is still hanging out in a liquid state. At this moment, the matrix of air bubbles and ice crystals suspended in liquid water and a network of fat particles is the most perfect it will ever be. It will be smooth and creamy, with the tiniest ice crystals melting on your tongue. Sadly, every second from there on will be downhill. After churning, the ice cream is put into a freezer where that liquid water will eventually freeze . . . key word being "eventually." But before then, these free-floating water molecules will find each other like long-lost soulmates and attach themselves to each other as well as the tiny ice crystals in the ice cream, forming bigger ice crystals.

> ## When Ice Cream Is at Its Most Perfect
>
> Whenever I bring someone into the Wanderlust Creamery kitchen to watch us make ice cream, I make them taste the ice cream right out of the machine. Right then is the best it will ever be. The ice crystals are at their tiniest, the air bubbles are uniform throughout. It will never be as smooth or creamy ever again, even with all our commercial equipment and efforts to keep it as cold as possible from the machine to the dipping case. The power of love between water molecules is just too strong.

Have you ever left your ice cream out too long and tried to refreeze it? You probably noticed it was icy, grainy, and generally not delicious. That's because in a liquid state, water molecules, much like Romeo and Juliet, love each other and will do anything to be together. So how do we prevent that? By freezing the ice cream as fast as possible before the water molecules have a chance to find each other, and keeping it as cold as possible after that.

At Wanderlust Creamery, we use a commercial batch freezer with a compressor so powerful that it freezes the ice cream in under eight minutes. We extrude it from the machine as quickly as possible, after which it immediately gets shoved into what we call a "blast freezer," which is –35°F (–37°C). At this frigid temperature, water is frozen so fast that any chance of water molecules hooking up ain't happening. These steps (in addition to stabilizers; see page 23) will *minimize* bigger ice crystals forming, but slight degradation of the perfect molecular structure of the ice cream is inevitable as time passes.

At home, churning can take up to twenty minutes, and the coldest your freezer will ever get is 0°F (−18°C). So what can be done to make sure you get the smallest ice crystals you can at home? Without commercial equipment there isn't much, but there are some helpful tricks and techniques (see page 39). Formula-wise, you can use proteins, sugars, other solids, or stabilizers to bind free water and keep it from roaming. Equipment-wise, choose an ice cream maker with a strong compressor for faster freezing time. Technique-wise, make the ice cream in the coldest environment possible (blast that air conditioning!) and work as quickly as possible when transferring the ice cream from machine to freezer or adding mix-ins. Lastly, you can use a block of dry ice (see Working with Dry Ice, page 262) to mimic commercial blast freezing to achieve the finest ice crystals at home.

Fat

Ice cream is rich in fat, as there is some fat in milk (3.5%) and plenty in cream (36% to 38%). In the world of ice cream, fat from dairy in an ice cream base is called "butterfat" and expressed in percentages, and it's generally in the range of 8% to 16% butterfat, also known as "economy" ice cream. Thrifty, Breyers, and Baskin-Robbins all fall into this category. "Premium" ice cream, like Häagen-Dazs, lies somewhere in the 12% to 14% range. "Super premium," or 15% to 17%, is what most would consider the artisanal or small-batch ice cream brands.

In the United States, there seems to be a belief that higher butterfat equals better ice cream. I wholeheartedly disagree. While ice cream should of course be rich and creamy, not all flavors benefit from high butterfat. For example, some fruit flavors would be better represented in a lower butterfat formula. This is because fat holds flavor. Without much fat to coat your tongue, an 8% butterfat mango ice cream would punch you in the face immediately with fruit flavor but diminish quickly with no lingering flavor. In contrast, in a 16% butterfat mango ice cream, the mango flavor would be hardly detectable until all the ice cream has melted on your tongue, after which any residual fat coating your mouth would hold on to the taste, making the flavor linger for a while. Of course taste is subjective, but a higher-butterfat formula dulls the freshness and intensity of fruit flavors.

Butterfat Is Cultural

In Mexico, or even some heladerías stateside, it's rare to see an ice cream with more than 12% butterfat. Maybe that's because the weather in parts of Mexico demands refreshment from ice cream (a lower-butterfat ice cream will be colder on the tongue). Likewise, the butterfat of Italian gelato can vary widely: In northern Italy near the Alps, you'll find some as high as 15%, whereas the gelato in the south of the country can go below 8%. Persian-style ice cream also tends to be on the lower end of the butterfat spectrum. Owning an ice cream business myself, I can attest to the wide range of butterfat preference in Los Angeles alone. One review will complain the ice cream isn't rich enough, while the next will say the same exact ice cream is too rich for them to finish the entire scoop. It all depends on preference and taste, which you can see are often correlated with culture and weather.

Fat also plays a structural role by trapping the air bubbles that get whipped into ice cream.

Having the smallest possible fat droplets in an ice cream base is important because it leads to a smoother and creamier texture. When fat globules are smaller, their outer membranes have more surface area relative to their interior fat, better trapping small air bubbles, which in turn creates a more homogeneous and stable emulsion. To achieve this, the fat needs to be mechanically beaten or broken up as it's warmed or heated—a process called homogenization.

By homogenizing the ice cream base, you are ensuring that the fat globules are uniformly sized and dispersed throughout the mixture.

The Importance of Homogenization

Hold up—if most store-bought milk and cream is already homogenized, do we really need to homogenize it again when making ice cream? Homogenization at the dairy plant breaks down the fat globules in the milk and cream into smaller particles, which helps to create a uniform texture and prevents the cream from separating and rising to the top of the milk. However, even with homogenized milk and cream, there can still be variations in the size and distribution of the fat globules. Furthermore, fat globules in cream are larger than those of milk. Remember: When it comes to the structure of ice cream, we want uniformity throughout.

Protein

The milk in ice cream provides proteins (casein and whey) to the structure. When these proteins are heated as we cook an ice cream base, their amino acid chains unravel to cross-link with each other to form a sort of mesh. This mesh will stall the movement of water, buying us time as we freeze the water in its tracks. In addition, these unraveled protein strands will bind to water molecules, preventing them from roaming even more.

As this is the case, wouldn't the easy-answer hack to ice cream simply be to add more milk to a recipe? Well, yes and no. More milk comes with *more water*, making that solution useless. But the answer is to add a concentration of milk proteins without the water. Many ice cream makers do this with something they call "MSNF" (milk solids not fat). Nonfat dry milk powder is the most common source of MSNF, because calculating it into a formulation is relatively uncomplicated, since it's not adding any fat or water to the mix. But with a little extra

calculation, MSNF can also come from other flavorful sources such as cream cheese, cheese powder, mascarpone, evaporated milk, or something you'll find in my recipes—sweetened condensed milk.

In addition to binding water, the proteins in milk also work as emulsifiers, making fat and water homogeneous in the matrix or structure.

The Lactose Factor

A caveat: While we need protein from MSNF, these additions almost always contain lactose—a sugar present in milk. While lactose has barely any detectable sweetness, it does contribute to the sugar content of an ice cream base (antifreezing power). Also, lactose is a sugar that tends to crystallize. In ice cream, too much lactose will result in a sandy texture. Most of my recipes contain a little condensed milk (which contains a lot of lactose), but not more than 7% of a recipe, which usually constitutes half of the total MSNF in a formulation.

Sugar

People ask me all the time: "Can you make a sugar-free ice cream?" My answer to that is always, "Girl, bye!" The question is almost always posed assuming sugar's only role in ice cream is providing sweetness. Yes, sugar provides sweetness (duh!), but structurally, sugar in ice cream is nonnegotiable. Aside from making ice cream sweet, sugar has another equally important role: It depresses the freezing point of the ice cream mix. Remember when I said that just after churning, ice cream is soft and pliable because some of it is still unfrozen water? It's sugar that keeps that water unfrozen. If all the water in an ice cream froze solid, the ice cream would never be scoopable.

However, in the world of ice cream, not all sugars are equal. Different sugars have varying abilities to bind water and not let it freeze (aka anti-freezing power). In its simplest form, sugars are a grouping of carbon, hydrogen, and oxygen atoms, known as saccharides. A monosaccharide is one grouping, a disaccharide is a chain of two groupings, and oligosaccharides are chains of three to ten monosaccharides. The chains are linked with something called glycosidic bonds. These bonds take up space on the carbon-hydrogen-oxygen grouping where water molecules in the ice cream base would have attached to.

So what does this mean? Longer sugar chains have less anti-freezing power than shorter, or simpler, sugars. For example, regular ol' granulated sugar as we know it (a disaccharide of glucose and fructose) will have less anti-freezing power than glucose (a lonely monosaccharide). This anti-freezing power is referred to as "AFP" in the world of ice cream and "PAC," potere anti-congelante, in the gelato world. Different sugars are often assigned a related (although entirely different) value called dextrose equivalence, or "DE." This is useful to ice cream making because the higher the DE a sugar has, the higher its anti-freezing ability.

Sticking to Sugar

So can I make a sugar-free ice cream? Of course something resembling ice cream can be made with non-caloric sweeteners, but it will need to be softened with other molecular gastronomy-ish ingredients. While I do like to consider myself a food scientist, I only want to use my skills to make delicious things. I leave the nutritional stuff to other people.

Let's throw another wrench into the mix: Not all sugars taste the same. Some are sweeter than others. This varying sweetness is known as "relative sweetness" in the ice cream world and "POD," or potere dolcificante, in gelato making. In professional ice cream recipes, including those in this book, you'll often find glucose called for. That's because to make an ice cream soft and scoopable, you'll need a certain amount

of sugar in the base. Well, if you're like me and a lot of people with nonstandard-American-diet palates, that amount in regular granulated sugar (sucrose) is just way too sweet. To remedy this, glucose—which is less sweet than sucrose, but with a higher anti-freezing power—replaces some of the sucrose. The result is a texturally effective formulation (enough sugar to make it soft), but with an improved taste (not too sweet).

"Not Too Sweet"

In general, the recipes in this book are much less sweet than standard American ice creams, which have a POD of 170 to 180. The majority of my recipes err on the side of "not too sweet"—a POD of 150 to 165, depending on the flavor. Note that POD measures sweetness only, and does not take into account sweetness compensating for bitter or sour flavors. For example, a lemon sorbet might have a POD of more than 200—which seems exorbitantly sweet—but will taste just fine because of the accompanying tartness. The same goes for chocolate or tannic tea flavors, which may be near 190 POD.

In relation to sugar (as well as salt and alcohol), the gelato world uses another value to indicate the softness or scoopabilty of an ice cream, called PAC. The average PAC values of the recipes in this book will be around 24 to 28, which means that the temperature at which they will be perfectly scoopable is around 8° to 10°F (–13° to –12°C)—a few minutes out of a home freezer.

Air

Air is present in every ice cream. Like sugar, without it, an ice cream would be rendered a hard, solid mass. Imagine not churning an ice cream base and just freezing it as is—it would freeze hard just like a paleta, or an ice pop. Air is necessary to ice cream. But as with all the other components of the structure of ice cream, we want the smallest air particles, or bubbles, in just the right amount.

In the world of ice cream, air is referred to as "overrun." Let's imagine a quart of liquid ice cream base gets poured into an ice cream machine and churned. During churning, the blade in the machine whips air into the mix, fluffing it up almost like whipped cream. You'll notice that when the ice cream has finished churning, it is no longer a quart—it'll be a quart and a half, or maybe even almost two quarts. While overrun is essential to making the ice cream soft and scoopable, many ice cream manufacturers also use overrun to increase the volume of their product, making it cheaper. You may notice that a pint of premium ice cream may be double the price of another ice cream brand. I dare you to weigh the two on a scale. You may find that while they're exactly the same size, they're not the same weight. The more expensive ice cream has less air and weighs more, which means you're actually getting *more* ice cream, hence the price. By this same principle, a small scoop of dense artisanal ice cream will cost more than a big cone of soft serve, half of which is just air.

Overrun affects taste. As ice cream melts in your mouth, you perceive aromas and flavors released from the melting butterfat, and sweetness as the tiny ice crystals dissolve and carry water-bound sugar onto the tongue. The more air that is present among all of that, the less intensely you'll taste it all, because air tastes like . . . nothing. Have you ever noticed how gelato, although generally lower in butterfat, seems creamier and more intensely flavored than run-of-the-mill ice cream? It's because the lower overrun creates a densely compact matrix of flavor-containing compounds on your palate. In general, the less overrun an ice cream has, the higher-quality it will be. This is why gelato has the highly regarded reputation it does—it has way less overrun than traditional American commercially produced ice cream. But what most people don't realize is that one of the foundational pillars of this new wave of "artisanal" ice cream is low overrun—just as low as gelato.

So how do we control overrun and make sure we don't have too much of it in our ice cream? Several things in the base (the amount of butterfat, proteins, and the presence of emulsifiers) contribute to that, but none so much as the speed of churning. The faster the rate of the churn, the more air that is incorporated into the ice cream. Luckily for you, most home ice cream machines don't churn at a very fast rate. Nonetheless, the churning speed is definitely something to consider when choosing equipment: If you can control the speed at which an ice cream machine churns, opting for a slower one will yield you a denser, and in turn creamier, product. However, churning ice cream at home takes significantly longer than it does commercially. And the longer your ice cream spends churning, the more air will get whipped in with every turn of the blade. Controlling churning time (more on how to do that later) will also help to control overrun.

Tomayto, Tomahto; Ice Cream, Gelato

The classic frozen dessert question: What's the difference between ice cream and gelato? Many will agree on three main differences—butterfat, overrun, and temperature. In most cases, gelato is lower in butterfat. But as mentioned earlier, the butterfat of gelato can vary widely depending on seasonality, region, or even flavor. I can confirm, however, that gelato is always dense and has minimal overrun—at around 25% to 30%. Sure, that's a lot less airy and fluffed up than your run-of-the-mill ice cream from a grocery store and most chain scoop shops. But in comparing gelato with artisanal ice cream, the overrun is about the same. The third difference is one most don't even think about: temperature. You may have noticed that ice cream is scooped, but gelato is smeared and spatula-ed onto a cone. That's because gelato is too warm to be scooped; it's served at around 12°F (–11°C), whereas ice cream is scooped at about 6°F (–14°C). The temperature of gelato gives it its intensity of flavor, because taste and aroma are perceived more strongly the warmer it is. But remember what I explained about water molecules and their shenanigans when left to their own devices, especially out of frigid temperatures? Certainly, the warmer an ice cream is held and served, the more it will need to be stabilized. This goes against a widely held assumption that gelato is more "natural" or "real"—whatever that means to the people who claim so. Italians, after all, perfected the science of ice cream/gelato, as the primary users of MSNF in a base, and the discoverers of stabilizers and texture-enhancing ingredients—the culprit of the "creamy mouthfeel" often cited by unaware consumers to differentiate gelato from standard ice cream. So what *is* gelato? It's simply the Italian word for "ice cream." To me, it's artisanal ice cream, served warmer.

The Stabilizers

In the world of ice cream (and even more so in the gelato world!), the structure of ice cream—no matter how vigilant we are about formulation, temperature control, etc.—isn't stable unless it's . . . well, stabilized. If you're hoping for someone to tell you that you can make the best ice cream without the help of some kind of stabilizer, you've got the wrong book. I can *tell* you that, but it'd be a lie. Unless you're planning on eating the ice cream straight out of the machine (there's nothing wrong with that though, like I said—it's the best!), you'll need to stabilize your ice cream.

Ice cream stabilizers have a shady reputation because they sound "unnatural" and seem foreign or unfamiliar to most people, largely because they often don't have any use in home cooking. Many common pantry items are stabilizers, too (flour, cornstarch, tapioca starch, pectin, etc.), but I rarely use them in ice cream because the dairy would have to be boiled or heated to such high temperatures to hydrate and activate them (which can alter the flavor of the cream and milk). Sure, there are some bad food additives out there, but most ice cream stabilizers are safe and a lot of claims I've seen against them are not scientifically substantiated. We're also talking 2 grams in an entire 1-quart (1 liter) batch. If you really can't shake off the brainwashing that stabilizers are bad, you can choose not to use them—but try to eat your ice cream the same day it's churned.

There are many different types of emulsifiers and stabilizers used in the world of ice cream. However, for the purpose of brevity (so you can get on to the fun part sooner—making ice cream!), I'll only address the ones used in this book.

EMULSIFIERS

Think of emulsifiers as peace-makers: They bring things that don't normally go together (like fat and water), together.

Egg Yolks

Egg yolks in ice cream tend to elicit polar opposite reactions in people. Some hate them, while others think their texture and flavor are necessities. Again, like butterfat level, sweetness, and other varying qualities of ice cream, it depends on preference and personal taste.

Egg yolks are used primarily as an emulsifier—by stripping the outer membranes off fat droplets to help them stick together. They add a creaminess and body to the ice cream as a direct result of the emulsification. But with that emulsifying power comes the fat and flavor that are present in an egg yolk. The fat, like butterfat, will bind to flavors in the ice cream and make them less immediately pronounced. The flavor—which is, um, egg-y—will either complement or compete with other flavors. For example, I almost never make a fruit ice cream with egg yolks because it dampens the vibrant, juicy, fresh taste of fruit. But I find that bitter and tannic tea and coffee infusions, or even floral lavender, need that custardy back note for balance.

The emulsifying agent in egg yolks is lecithin, which brings us to the next topic . . .

Lecithin

Let's say for flavor purposes, you don't want to use egg yolks. Conveniently, you can get the emulsifying agent that's present in egg yolks in pure form—from soybeans or sunflower seeds. Powdered lecithin is a powerful emulsifying tool for eggless bases. Adding 3 grams of lecithin to a 1-kilogram batch of ice cream base will have the same emulsifying effect as two egg yolks.

HYDROCOLLOIDS

Hydrocolloids are ingredients that bind water, preventing water molecules from running off into the sunset together, ultimately helping to maintain the original structure of freshly churned ice cream.

Guar Gum

An all-natural ingredient made from guar beans, a vegetable that has been used in Indian and Pakistani cooking for centuries. Guar gum thickens and adds body, or substantiality, to the ice cream when it melts in your mouth. Guar is most often paired with locust bean gum (see below) because the two work synergistically. Guar gum hydrates (binds water) at cold temperatures, therefore it doesn't need heat to be activated.

Tara Gum

Made from the seeds of the South American tara tree, this all-natural ingredient is getting a lot of attention right now in the ice cream world because it has similar properties to a mix of guar gum and locust bean gum, widely used together in ice cream. Tara gum hydrates at 165°F (75°C).

Cellulose Gum

Made from the cell walls of plants, this hydrocolloid is also known as "CMC," or carboxymethyl cellulose. This gum has all the anticrystalline power of locust bean gum, the thickening power of guar gum, and it forms a gentle gel in the presence of carrageenan (see below). It's cold soluble, making it perfect for sorbets where you wouldn't want to ruin fruits with heat.

Carrageenan

Carrageenan is a naturally occurring polysaccharide that is derived from red seaweed. There are three types of carrageenan: iota, kappa, and lambda. Each type has varying strengths of thickening properties in the presence of calcium (perfect for dairy). Iota is often used in ice cream because it forms a strong gel in the presence of calcium (dairy), however lambda has the softest and gentlest thickening of the three. It adds a custard-like but clean-finishing mouthfeel during the ice cream's meltdown. Other stabilizers, such as locust bean gum and cellulose gum, despite their helpful properties, have a small side effect on the ice cream base called "wheying-off," which means they sometimes cause proteins to gather and separate from the water in the base. Carrageenan keeps the peace by preventing this separation through its slight emulsifying properties. The kind of carrageenan (lambda) used in this book is cold soluble.

A Note on Stabilizers

Concerns have been raised about the potential health effects of consuming large quantities of carrageenan. These concerns are primarily related to degraded carrageenan—a form of carrageenan that is not used in food production and is different from the lambda form. Overall, lambda carrageenan is considered safe for consumption in small quantities. However, if you have any concerns or gastrointestinal issues that can be affected by carrageenan (colitis or inflammatory bowel disease), you may opt not to use it.

Terminology

Base: The liquid form of ice cream or sorbet, before it's churned and frozen.

Brix: A measurement of the sugar percentage in a liquid. Example: 5 Brix = 5% sugar.

Freckle/stracciatella: Melted chocolate that is added to churning ice cream to create tiny "freckles" or "fine shreds" of chocolate in the ice cream.

Mix-in: A solid addition to churned ice cream. Think cookie pieces, honeycomb, or mochi pieces.

MSNF: "Milk solids not fat"—all the solids present in a milk product, minus the butterfat. Nonfat dry milk powder is a source of MSNF in pure form.

PAC: The freezing point depression of the water in a recipe, expressed as a number. The higher the PAC of an ice cream, the softer it will be and the colder it will need to be to be served. Generally, you can take the PAC of an ice cream and divide it by 2 to 2.5, and it will give you the temperature (in Celsius) at which it will be perfectly scoopable.

POD: The perceived sweetness of an ice cream.

Tempering: Bringing something to a specific temperature through gentle or gradual heating or cooling.

Variegate: A liquid addition to churned ice cream, like fruit jams, chocolate fudge, or caramel swirls, etc.

CHAPTER 2

mak
ice

Now that you know more about the science of ice cream, it's clear that ingredient selection and technique are what set apart great ice cream from average ice cream. The creaminess and flavor are dependent on the quality of ingredients you select. Using quality dairy that has a rich yet clean-tasting butterfat will carry flavors on the tongue without interfering

ing cream

or leaving a lingering aftertaste. Next, every step taken during the process of making the ice cream base should ensure that you're unlocking the most emulsifying and water-binding power from all of your ingredients. And last, being vigilant about ice crystal formation during the churning, freezing, and storage of the ice cream will ensure the smoothest texture possible.

INGREDIENTS

Milk

Cream

Sugar

Glucose Powder

Egg yolks/Whites

Nonfat Dry Milk Powder

Nonfat Yogurt Powder

Sweetened
Condensed Milk

Coconut Cream

The recipes in this book will frequently call for the following ingredients.

Milk

Use whole milk, and whole milk only. The recipes were formulated with the specific fat percentage (3.5%) of whole milk in mind. I personally don't find a taste difference between regular and organic milk, *but* grass-fed milk (from cows that only forage on grass) makes all the flavor difference.

Cream

Most of the recipes in this book leave the cream unheated to maintain its pure, "fresh" flavor, so use the highest quality of heavy cream you can find (again, grass-fed is delicious). Don't use "whipping cream," which is lower in fat—30% as opposed to 36% in heavy cream. And stay away from UHT (ultra-high temperature) cream, which has a distinctively cooked flavor.

Sugar

This refers to regular granulated cane sugar. If you're looking to make one of the nondairy recipes here completely vegan, use organic cane sugar. Do not attempt to reduce the sugar in a recipe unless you replace it with another sugar with similar antifreezing power. Most of the recipes in this book will be on the lower end of the sweetness spectrum anyway—not too sweet. To increase the sweetness of any of the recipes, replace 5 to 10 grams of the glucose with sugar.

Glucose Powder

For the recipes in this book, I use glucose powder or atomized glucose with a DE (dextrose equivalence) of 38 to 40. Glucose powder can be purchased at baking supply stores or online (see sources). If glucose powder is not available to you, you can use glucose syrup or corn syrup by taking the weight of powder called for and multiplying it by 1.5 (you'll need a scale for this). Using syrup instead of powder will add a tiny percentage of water to the recipe, but nothing significant enough to make major changes. In the ice cream world, the word "glucose" can be confusing because it is sometimes also used to refer to dextrose, another sugar in powdered form. Do not use dextrose where glucose is called for in these recipes; the ice cream will be too sweet and too soft.

Egg Yolks/Whites

When egg yolks or egg whites are called for, a gram weight is given followed by the number of standard large eggs you would need for that amount.

Nonfat Dry Milk Powder

Aka skim milk powder—from spray-dried nonfat milk. Do not use whole milk powder or full cream powder in its place, as it will throw off the balance of the recipe's formulation.

Nonfat Yogurt Powder

This is essentially the yogurt version of dry milk powder, giving a little tang in specific recipes where it's needed with the added benefit of MSNF. Like dry milk powder, make sure to use one labeled "nonfat."

Sweetened Condensed Milk

You know, the delicious stuff that comes in a can! However, not all of them are the same. Look for the ones that only list sugar and milk as ingredients, because additions like hydrogenated oils can throw the balance of a recipe off. I like Eagle Brand from Borden.

Coconut Cream

Be snobby about your coconut cream; not all of them are made equal. Especially for Asian flavors, I only use Mae Ploy, Aroy-D, or Savoy coconut cream. Stay away from coconut products with UHT (ultra-high temperature) on the label, as they have a slightly oxidized flavor that doesn't work well in many recipes. And be sure to use full-fat coconut cream—not coconut milk.

Refined Coconut Oil

Different from "virgin coconut oil," refined coconut oil is deodorized and has a neutral flavor, meaning it doesn't taste like coconut. In this book, it's used to replace butterfat in nondairy ice cream bases and will turn chocolate into melt-in-your-mouth freckles, stracciatella, or a dip for coating ice cream novelties.

Glutinous Rice Flour

Glutinous rice flour, aka "sweet rice flour," is not to be confused with regular rice flour—it has a discernible sweet flavor, and when cooked it creates a thick, glue-like texture that adds to the body of our signature ice cream base. At Wanderlust Creamery, we use Koda Farms mochiko, which is widely available at most specialty food stores like Whole Foods. However, any brand can be used, as long as it's labeled "glutinous rice" or "sweet rice."

Agar-Agar

A gelling agent made from seaweed that's a little more freeze-stable than gelatin. Use the powdered form, which is available at Asian supermarkets and online.

Cocoa Powder

There are two kinds of cocoa powder: Dutch process and natural. Dutch process cocoa powder goes through an alkalinization process that results in a cocoa powder darker in color with a simple, straightforward and one-dimensional chocolate flavor. Natural cocoa powder won't color or flavor your ice cream as intensely, but it's brighter and more nuanced with flavors that vary, like tannic and citric notes. Think of cocoa powder like coffee: the darker the roast, the more pronounced "coffee" flavor you'll instantly recognize, but the harder it will be to discern the subtleties and nuances of the coffee bean. The lighter the roast, the more acidic the coffee will be, but you'll more easily pick up distinct flavor notes and terroir. So which to use? It depends. For a classically flavored chocolate base, use cocoa that has been Dutched. For a more complex chocolate ice cream, like Ruby Chocolate (page 78), use natural. Or you can mix a blend of the two for the best of both worlds. At Wanderlust Creamery, we use mostly Dutch process cocoa from Callebaut or Bensdorp.

Chocolate

When chocolate is called for, always use couverture chocolate, which is higher-quality chocolate used by pastry chefs. Couverture chocolate has a higher cocoa butter percentage, which makes for chocolate freckles, or stracciatella, that instantly harden upon contact with cold ice cream and last just a little longer before completely melting in your mouth. It also gives more structure to ice cream coatings for that "snap" when you bite in. Valrhona, Callebaut, and Guittard are some brands of couverture chocolate. If you have to use Hershey's, fine—just don't call it *my* recipe!

STABILIZERS AND EMULSIFIERS

Stabilizers and emulsifiers are optional, especially if you plan to eat the ice cream just shortly after churning. However, if you plan to store your ice cream for more than a few hours past churning, then I urge you to use a stabilizer. If making a nondairy recipe, understand that stabilizers and emulsifiers are essential to the body and cohesion of the ice cream or sorbet and opting to go without them will certainly affect the final texture.

Tara Gum

This is my choice of stabilizer because of its low hydration temperature (which means less heating and preserving fresh dairy flavor). You can find it widely available online.

Refined Coconut Oil

Glutinous Rice Flour

Agar-Agar

Cocoa Powder

Tara Gum

Chocolate

Sorbet Stabilizer

Nondairy Stabilizer

Lecithin

Inulin

Sorbet Stabilizer

For sorbets, I use a blend of three stabilizers: cellulose gum, guar gum, and lambda carrageenan—all of which are widely available online. See Stabilizer Blends (page 33).

Nondairy Stabilizer

Nondairy formulations need a little extra help from stabilizers. I combine one emulsifier and three hydrocolloids for a synergistic effect: lecithin, tara gum, guar gum, and lambda carrageenan—all of which are widely available online. See Stabilizer Blends (page 33).

Lecithin

Lecithin powder gives us the emulsifying power of egg yolks without having to actually use them. Although brands vary in taste, soy lecithin has a more neutral flavor than sunflower lecithin. It can be found widely online.

Inulin

Inulin is a powder made from chicory fiber, sold as a fiber supplement and prebiotic, widely available in health food stores and online. Incidentally, it's also a useful tool for thickening watery sorbets. Be sure to use a flavorless inulin.

STABILIZER BLENDS

SORBET STABILIZER
Makes 110 grams
(enough to stabilize 30 quarts)

This stabilizer blend is designed to give body and the slightest hint of creamy mouthfeel to sorbets, without altering or masking the flavor of fresh fruit. All of the ingredients can be found in baking supply stores and online. Cellulose gum is sometimes referred to as "carboxymethyl cellulose" or "CMC powder." Recommended dosage: 0.5% to 0.75% (by weight) of the water in your recipe.

5 tablespoons (45 g) cellulose gum

3 tablespoons + 2 teaspoons (35 g) guar gum

2 tablespoons + 1 teaspoon (20 g) lambda carrageenan

1 tablespoon + ½ teaspoon (10 g) glucose powder

Mix all the ingredients together and store in an airtight container in a cool and dry place. Mix well before each use.

NONDAIRY STABILIZER
Makes 110 grams
(enough to stabilize 36 quarts)

This synergistic blend of emulsifiers and stabilizers gives ice cream recipes made with nondairy milk alternatives (like coconut cream, rice milk, or pea milk) a rich texture and smooth meltdown, but with a clean finish. All of the ingredients can be found in baking supply stores and online. Recommended dosage: 0.025% to 0.04% (by weight) of total recipe.

½ cup (36 g) soy lecithin

3 tablespoons (36 g) tara gum

1 tablespoon + 2 ½ teaspoons (18 g) guar gum (optional)

1 tablespoon + ½ teaspoon (9 g) lambda carrageenan

1 tablespoon + ½ teaspoon (10 g) glucose powder

Mix all the ingredients together and store in an airtight container in a cool and dry place. Mix well before each use.

TOOLS & EQUIPMENT

Some would argue that you don't need fancy equipment to make the best ice cream. Knowing what you know now about the science of ice cream, you'll understand that there's only so much you can do with noncommercial equipment to make the smoothest ice cream possible. *But* that doesn't mean you can't come close at home. Here's my short list of everything you'll need to start churning in your own kitchen.

NONNEGOTIABLES

Ice Cream Maker

There are several types of ice cream makers. While any of them can make ice cream, some will be more beneficial than others, so my choice of home ice cream machine is one with a built-in compressor. These are less-sophisticated versions of what most professional ice cream makers use. They contain their own compressor inside the unit that chills the ice cream directly as it churns. Because there is no prechilling of any parts, there's no downtime between batches, which means you can churn a few batches per hour.

Some even have the option of controlling the churning speed, allowing you to opt for lower overrun.

The next best option in my opinion would be a Ninja Creami, which is a home version of a restaurant pastry chef's Pacojet. Instead of pouring a base into a machine where it's churned, the base is frozen into a hard solid block inside a canister. The canister is then inserted into the machine, where a spiral blade drills into the block and shaves the frozen mass into very tiny ice crystals while injecting a minimal amount of air into the ice cream. Because of the way the ice cream is made, it's very forgiving for unbalanced and unstabilized formulations. You can literally throw anything into the base (even a sugar-free ice cream attempt) and it will turn it into an ice cream form. A caveat, though, is that it only makes a few servings at a time and the ice cream is meant to be eaten right away, or soon after churning (or shaving). If you're looking to store the ice cream in the freezer for a while after it's made, you'll still need to stabilize the base and have a well-balanced formula (sugar included) as the free-flowing water will do its thing and get together during storage.

Precision Kitchen Scale

The recipes in this book indicate measurements in volume because that's what most cookbooks published in North America require. But since you picked up a book on "The World" of ice cream, it's best you know that **the ice cream**

world speaks in weights and formulates recipes by weight. Please do yourself a favor and get a good kitchen scale that can accurately weigh down to 1 gram. Weigh the ingredients. Not only will you get the best accuracy for the formula, you'll save yourself having to wash measuring cups and spoons.

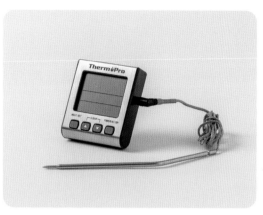

Whisk
Make sure that your whisk's wires are sealed into the handle, as any open crevices may accumulate gunk and be difficult to clean.

Instant-Read Thermometer
Most of the recipes in this book will call for the ice cream bases to be heated to specific temperatures in order to hydrate stabilizers. Even if you're not using stabilizer, it would be essential to know what temperature you're heating your base to because overheating can cause unwanted flavors and textures—especially if using egg yolks. I like to use a digital probe thermometer that can go up to candy temperatures (up to 360°F/180°C) for making caramel and brittles.

Small-ish Saucepan
A 2- to 3-quart (2 to 3 liter) stainless steel saucepan will be your best friend in cooking most of the bases in this recipe. For making caramel or doubling the recipes, opt for a 4-quart (4 liter) saucepan.

Heatproof Spatula
For cooking, scraping your saucepan clean, and folding variegates and solid mix-ins into churned ice cream.

OTHER TOOLS & EQUIPMENT

Metal Loaf Pan

At home, I like to store and scoop my ice cream in an 8½ by 4½-inch (21 by 11 cm) aluminized steel loaf pan, which is a standard 1-pound (450 g) pan. It's a mini-version of what we serve our ice creams out of at Wanderlust Creamery. A loaf pan gets very cold fast, which makes it easy to prechill while churning your ice cream. Its length makes for easy glide scooping.

Tall Cylindrical Mixing Vessel

If using a hand blender, you'll definitely need a tall cylindrical mixing vessel to immerse the blending tip in the ice cream base. Most hand blenders come with a plastic one, however, they don't hold enough liquid for the recipes in this book. Instead, I find that 1½-quart (1.5 liter) stainless steel bain-marie pots are handy to have around for mixing and homogenizing ice cream. They also come in handy for ice baths to quickly cool cooked bases. You can buy one for under $2 at any restaurant supply store, or online. Alternatively, you can use the canister insert of your ice cream maker—a tip suggested by the very people who tested these recipes.

Hand Blender

Also known as an immersion blender, this gadget will be essential in properly dispersing clumpy stabilizers and homogenizing your ice cream base (to break up those fat droplets). A standard stand blender will work for this purpose, too, but most of the recipes in this book are written with a hand blender in mind.

Brix Refractometer
Use this to take the guessing game out of sorbet base formulating and adjusting. You don't need a fancy one—a $15 one from Amazon will work just fine.

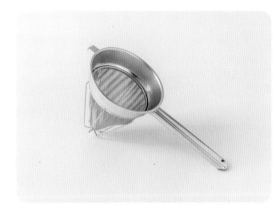

Fine-Mesh Sieve
Not just any sieve—a *fine-mesh* sieve, aka a chinois or bouillon sieve. These will be necessary for straining infused bases, and also filtering out any curdled yolks (it happens!) or unblended clumps of stabilizer. The conical shape is best.

Stand Mixer
Many of the mix-ins, like marshmallow crème and various baked goods, will require this. Additionally, this book gives a method for making carbonated ice cream (see Ramune Sherbet, page 261) using a stand mixer and dry ice!

Sheet Pans
Most of the baking in this cookbook will require a sheet pan. For most of the recipes, a quarter-sheet (13 by 9 inches/33 by 23 cm) or a half-sheet (18 by 13 inches/46 by 33 cm) are called for.

Small Baking Dish
Many mix-ins that need to be set, like Namelaka Cubes (page 278), Jellies (pages 280 to 281), or Ice Cream "Boba" (page 284), will require a small, shallow freezer-safe baking dish.

Glass Measuring Cup
You'll use this to temper chocolate without fuss in a microwave. I prefer one with a spout for pouring liquid chocolate into a batch of churning ice cream, to make "freckles" or stracciatella.

Electric Spice Grinder
For pulverizing freeze-dried fruit and other ingredients into fine powders and crushing small amounts of spices.

Ice Cream Spade
A rubber spatula isn't sturdy enough for scraping freshly frozen ice cream from the machine's paddle or blade. Instead, you'll need an ice cream spade—the kind used to serve gelato.

Thermometer Gun
While this isn't necessary, it would be helpful in determining the doneness of your ice cream, for timing when to churn in small mix-ins or chocolate freckles.

TECHNIQUES

THE BASE

A step-by-step guide to making ice cream bases.

1. Prepare an ice bath. You have a few options here.

- You can place a shallow baking dish nestled inside a roasting pan filled with ice and a little cold water. The ice and water should not go more than halfway up the pan. Add ice as it melts, but do not let the water rise to the level of the top of the baking dish. This option is the quickest, as it provides a large surface for cooling and heat escape.

- Place a stainless-steel bain-marie pot inside a large bowl or stockpot filled with ice and a little cold water. The ice and water should not go more than three-quarters of the way up the bain-marie pot. Add ice as it melts, but do not let the water rise to the level of the top of the bain-marie pot. This option provides the slowest cooling of the three, but poses the least risk of water going into the base.

- Line a tall cylindrical vessel, such as a 1½-quart (1.5 liter) stainless-steel bain-marie pot, with a zip-top plastic bag. Fold the edges of the bag over the sides of the bain-marie pot. Fill the bag with hot ice cream base and seal it with the zip-top. Submerge the bag in a bowl or shallow pan of ice and water. (The recipes in the book don't really call for this method, because I often require you to add ingredients after cooling—tricky to do when the base is in a bag.)

2. In a small bowl, whisk together the dry ingredients.

3. In a tall cylindrical mixing vessel, blend the liquid ingredients except the heavy cream (or any other ingredients listed after heavy cream) with a hand blender.

4. While blending, add the dry ingredients, blending until completely smooth.

5. Pour the mixture into a small saucepan and cook over medium-low heat, whisking constantly, until it reaches the temperature designated in the recipe. If not using stabilizers, any creamy bases should be heated to 165°F (75°C) unless otherwise stated. Sorbet bases should only be heated enough to dissolve any sugars.

6. Once the base reaches temperature, pour it back into the tall mixing vessel.

7. Pour in the heavy cream and any additional ingredients indicated at this step in the recipe.

8. Blend the mixture for 2 minutes to fully homogenize and get those fat droplets as small as possible. This also helps drop the temperature of the base before moving on to the ice bath.

10. Once completely cool, stir in any extracts or additional ingredients that the recipe calls for at this step.

9. Pour the base through a fine-mesh sieve into the prepared ice bath to cool. If the base is to be steeped overnight, skip the straining and go directly into the ice bath. Occasionally stir the base in the ice bath to hasten cooling.

11. Transfer the ice cream base to an airtight container. Cover and refrigerate for at least 12 hours. This is the "aging" process, where the proteins and solids bind water, the stabilizers hydrate, the emulsifiers strip fat droplets of their outer membrane, and the fat droplets partially crystallize to form stronger bonds to trap air when they're churned.

ALL ABOUT CHURNING

Your main goal when churning ice cream is to keep everything cold. The room must be cool . . . the container you put the ice cream in should be cold . . . any ingredients you add (except for liquid chocolate) should be cold. First, make sure the room you're churning the ice cream in is cool. Don't try to churn ice cream in an 85°F (30°C) kitchen—your machine will struggle and the ice cream will take longer to finish churning, resulting in bigger ice crystals.

   If the ice cream has mix-ins or variegates, have them ready to go, chilling them briefly in the freezer just before you start churning. Take them out of the freezer just before they're about to be used. Make sure to clear out space in your freezer and make a landing spot for your ice cream *before* you start churning.

   As soon as the ice cream is done churning, MOVE QUICKLY. When folding in mix-ins or variegates, move in as few movements as possible. Remember, this is when the ice cream is in its most perfect state and every second after that is a race to the freezer to maintain the structure as much as possible!

The Basics

1. Just before churning, quickly blend the chilled base once more with a hand blender or whisk in order to loosen any thickness or coagulation from the stabilizers. Strain out any infusions if necessary.

2. Fill your machine no higher than the top of the churning blade. Remember, you'll be whipping air into the base, and the finished volume will be more than what you put in. Smaller batches also will freeze faster, making a smoother ice cream. Most of the recipes will account for this specific volume, but anytime you have more base than will fit, churn it in two separate batches.

3. As your ice cream churns and thickens, you'll start to notice small ice crystals begin to form. Soon after, you may notice a milkshake texture. After that, you'll see the surface of the ice cream begin to lose its shine because as the water freezes, the ice cream will begin to look drier. When the surface of the ice cream looks dry and has the texture of very stiff soft-serve, it's just a few moments away from being ready.

4. If you are not adding any chocolate freckles or dry mix-ins (see below), continue churning until the machine starts to slow down against the stiffness of the ice cream, about 25°F (–5°C) or colder on a thermometer gun. For sorbets, the mix should never be churned to a "dry" look. It will be finished when it looks like a thick milkshake or freshly extruded slushy, still glistening with wetness.

5. Quickly transfer the ice cream to the pre-chilled loaf pan, spreading it into the bottom of the pan as evenly as possible.

6. Press a piece of wax paper directly on top of the ice cream and freeze for at least 4 hours before serving.

Chocolate Freckling

When the ice cream looks like it's almost done churning (step 3 above), quickly pour in the liquid chocolate in a steady stream (see Note), away from the center of the churning paddle or blade. After all the chocolate has been added, let the churning blade rotate three or four more turns, then *immediately* stop the machine.

Note: Do not pour the chocolate in *too* thin of a stream, because this will take too long. The longer the chocolate spends churning, the more it will get mixed in or dissolve into the ice cream, which may affect the consistency and texture. After all the chocolate has been added, let the churning blade rotate three or four more turns, then *immediately* stop the machine.

When to Add Mix-Ins

You're going to want to time adding the mix-ins just right. If you add them too early, before the ice cream is ready, you'll risk either under-churning the ice cream or overmixing the mix-ins. If you wait too late to add them, your machine may stop churning (because the ice cream is too hard or frozen) and you'll have to wait for the ice cream to melt a little so that the motor can start churning again (resulting in larger ice crystals). The optimal time to start churning in solid mix-ins or liquid chocolate (for freckling) will be 30 seconds before the surface of the ice cream reaches 25°F (–5°C). This is where a thermometer gun will come in handy. If you don't have a thermometer gun, simply use the visual cues: dry surface, stiff texture.

Small-Scale Mix-Ins

If you have a small amount of mix-ins that will fit into the machine without overflowing, add them in the last few seconds of churning (in step 3). After all the mix-ins have been added, let the churning blade rotate three or four more turns, then *immediately* stop the machine. For larger quantities of mix-ins, see Large-Scale Mix-Ins below.

Large-Scale Mix-Ins and Variegates

- Have a loaf pan chilled and ready to go.
- Stop the machine. Quickly scrape half of the ice cream into the prechilled loaf pan and spread it evenly onto the bottom.

- Add half of the mix-ins or variegate on top of the ice cream.

- Spread the remaining ice cream on top.

- Add the remaining mix-ins or variegate as the final layer.
- Place the ice cream pan into the freezer for 15 minutes to firm up before folding.

- Quickly, but carefully, fold the ice cream in three or four folds. If folding in variegates, fold just enough to create swirls or ribbons. Overmixing the variegate into the ice cream can ruin the texture of the ice cream.

- After folding, lightly press a sheet of wax paper on top of the ice cream.
- Immediately place the pan in the coldest part of your freezer (which will be located at the very back and center), allowing breathing room on all sides of the pan. Don't open the freezer again for a few hours!

Making Sliced Ice Creams

This technique is used for ice cream terrines (Thai Candy Corn, Sapin Sapin) and ice cream novelties (Nanaimo Bars, Kaya Toast, Tita's Fruit Salad).

1. Cut four pieces of wax or parchment paper to line two metal loaf pans so that they come up the walls of the pan with some overhang (for pulling out the ice cream).
2. Churn the ice cream as usual, and divide it between the two prepared metal loaf pans.
3. If possible, blast freeze the ice cream until hard enough to unfold, 30 to 45 minutes. Alternatively, place the ice cream in the coldest part of your freezer for at least 12 hours.
4. Using a wet knife, slice the ice cream as directed in the recipe.

TEMPERING ICE CREAM

Tempering your ice cream so that it is soft enough to scoop, yet not melted, will ensure that you maintain the integrity of the ice cream structure for as long as possible. See Steps for a Perfect Scoop (below).

Steps for a Perfect Scoop

1. Remove the ice cream pan from the freezer and place it in the fridge for 8 to 12 minutes.

2. After 8 to 12 minutes, take the ice cream out of the fridge and put it out on the counter. In just a few moments, it will warm up to scooping temperature.

3. Peel off the sheet of wax or plastic wrap covering the ice cream.

4. Wet your ice cream scooper with cold water and shake off as much excess water as you can. Position the pan vertically on the counter, with a short side of the pan facing you. Starting at the opposite end of the pan, farthest away from you, hold the scooper perpendicular to the ice cream and slowly

Blast Freezing

If you want to "blast freeze" your ice cream in its most perfect state, as we do in our kitchen, you can use a block of dry ice to mimic a commercial blast freezer at home. You can get 5- to 10-pound (2.3 to 4.5 kg) blocks of dry ice at many chain groceries. Note: Do not attempt to blast freeze your ice cream pan before folding in any mix-ins or variegates—it will freeze too hard to mix anything in.

Important: Before you start, be sure you read Working with Dry Ice (page 262).

1. Place your finished ice cream pan in an insulated container like a cooler or Styrofoam box with a lid.
2. Place a 5-pound (2.3 kg) or greater block of dry ice on top of the ice cream. Close the cooler and let it sit for 30 to 45 minutes.
3. After the ice cream has frozen solid, use well-insulated hands (cloth oven mitts work well) to transfer the ice cream pan to the freezer.

scoop in one long motion, pulling the ice cream toward yourself. Bring the scoop back to the top of the pan where you started, and roll the scoop again, gathering more ice cream around it.

5. Place your scoop in a cup or on a cone . . . but hold on! Before you eat it, press a fresh sheet of wax paper or plastic wrap onto any remaining ice cream in the pan and return it to the freezer.

CHAPTER 3

ice cr

Ice cream flavors are like people—each one has its own unique qualities and traits. That's why I don't believe in a perfect base that fits all flavors. In online ice cream geek forums, I see people go on about how they found the best, balanced base recipe. That base might be good for vanilla or coffee, but what about strawberry? Or a floral honey lavender? In my experience, eggless bases are best suited for fresh flavors. Coffee and tea ice creams need

ream
bases

a little egg yolk present in the base to round out bitterness and tannins. Other flavors need an even more custardy base. At Wanderlust Creamery, we use about six proprietary bases—each one fulfills a different flavor purpose.

The following recipes for these bases (which are geared toward the home cook) are minimally sweet and lower on solids, allowing you to add ingredients and flavors to make them your own.

BLANK BASE

Makes about 1 quart (1 liter)

Think of this base as a blank canvas for ice cream flavors, to let the star ingredients shine. It works best with fresh fruit or mint, and with very delicate flavors such as olive oil. This recipe has a minimal amount of sugar so that you can add other ingredients and flavors to your liking. The secret ingredient here is condensed milk. It lends a milky sweetness that comes from slightly toasted milk proteins. It also provides some essential sugars, solids, and fat to the recipe, but I cap it at 7% of the formula to prevent any sandiness from lactose crystallization.

2 tablespoons + 2 ½ teaspoons (20 g) nonfat dry milk powder

½ cup (100 g) granulated sugar

⅓ cup + 1 teaspoon (50 g) glucose powder

½ teaspoon (2 g) tara gum (optional; see page 24)

Scant ½ teaspoon (2 g) lecithin

1¾ cups (425 g) whole milk

3 tablespoons + 1 teaspoon (65 g) sweetened condensed milk

1½ cups + 2 tablespoons (375 g) heavy cream

1. Prepare an ice bath (see page 39).

2. In a small bowl, whisk together the milk powder, sugar, glucose, tara gum (if using), and lecithin. In a tall cylindrical 1½-quart (1.5 liter) mixing vessel, blend the whole milk and condensed milk with a hand blender. Add the dry ingredients, then blend again thoroughly to dissolve all the solids.

3. Pour the mixture into a small saucepan and cook over medium-low heat, whisking constantly, until it reaches 165°F (75°C) on an instant-read thermometer.

4. Once the base reaches 165°F (75°C), immediately remove from the heat and pour it back into the tall mixing vessel. Add the heavy cream and blend the mixture with a hand blender for 2 minutes to fully homogenize it.

5. Pour the base through a fine-mesh sieve into the prepared ice bath to cool. Once completely cool, transfer the base to an airtight container and refrigerate it for at least 12 hours and up to 3 days.

6. Quickly blend the ice cream base once more with a hand blender or whisk before processing it in an ice cream machine according to the manufacturer's instructions.

BALANCED BASE

Sometimes ice cream just needs eggs for a velvety texture that can carry strong flavors. A bitter coffee or tea, floral notes like lavender, and some chocolate require egg yolks to round out the flavor. In my experience, I've found that three yolks is the magic number for an ice cream base that is balanced and not too "eggy."

1 tablespoon + 1¼ teaspoons (10 g) nonfat dry milk powder

½ cup (100 g) granulated sugar

¼ cup + 1 tablespoon (45 g) glucose powder

½ teaspoon (2 g) tara gum (optional; see page 24)

1⅔ cups (400 g) whole milk

3 tablespoons + 1 teaspoon (65 g) sweetened condensed milk

50 grams egg yolks (about 3 large eggs)

1¼ cups + 3½ tablespoons (340 g) heavy cream

1. Prepare an ice bath (see page 39).

2. In a small bowl, whisk together the milk powder, sugar, glucose, and tara gum (if using). In a tall cylindrical 1½-quart (1.5 liter) mixing vessel, blend the whole milk, condensed milk, and egg yolks with a hand blender. Add the dry ingredients, then blend again thoroughly to dissolve all the solids.

3. Pour the mixture into a small saucepan and cook over medium-low heat, whisking constantly, until it reaches 165°F (75°C) on an instant-read thermometer.

4. Once the base reaches 165°F (75°C), immediately remove from the heat and pour it back into the tall mixing vessel. Add the heavy cream, then blend the mixture with a hand blender for 2 minutes to fully homogenize it.

5. Pour the base through a fine-mesh sieve into the prepared ice bath to cool. Once completely cool, transfer the base to an airtight container and refrigerate it for at least 12 hours and up to 3 days.

6. Quickly blend the ice cream base once more with a hand blender or whisk before processing it in an ice cream machine according to the manufacturer's instructions.

CUSTARD BASE

Makes about 1 quart (1 liter)

Sometimes an ice cream will call for a very rich custard base: Let's say you want to make a flan, egg tart, or zabaglione ice cream flavor where the egg note needs to be strong. But there are only so many egg yolks you can add to the recipe before the texture is significantly affected. My solution is to cheat with kala namak, aka Indian black salt. It's a volcanic salt used in South Asian cooking that contains a trace amount of sulfur compounds, which lend a distinct cooked egg yolk flavor and aroma of its own. It's so "eggy" that it's a known trick vegan chefs use to make faux egg dishes, like tofu scramble. This recipe utilizes 8 egg yolks (which is what I consider the maximum for optimal texture), but if you find that the egg flavor isn't as strong as you'd like, go ahead and add this secret ingredient.

3½ teaspoons (8 g) nonfat dry milk powder

½ cup (100 g) granulated sugar

⅓ cup + 1 teaspoon (50 g) glucose powder

¼ teaspoon (1 g) tara gum (optional; see page 24)

1½ cups + ½ tablespoon (375 g) whole milk

3½ tablespoons (70 g) sweetened condensed milk

140 grams egg yolks (from 8 to 9 large eggs)

1¼ cups (290 g) heavy cream

½ teaspoon (3 g) kala namak (Indian black salt), plus more to taste (optional)

1. Prepare an ice bath (see page 39).

2. In a small bowl, whisk together the milk powder, sugar, glucose, and tara gum (if using). In a tall cylindrical 1½-quart (1.5 liter) mixing vessel, blend the whole milk, condensed milk, and egg yolks with a hand blender. Add the dry ingredients, then blend again thoroughly to dissolve all the solids.

3. Pour the mixture into a small saucepan and cook over medium-low heat, whisking constantly, until it reaches 165°F (75°C) on an instant-read thermometer.

4. Once the base reaches 165°F (75°C), immediately remove from the heat and pour it back into the tall mixing vessel. Add the heavy cream, then blend the mixture with a hand blender for 2 minutes to fully homogenize it.

5. Pour the base through a fine-mesh sieve into the prepared ice bath to cool. Taste the base to check if the flavor is "eggy" enough for you. Whisk in the kala namak (if using), adding a little more at a time until the desired flavor is achieved. Remember that the final flavor of the ice cream will be muted once frozen.

6. Once completely cool, transfer the base to an airtight container and refrigerate it for at least 12 hours and up to 3 days.

7. Quickly blend the ice cream base once more with a hand blender or whisk before processing it in an ice cream machine according to the manufacturer's instructions.

MASCARPONE BASE

Makes about 1 quart (1 liter)

This is my favorite ice cream base. When researching and developing the recipes for Wanderlust Creamery, I wanted a base that tasted simply of rich, sweet cream, and I immediately thought of mascarpone cheese. Unlike the Blank Base (page 48), which serves as more of a blank canvas to which other ingredients would be added, this mascarpone base is meant to be a flavor in its own right. It is, nonetheless, very versatile. Something as simple as a bit of vanilla, zest of citrus, a teaspoon of matcha, or fruit jam swirled in can magically transform it into a wide range of entirely different flavors.

⅓ cup + 2 teaspoons (40 g) nonfat dry milk powder

¾ cup + 1 tablespoon (160 g) granulated sugar

⅓ cup + 2½ teaspoons (55 g) glucose powder

½ teaspoon (2 g) tara gum (optional; see page 24)

Generous ¼ teaspoon (1.5 g) lecithin (optional)

2⅔ cups (575 g) whole milk

¼ cup + 3 tablespoons (100 g) heavy cream

9 ounces (260 g) mascarpone cheese

1. Prepare an ice bath (see page 39).

2. In a small bowl, whisk together the milk powder, sugar, glucose, tara gum (if using), and lecithin. In a tall 1½-quart (1.5 liter) mixing vessel, blend the milk with a hand blender while slowly adding the dry ingredients. Blend thoroughly to dissolve all the solids.

3. Pour the mixture into a small saucepan and cook over medium-low heat, whisking constantly, until it reaches 165°F (75°C) on an instant-read thermometer.

4. Once the base reaches 165°F (75°C), immediately remove from the heat and pour it back into the tall mixing vessel. Add the heavy cream and mascarpone cheese, then blend the mixture with a hand blender for 2 minutes to fully homogenize it.

5. Pour the base through a fine-mesh sieve into the prepared ice bath to cool. Once completely cool, transfer the base to an airtight container and refrigerate it for at least 12 hours and up to 3 days.

6. Quickly blend the ice cream base once more with a hand blender or whisk before processing it in an ice cream machine according to the manufacturer's instructions.

RICE CREAM BASE

I developed this ice cream base formula when creating Wanderlust's famous Sticky Rice & Mango ice cream (page 169). I quickly found it has so much more versatility. There are two options here: One is made with coconut cream, and can be the nondairy base for so many iterations of Southeast Asian sticky rice desserts. Black or purple sticky rice can also be used for a stunning color. The second option is made with dairy instead of coconut cream; it can taste like mochi, tteok, horchata, or rice pudding.

For the coconut rice cream base

Sticky Rice Milk (recipe follows)

½ cup + 2½ teaspoons (110 g) granulated sugar

1¼ cups (180 g) glucose powder

1 teaspoon (3 g) Nondairy Stabilizer (page 33)

1¾ cups (385 g) coconut cream (see Note)

Heaping ¼ teaspoon (1 g) tapioca flour

3 tablespoons (45 g) water

2 tablespoons + 1 teaspoon (30 g) virgin coconut oil

For the rice cream base with dairy

Sticky Rice Milk (recipe follows)

½ cup + 1 tablespoon + 2 teaspoons (120 g) granulated sugar

1¼ cups (180 g) glucose powder

½ teaspoon (2 g) tara gum (optional; see page 24)

Scant ¾ teaspoon (3 g) lecithin (optional)

2 tablespoons (30 g) whole milk

1½ cups (350 g) heavy cream

Heaping ¼ teaspoon (1 g) tapioca flour

3 tablespoons (45 g) water

2 tablespoons + 1 teaspoon (30 g) refined coconut oil (see Tip)

1. Prepare an ice bath (see page 39).

2. For both versions: Make the sticky rice milk as directed and set aside.

3. In a small bowl, whisk together the sugar, glucose powder, and stabilizer blend (for the nondairy version) or tara gum and lecithin (for the dairy version). In a tall cylindrical 1½-quart (1.5 liter) mixing vessel, blend the coconut cream (for the nondairy version) or milk and heavy cream (for the dairy version) with a hand blender. Add the dry ingredients, then blend again thoroughly to dissolve all the solids.

4. Pour the mixture into a small saucepan and cook over medium-low heat, whisking constantly, until it reaches 165°F (75°C) on an instant-read thermometer.

5. Meanwhile, in a small bowl, whisk together the tapioca flour and water to make a slurry.

6. When the mixture reaches 165°F (75°C), whisk in the tapioca slurry. Bring to a boil and cook, stirring, until thickened, about 1 minute. Immediately remove from the heat and pour it back into the tall mixing vessel. Add the sticky rice milk and coconut oil and blend with a hand blender for 2 minutes to fully homogenize.

7. Pour the base through a fine-mesh sieve into the prepared ice bath to cool. Once completely cool, transfer the base to an airtight container and refrigerate it for at least 12 hours and up to 3 days.

NOTE: Be sure to use full-fat coconut cream, not coconut milk. And be snobby about your coconut cream; not all of them are made equal. Non-Asian brands of coconut milk can taste overly coconut-y (like the kind meant for piña coladas), which can mask the delicate rice flavor. I specifically use only these brands: Mae Ploy, Aroy-D, and Savoy. Also stay away from coconut products with UHT (ultra-high temperature) on the label, as they have a slight oxidized flavor.

TIP: The reason for using refined coconut oil in the dairy version is that the oil is neutral in flavor, as you don't want to add any unwanted coconut flavor here. The nondairy version, on the other hand, can use the more prominently flavored virgin coconut oil.

STICKY RICE MILK
Makes about 1½ cups

3 tablespoons + 1 teaspoon (33 g) glutinous or sweet rice flour (see Note)

½ teaspoon + ⅛ teaspoon (2 g) kosher salt

1½ cups + 1½ tablespoons (375 g) water

In a small saucepan, whisk together the glutinous rice flour, salt, and water. Cook over medium heat until the mixture reaches 150°F (65°C), whisking frequently so that rice flour doesn't clump together at the bottom of the pot. The final mixture should be a thick, semitranslucent liquid. Remove from the heat and set aside until ready to use, up to 24 hours.

NOTE: Glutinous or sweet rice flour is not to be confused with regular rice flour. It has a discernible sweet flavor and when cooked, creates a thick glue-like texture that adds to the body of this ice cream. At Wanderlust Creamery, we use Koda Farms Mochiko, which is widely available at most specialty food stores like Whole Foods. However, any brand can be used as long as it's labeled "glutinous" or "sweet rice."

VARIATION: Black or purple sticky rice grains can be used instead of sweet rice flour. Substitute an equal weight (or 2⅓ tablespoons) of black or purple sticky rice grains for the rice flour. Instead of the method above, in a saucepan, combine the rice with 1½ cups + 1½ tablespoons (375 g) water and cook the rice until tender, 22 to 25 minutes. Puree the cooked rice with its cooking water to make the sticky rice milk.

VEGAN BASE

Makes about 1 quart (1 liter)

I never set out to make a vegan version of ice cream just for the sake of offering a vegan option. I want to make amazing ice cream, period. Not "pretty good ice cream, considering it's vegan." If a flavor just so happened to taste better without dairy (like Sticky Rice & Mango, page 169, or a deep, dark gianduja), it'd serve as our vegan option at Wanderlust Creamery. One of the reasons for this was because many alternative ingredients commonly used in vegan ice cream—cashews, coconut, nut milks, and oat—add flavors that are out of place. For example, a strawberry ice cream, vegan or not, should taste like strawberry ice cream, not coconut-strawberry ice cream. Enter pea milk. It was the first time anything had changed my mind about dairy-free alternatives. It's blank in flavor; there's no distracting back note of anything. And unlike watery nut milks, it almost has the body to stand in the place of real milk. Combined with flavorless coconut oil, it can be just as creamy as any of the other mother ice cream bases in this chapter.

¼ cup (50 g) granulated sugar

2¼ cups + 2½ tablespoons (345 g) glucose powder (see Note)

1 teaspoon (3 g) Nondairy Stabilizer (page 33)

2⅓ cups (555 g) unsweetened pea milk

½ cup + 3½ tablespoons (150 g) refined coconut oil

NOTE: That's not a typo—this recipe really calls for 345 grams of glucose. Without the proteins, fat, and natural sugars from dairy, a vegan recipe requires that much more sugar to be scoopable.

1. Prepare an ice bath (see page 39).

2. In a small bowl, whisk together the sugar, glucose, and stabilizer. In a tall cylindrical 1½-quart (1.5 liter) mixing vessel, blend the pea milk with a hand blender while slowly adding the dry ingredients. Blend to thoroughly dissolve all the solids.

3. Pour the mixture into a small saucepan and cook over medium-low heat, whisking constantly, until it reaches 165°F (75°C) on an instant-read thermometer.

4. Once the base reaches 165°F (75°C), immediately remove from the heat and pour it back into the tall mixing vessel. Add the refined coconut oil and blend the mixture with a hand blender for 2 minutes to fully homogenize it.

5. Pour the base through a fine-mesh sieve into the prepared ice bath to cool. Once completely cool, transfer the base to an airtight container and refrigerate it for at least 12 hours and up to 3 days.

6. Quickly blend the ice cream base once more with a hand blender or whisk before processing it in an ice cream machine according to the manufacturer's instructions.

CHAPTER 4

cust

Custard ice cream, referred to sometimes as "French ice cream," relies heavily on egg yolks as an emulsifier and thickener. Over the years, I've relied on a rich, high-yolk custard base to translate many of the world's most loved egg desserts. Doused with pastry flakes, it's evocative of an egg tart from Portugal. Made the same way, but with salted duck egg yolks, it transforms into a version found in Macau, China. Adding pandan and coconut makes it the frozen version of Singaporean kaya jam. I've spiked a

ards

few custard bases with booze: sweet wine to make zabaglione ice cream, rum with coconut cream to make Puerto Rican Christmas coquito, or Cognac with honey and espresso for a Viennese Kaisermelange. Simply churned on its own, then swirled into another ice cream flavor—like Vietnamese coffee to make Hanoi egg coffee, or a simple marshmallow-flavored ice cream for brazo de Mercedes—spawns another subset of possibilities.

PASTEIS DE NATA

Makes about 1 quart (1 liter)

For the caramel

½ cup + 1 tablespoon (115 g) granulated sugar

2 tablespoons (30 g) water

1¼ cups (290 g) heavy cream

For the base

1 tablespoon + ½ teaspoon (8 g) nonfat dry milk powder

½ teaspoon (2 g) tara gum (optional; see page 24)

⅓ cup + 1 teaspoon (50 g) glucose powder

1½ cups + ½ tablespoon (375 g) whole milk

3½ tablespoons (70 g) sweetened condensed milk

136 grams egg yolks (from about 8 large eggs)

1 vanilla bean, split lengthwise

Heaping ¼ teaspoon (1.5 g) kala namak (Indian black salt), plus more to taste (optional)

For the ice cream

½ cup (150 g) puff pastry flakes (see Note)

NOTE: Puff pastry flakes can be made from either homemade or store-bought frozen puff pastry dough. Bake the dough as directed, until a deep golden brown. Once cooled, break the puff pastry into flakes.

In Portugal, I unregretfully ate a box of pasteis de nata every day. Visitors lined up for blocks for these little egg tarts—custardy bites with blackened tops, encased in shattering layers of flaky pastry. Luckily, the line moved along quickly. Dozens of tarts were baked briefly in a 600°F (315°C) oven, after which they were boxed and then sold in half the time it took to bake them. This ice cream version utilizes an eight-egg custard base, burnt sugar, sulfuric black salt (to fortify the eggy flavor), and shards of buttery pastry to achieve the distinct experience of biting into a pasteis de nata on a steep cobblestoned street in Lisbon.

1. Prepare an ice bath (see page 39).

2. **Make the caramel:** In a medium saucepan, melt the sugar over medium-high heat. Do not stir; pick up the pot and swirl it around occasionally as it melts. Continue heating until the sugar caramelizes, 10 to 12 minutes. Once the sugar is approaching 365°F (185°C) on an instant-read thermometer, keep a *very* close eye on it. As soon as the temperature hits 375°F (185°C), turn off the heat and add the water and heavy cream; the mixture will violently bubble up and create a lot of steam. Whisk to dissolve the caramel completely. Set aside.

3. **Make the base:** In a small bowl, whisk together the milk powder, tara gum (if using), and glucose powder. In a tall cylindrical 1½-quart (1.5 liter) mixing vessel, blend the milk, condensed milk, and egg yolks with a hand blender. Add the dry ingredients

4. and blend again to dissolve all the solids.

5. Pour the mixture into a medium saucepan. Scrape the vanilla seeds into the pan and add the vanilla pod. Cook over medium-low heat, whisking constantly, until it reaches 165°F (75°C) on an instant-read thermometer. Meanwhile, pour the caramel into the tall mixing vessel.

6. Once the base reaches 165°F (75°C), immediately remove from the heat, fish out the vanilla pod, and pour the hot milk mixture over the caramel in the tall mixing vessel. Blend with a hand blender for 2 minutes to fully homogenize.

7. Pour the base through a fine-mesh sieve into the prepared ice bath to cool. Whisk in the kala namak (if using), adding a little more at a time until the desired flavor is achieved. Remember that the final flavor of the ice cream will be muted once frozen.

8. Once completely cool, transfer to an airtight container and refrigerate for at least 12 hours and up to 3 days.

9. **Churn the ice cream:** When ready to begin, place a loaf pan and the pastry flakes in the freezer to chill. Quickly blend the ice cream base once more with a hand blender or whisk before pouring it into an ice cream machine. Churn the ice cream until it reaches the texture of very stiff soft-serve and the surface looks dry, about 25°F (-5°C) or colder on a thermometer gun. Add the pastry flakes in the last few seconds of churning.

10. Transfer the ice cream mixture to the chilled loaf pan. Press a piece of wax paper directly on top of the ice cream and freeze for at least 4 hours before serving.

SALTED EGG TART

Makes about 1 quart (1 liter)

For the base

9 salted duck egg yolks (110 g total; see Note)

1½ cups + ½ tablespoon (375 g) whole milk

½ cup (100 g) granulated sugar

1 tablespoon + 1¼ teaspoons (10 g) nonfat dry milk powder

3 tablespoons + 1 teaspoon (30 g) glucose powder

¾ teaspoon (3 g) tara gum (optional; see page 24)

3½ tablespoons (70 g) sweetened condensed milk

1⅓ cups (300 g) heavy cream

½ teaspoon (2 g) vanilla extract

For the ice cream

½ cup (150 g) puff pastry flakes (see Note, page 58)

In 2017, when a friend brought back a precious bag of salted-egg potato chips from Asia, sparks flew in my mouth and brain. Salted duck eggs are essentially salt-cured duck eggs (which taste kind of like the chicken eggs we know), leaving the yolk semitranslucent, savory, and concentrated in flavor. Those yolks were Asia's latest obsession, used to dust fried chicken and McDonald's fries, emulsified into savory sauces, and flavoring thick custards that oozed out of steamed or fried buns at dim sum. I set out to make a salted-egg dan tat ice cream, a riff on Chinese-style egg tarts. The ice cream tasted like crème brûlée or custard, with that distinctive sweet/salty/savory note from the salted egg not too far off from something like a salted caramel.

NOTE: Store-bought parcooked salted egg yolks are available frozen or refrigerated at most Asian supermarkets.

VARIATION: Swirl this ice cream (without the puff pastry flakes) with the Vietnamese coffee ice cream from Vietnamese Rocky Road (page 247) for a salted Hanoi egg coffee flavor.

1. Prepare an ice bath (see page 39).

2. **Make the base:** In a stand blender, blend the salted egg yolks with 1 cup (250 g) of the milk until completely smooth. Add the remaining milk, the sugar, milk powder, glucose, and tara gum (if using) and blend again to dissolve the solids.

3. Pour the mixture into a medium saucepan and cook over medium-low heat, whisking constantly, until it reaches 165°F (75°C) on an instant-read thermometer. Set the blender aside.

4. Once the base reaches 165°F (75°C), immediately remove it from the heat and pour it back into the blender. Add in the heavy cream and blend on high for 2 minutes to fully homogenize.

5. Pour the base through a fine-mesh sieve into the prepared ice bath to cool. Once completely cool, stir in the vanilla and transfer the base to an airtight container and refrigerate for at least 12 hours and up to 3 days.

6. **Churn the ice cream:** When ready to begin, place a loaf pan and the pastry flakes in the freezer to chill. Quickly blend the ice cream base once more with a hand blender or whisk before pouring it into an ice cream machine. Churn the ice cream until it reaches the texture of very stiff soft-serve and the surface looks dry, about 25°F (−5°C) or colder on a thermometer gun. Add the pastry flakes in the last few seconds of churning.

7. Transfer the ice cream mixture to the chilled loaf pan. Press a piece of wax paper directly on top of the ice cream and freeze for at least 4 hours before serving.

SALTED KAYA TOAST

My grandfather, an expat from the Philippines, and my grandmother, an immigrant from Guangzhou, met in Malaysia while working at an ice cream and dairy plant. The company they worked for later moved the factory to present-day Singapore, where my grandparents would eventually start a family. My grandmother's favorite topic of conversation was food, especially the cuisine of the place my father grew up. Detailed stories of noodle soups sold on the sidewalk outside my father's kindergarten and descriptions of the dishes born of working immigrants embracing local Malay ingredients fill my memories of her. From the few I have, I often imagine my family's history visually like a Wong Kar-wai film, in vignettes of Singaporean food. Whenever I learn about a Malay dish, I instantly wonder whether it would have brought nostalgia to my father or grandmother. One such dish I imagine they might've eaten daily for breakfast is toast slathered with kaya—a custardy jam of coconut, yolks, and pandan leaf—perhaps paired with soft-boiled eggs, as part of a customary Singaporean morning. In this ice cream, the kaya custard is translated into one with salted duck eggs, and the "toast" is represented by a piece of bread wrapped around a brick of the ice cream—an ice cream loti, the famous ice cream sandwich served on the streets of Singapore today.

For the base

1 pandan leaf, fresh or frozen

9 salted duck egg yolks (110 g total); see Note

1 cup (250 g) whole milk

1¼ cups (270 g) coconut cream

1 tablespoon + 1¼ teaspoons (10 g) nonfat dry milk powder

3 tablespoons + 1 teaspoon (30 g) glucose powder

¾ teaspoon (3 g) tara gum (optional; see page 24)

½ teaspoon (1 g) salt

½ cup (115 g) packed light brown sugar

3 tablespoons + 1 teaspoon (65 g) sweetened condensed milk

35 grams egg yolks (from about 2 large eggs)

½ cup + 1 teaspoon (120 g) heavy cream

For the sandwiches

6 large slices Asian-style milk bread, Hawaiian bread, or brioche

NOTE: Store-bought parcooked salted duck egg yolks can be found at most Asian supermarkets. If you prefer, omit the salted eggs and simply blend the pandan leaf with the milk and coconut cream. Then in step 3, when adding the brown sugar and condensed milk, use 8 regular egg yolks instead of 2.

TIP: The ice cream must be extremely cold and hardened when slicing, which may be difficult to achieve with a home freezer if you live in a warmer climate. The quick-freezing method using dry ice (see Blast Freezing, page 45) is very useful for this recipe.

1. **Make the base:** In a stand blender, process the pandan leaf and salted duck egg yolks with the milk and coconut cream until completely smooth. Transfer the puree to a tall 1½-quart (1.5 liter) mixing vessel.

2. Prepare an ice bath (see page 39).

3. In a small bowl, whisk together the milk powder, glucose powder, tara gum (if using), and salt. To the tall mixing vessel with the puree, add the brown sugar, condensed milk, and the 2 raw egg yolks and blend with a hand blender while slowly adding the dry ingredients. Blend thoroughly to dissolve all the solids.

4. Pour the mixture into a medium saucepan and cook over medium-low heat, whisking constantly, until it reaches 165°F (75°C) on an instant-read thermometer.

5. Once the base reaches 165°F (75°C), immediately remove from the heat and pour into the tall mixing vessel. Add the heavy cream and blend with a hand blender for 2 minutes to fully homogenize.

6. Pour the base through a fine-mesh sieve into the prepared ice bath to cool. Once completely cool, transfer the base to an airtight container. Cover and refrigerate for at least 12 hours and up to 3 days.

7. **Churn the ice cream:** When ready to begin, line a metal loaf pan with wax or parchment paper (see page 45). (Alternatively, you can use a silicone loaf pan.) Place the loaf pan in the freezer to chill.

8. Quickly blend the ice cream base once more with a hand blender or whisk before pouring into an ice cream machine. Churn the ice cream until it reaches the texture of very stiff soft-serve and the surface looks dry, about 25°F (-5°C) or colder on a thermometer gun.

9. Transfer the ice cream to the chilled loaf pan. Press a piece of wax paper directly on top of the ice cream and freeze for at least 8 hours. (Alternatively, use dry ice to quick-freeze the ice cream; see Blast Freezing, page 45.)

10. **Make the "sandwiches":** When the ice cream has completely hardened, in an ungreased skillet or griddle, very lightly toast the bread slices (so that they are still soft and pliable) on one side only. Leave the other side of the bread completely untoasted.

11. Remove the ice cream loaf from the freezer and unmold the ice cream onto a piece of parchment or wax paper. Using a wet chef's knife, slice the ice cream crosswise into 6 equal slices, a little less than 1½ inches (4 cm) thick. Place a slice of ice cream onto the untoasted side of each piece of bread. Carefully fold the bread around the ice cream (like a taco) and serve.

NANAIMO BARS

These ice cream bars—a frozen rendition of a famous Northwestern Canadian dessert named after the Canadian city Nanaimo—are incidentally inspired by another frozen treat named after another Canadian landmark: the Klondike Bar. But instead of plain vanilla ice cream encased in milk chocolate, this is a yolky custard vanilla ice cream enriched with ghee (to imitate a Nanaimo bar's buttercream) with a graham/coconut/almond crust, encased in a crispy shell of salted dark chocolate.

1. Prepare an ice bath (see page 39).

2. **Make the base:** In a small bowl, whisk together the sugar, milk powder, tara gum (if using), and glucose powder. In a tall cylindrical 1½-quart (1.5 liter) mixing vessel, blend the milk, condensed milk, and egg yolks with a hand blender. Add the dry ingredients and blend again to dissolve all the solids.

3. Pour the mixture into a medium saucepan. Scrape the vanilla seeds into the mixture and add the pod. Cook over medium-low heat, whisking constantly, until it reaches 165°F (75°C) on an instant-read thermometer.

4. Once the base reaches 165°F (75°C), immediately remove it from the heat, fish out the vanilla pod, and pour the mixture back into the tall mixing vessel. Add the heavy cream and ghee and blend with a hand blender for 2 minutes to fully homogenize.

5. Pour the base through a fine-mesh sieve into the prepared ice bath to cool. Whisk in the kala namak (if using), adding a little more at a time until the desired flavor is achieved. Remember that the final flavor of the ice cream will be muted once frozen.

6. Once completely cool, transfer to an airtight container and refrigerate for at least 12 hours and up to 3 days.

For the base

½ cup + 1 teaspoon (105 g) granulated sugar

1 tablespoon + ½ teaspoon (8 g) nonfat dry milk powder

½ teaspoon (2 g) tara gum (optional; see page 24)

½ cup (70 g) glucose powder

1 cup + 2 tablespoons (280 g) whole milk

3½ tablespoons + 1 teaspoon (75 g) sweetened condensed milk

135 grams egg yolks (from about 8 large eggs)

1 vanilla bean, split lengthwise

¾ cup + 3½ tablespoons (225 g) heavy cream

1 tablespoon + 1½ teaspoons (20 g) ghee

Heaping ¼ teaspoon (1.5 g) kala namak (Indian black salt), plus more to taste (optional)

For the Nanaimo crust

3¼ ounces (90 g) semisweet chocolate

2 tablespoons (40 g) corn syrup

⅓ cup + 1 tablespoon (90 g) whole milk

¾ cup + ½ tablespoon (180 g) heavy cream

½ teaspoon (1 g) agar-agar powder

½ cup (60 g) graham cracker crumbs

½ cup (80 g) toasted coconut

½ cup (60 g) slivered almonds

For the ice cream bars

Dark Chocolate Freckles (page 279)

Flaky sea salt, for sprinkling

Method continued on next page

7. **Churn the ice cream:** When ready to begin, line two metal loaf pans with wax or parchment paper (see page 45). (Alternatively, you can use silicone loaf pans.) Place the loaf pans in the freezer to chill. Quickly blend the ice cream base once more with a hand blender or whisk before pouring it into an ice cream machine. Churn the ice cream until it reaches the texture of very stiff soft-serve and the surface looks dry, about 25°F (-5°C) or colder on a thermometer gun.

8. Divide the ice cream evenly between the chilled loaf pans. Press a piece of wax paper directly on top of the ice creams and place them in the freezer while preparing the crust.

9. **Make the nanaimo crust:** Place the dark chocolate in a small heatproof bowl. In a small saucepan, bring the corn syrup, milk, heavy cream, and agar-agar to a boil. Remove the mixture from the heat and pour it into the bowl over the chocolate. Let the mixture sit for 1 minute, then using a whisk or flexible spatula, stir the mixture until all the chocolate has melted. Let the chocolate cool to room temperature.

10. Stir in the graham cracker crumbs, toasted coconut, and slivered almonds. Allow the mixture to cool.

11. Take the ice cream pans out of the freezer and spread the chocolate mixture evenly on top of each pan. Be sure to cover the top of the ice cream completely. Return the pans to the freezer and let the ice cream harden completely, 6 to 8 hours.

12. **Make the ice cream bars:** Line a small baking sheet with parchment or wax paper. Take one loaf pan out of the freezer (leave the other pan in). Carefully unmold the ice cream from the pan onto a cutting board, with the crust-side down. Working quickly, slice the ice cream block crosswise into 4 slices. Place the slices on the parchment-lined baking sheet and return them to the freezer. Repeat with the second loaf pan.

13. Make the dark chocolate freckles as directed. Transfer the chocolate to a tall mixing vessel and allow it to temper to 80°F (25°C).

14. Working with one ice cream bar at a time (leaving the others in the freezer), coat the bar completely in the chocolate by picking up the container of chocolate with one hand and tilting it at a 45-degree angle (to get a deeper amount of chocolate to dip into) and use a fork in the other hand to pierce the ice cream bar and dip it in the coating to fully cover it. Working quickly before the coating hardens, sprinkle the top of the ice cream bar with sea salt, then return it to the lined baking sheet in the freezer.

15. Once the chocolate coating has hardened, individually wrap each Nanaimo bar in plastic wrap until ready to serve.

NOTE: The ice cream bars must be extremely cold and hardened when dipping. If not cold enough during dipping, any melting ice cream can break the emulsion of the liquid chocolate. This may be very difficult to achieve with a home freezer if you live in a warmer climate. Instead, I urge you to use the quick-freezing method using dry ice (see Blast Freezing, page 45).

CHAPTER 5

choc

olate

Don't hate me for this confession: I'm not a chocolate person. As I've grown older, chocolate has slid into last place when it comes to my pick of ice cream flavors. But maybe this chocolate ambivalence gives me a unique advantage: I'm always exploring new and innovative ways to use chocolate in ice cream.

NAMELAKA CHOCOLATE

Makes 1 quart (1 liter)

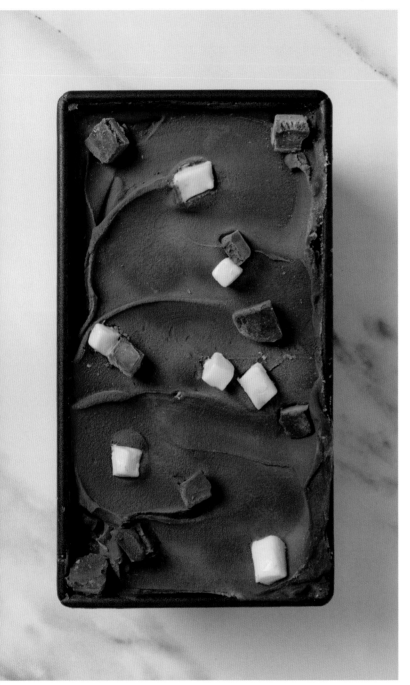

For the base

¼ cup + 2½ tablespoons (40 g) cocoa powder

¼ cup (60 g) boiling water

½ cup + 2½ tablespoons (130 g) granulated sugar

½ cup + 3 tablespoons (100 g) glucose powder

½ teaspoon (2 g) tara gum (optional; see page 24)

Scant ¾ teaspoon (3 g) lecithin (optional)

1½ cups + ½ tablespoon (375 g) whole milk

3½ ounces (100 g) dark chocolate (70% cacao or greater), coarsely chopped

1 cup + 1½ tablespoons (250 g) heavy cream

For the ice cream

½ cup (110 g) White Chocolate Namelaka Cubes (page 278)

½ cup (110 g) Milk Chocolate Namelaka Cubes (page 278)

½ cup (110 g) Dark Chocolate Namelaka Cubes (page 278)

This ice cream is my answer to the kind of indulgent fudgy, chunky, American-style chocolate ice creams I can't seem to enjoy. Bittersweet chocolate ice cream is contrasted with surprise cubes of soft and silky white chocolate, milk chocolate, and dark chocolate namelaka cubes. Namelaka—Japanese for *smooth*—is a sort of dense yet subtly sweet mousse-like crémeux that melts in your mouth.

1. Prepare an ice bath (see page 39).

2. **Make the base:** In a small bowl, whisk together the cocoa and boiling water to dissolve and set aside.

3. In another small bowl, whisk together the sugar, glucose powder, tara gum (if using), and lecithin. In a tall cylindrical 1½-quart (1.5 liter) mixing vessel, blend one-quarter of the milk and the dry ingredients together with a hand blender to dissolve all the solids. Add the remaining milk and blend again to combine.

4. Pour the mixture into a small saucepan (set the tall mixing vessel aside) and cook over medium-low heat, whisking constantly, until it reaches 165°F (75°C) on an instant-read thermometer. Meanwhile, place the cocoa paste and chopped dark chocolate into the reserved tall mixing vessel.

5. Once the base reaches 165°F (75°C), immediately remove it from the heat and pour it back into the tall mixing vessel with the chocolate. Blend the base to dissolve the chocolate. Add the heavy cream and blend for 2 minutes to fully homogenize.

6. Pour the base through a fine-mesh sieve into the prepared ice bath to cool. Once completely cooled, transfer the base to an airtight container and refrigerate for at least 12 hours and up to 3 days.

7. **Churn the ice cream:** When ready to make the ice cream, place a loaf pan and the namelaka cubes in the freezer to chill. Quickly blend the chilled base once more with a hand blender or whisk before transferring it to an ice cream machine. Churn the ice cream until it reaches the texture of very stiff soft-serve and the surface looks dry, about 25°F (–5°C) or colder on a thermometer gun.

8. Spread half of the ice cream into the chilled loaf pan. Place half of the namelaka cubes evenly on top of the ice cream. Repeat the layering process once more. Immediately place the ice cream into the freezer for 15 minutes to firm it up.

9. Using a spatula, fold the ice cream to evenly distribute the namelaka cubes throughout the pan. Three or four folds should be sufficient.

10. Press a piece of wax paper directly on top of the ice cream and freeze for at least 4 hours before serving.

ABUELITA MALTED CRUNCH

Makes about 1 quart (1 liter)

This flavor is made from childhood memories. My brother's first job was as an ice cream scooper at Thrifty's. After school my mother would often bring us to visit him at work. My Thrifty flavor of choice (and apparently that of many others who grew up in Southern California) was Chocolate Malted Krunch. It's a malted milk chocolate ice cream flecked with darker chocolate and dotted with tiny, crunchy malt balls. In an unrelated memory, I begged my mom for a box of powdered hot chocolate at the grocery store. She shook her head in disapproval: "That's not hot chocolate." We drove to a Mexican market, and she took a hexagonal box off the shelf with a photo of someone's grandma on it. "This! This is hot chocolate." It was the closest thing she had found to tablea—the kind of drinking chocolate she grew up with in the Philippines, made of pure ground cacao, raw sugar, and spicy cinnamon. So I re-created a milky chocolate ice cream that reminds me so much of the only kind of hot chocolate I've ever known and the malted crunch flavor I loved as a kid.

For the base

2 ½ tablespoons (15 g) cocoa powder

2 tablespoons (30 g) boiling water

3 tablespoons + 2 ½ teaspoons (45 g) malted milk powder

1 tablespoon (6 g) ground cinnamon

½ cup (100 g) granulated sugar

¼ cup + 1 ½ teaspoons (40 g) glucose powder

½ teaspoon (2 g) tara gum (optional; see page 24)

Scant ¾ teaspoon (3 g) lecithin (optional)

1 ¼ cups + 1 tablespoon (320 g) whole milk

3 ½ tablespoons (70 g) sweetened condensed milk

1 ½ ounces (40 g) Mexican tablet chocolate, such as Abuelita, chopped

1 ½ cups (350 g) heavy cream

For the ice cream

Dark Chocolate Freckles (page 279), tempered to 80°F (25°C)

1 ½ cups (150 g) Malted Crunch (page 272)

1. **Make the base:** In a small heatproof bowl, stir the cocoa and boiling water together to make a paste. Set aside.

2. Prepare an ice bath (see page 39).

3. In a small bowl, whisk together the malted milk powder, cinnamon, granulated sugar, glucose powder, tara gum (if using), and lecithin (if using). In a tall cylindrical 1½-quart (1.5 liter) mixing vessel, blend the milk and condensed milk together with a hand blender. Add the dry ingredients and blend once more to thoroughly dissolve all the solids.

4. Pour the mixture into a small saucepan and cook over medium-low heat, whisking constantly, until it reaches 165°F (75°C) on an instant-read thermometer. Meanwhile, place the cocoa paste and chopped Mexican tablet chocolate into the tall mixing vessel.

5. Once the base reaches 165°F (75°C), immediately remove it from the heat and pour it back into the tall mixing vessel containing the cocoa paste and chocolate. Blend with a hand blender to melt the chocolate, then add the heavy cream. Blend for 2 minutes to fully homogenize.

6. Pour the base through a fine-mesh sieve into the prepared ice bath to cool. Once completely cool, transfer to an airtight container and refrigerate for at least 12 hours and up to 3 days.

7. **Churn the ice cream:** When ready to begin, place a loaf pan in the freezer to chill. Quickly blend the chilled base once more with a hand blender or whisk before pouring it into an ice cream machine. Churn the ice cream until it reaches the texture of very stiff soft-serve and begins to look drier, about 25°F (−5°C) or colder on a thermometer gun. Pour in the dark chocolate to create freckles.

8. Spread half of the ice cream into the bottom of the chilled loaf pan. Sprinkle half of the malted crunch on top. Repeat the layering process once more. Immediately place the ice cream into the freezer for 15 minutes to firm it up. Using a spatula, gently fold the ice cream to mix in the malted crunch. Three or four folds should be sufficient.

9. Press a piece of wax paper directly on top of the ice cream and freeze for at least 4 hours before serving.

CARAMELIZED MILK CHOCOLATE & PLANTAIN BRITTLE

Makes about 1 quart (1 liter)

Silky milk chocolate ice cream made with caramelized milk gives this flavor an unexpected umami-butter finish with notes of toffee and burnt cream. The silkiness is interrupted with shards of crispy plantains candied in dulce de leche brittle.

For the caramelized dairy

½ cup (100 g) granulated sugar

2 tablespoons + ½ teaspoon (15 g) nonfat dry milk powder

½ teaspoon (2 g) baking soda

1½ cups + 1½ teaspoons (375 g) whole milk

1¼ cups + 3 tablespoons (330 g) heavy cream

3½ tablespoons + 1 teaspoon (75 g) sweetened condensed milk

For the base

2 tablespoons (30 g) boiling water

2½ tablespoons (15 g) cocoa powder

½ teaspoon (1 g) salt

½ cup + 1 tablespoon (80 g) glucose powder

½ teaspoon (2 g) tara gum (optional; see page 24)

Scant ¾ teaspoon (3 g) lecithin (optional)

1 ounce (30 g) semisweet chocolate, chopped

For the plantain brittle

5 ounces (140 g) sweet plantain chips

Vegetable oil, for greasing

½ cup (100 g) granulated sugar

1 tablespoon (15 g) unsalted butter

⅓ cup (100 g) sweetened condensed milk

¼ teaspoon salt

1. **Caramelize the dairy:** In a tall cylindrical 1½-quart (1.5 liter) mixing vessel, mix the sugar, dry milk powder, and baking soda together. Pour in one-quarter of the milk and blend with a hand blender to dissolve. Add the remaining milk, the heavy cream, and condensed milk and blend once more to combine. Split the mixture between two to three canning jars that will fit into the basket or steamer rack of your pressure cooker, lightly closing them so that the lids are just fingertip tight. Make sure the glass of the jars is not touching the walls of the pressure cooker at all. Cook with 1 inch of water on high pressure for 2½ hours. Let the pressure naturally dissipate, and allow the jars to cool completely before handling, about 1 hour. The mixture should have caramelized into a dark golden brown color.

2. Prepare an ice bath (see page 39).

3. **Make the base:** In a small heatproof bowl, stir together the boiling water and cocoa powder to make a paste. Set aside.

4. In a small bowl, whisk the salt, glucose powder, tara gum (if using), and lecithin (if using) together. In a tall cylindrical 1½-quart (1.5 liter) mixing vessel, blend one-quarter of the caramelized dairy and the dry ingredients with a hand blender to thoroughly dissolve all the solids. Add the remaining caramelized dairy and blend again to combine.

Method continued on next page

5. Pour the mixture into a medium saucepan and cook over medium-low heat, whisking constantly, until it reaches 165°F (75°C) on an instant-read thermometer. Meanwhile, place the cocoa paste and chopped semisweet chocolate into the tall mixing vessel.

6. Once the base reaches 165°F (75°C), immediately remove from the heat and pour it back into the tall mixing vessel. Blend with a hand blender for 2 minutes to fully homogenize.

7. Pour the base through a fine-mesh sieve into the prepared ice bath to cool. Once completely cool, transfer to an airtight container and refrigerate for at least 12 hours and up to 3 days.

8. **Make the plantain brittle:** Using your hands or a rolling pin, lightly crush the sweet plantain chips in their bag, into ¼- to ½-inch (.75 to 1.25 cm) pieces. Set aside.

9. Line a baking sheet with parchment and brush the parchment liberally with oil.

10. In a medium saucepan, melt the sugar over medium heat. Continue heating until the sugar reaches a dark amber color and begins to smoke. Immediately add the butter, condensed milk, and salt. Whisk to combine. Don't worry if the mixture looks nonuniform and partly burned; if you continue whisking, it should all come together into a golden brown mixture. Let the caramel come to a boil and continue whisking for 30 seconds.

11. Remove the caramel from the heat and immediately stir in the crushed plantain chips with a wooden spoon or heatproof spatula, stirring to coat the plantain chips evenly.

12. Spread the mixture out on the prepared baking sheet. As the brittle cools, gently separate it into small pieces. Allow the brittle to cool completely, then transfer to an airtight container and store in a cool and dry place for up to 3 days. Ensure that the pieces have not melted back together before using. If so, gently break them apart with your hands again.

13. **Churn the ice cream:** When ready to begin, place a loaf pan in the freezer along with the plantain brittle to chill. Quickly blend the chilled base once more with a hand blender or whisk before pouring it into an ice cream machine. Churn the ice cream until it reaches the texture of very stiff soft-serve and the surface looks dry, about 25°F (−5°C) or colder on a thermometer gun.

14. Spread half of the ice cream onto the bottom of the chilled loaf pan. Sprinkle half of the plantain brittle on top. Repeat this layering process once more. Immediately place the ice cream into the freezer for 15 minutes to firm it up. Using a spatula, gently fold the ice cream to evenly distribute the mix-ins throughout. Three or four folds should be sufficient.

15. Press a piece of wax paper directly on top of the ice cream and freeze for at least 4 hours before serving.

RUBY CHOCOLATE

Makes 1 quart (1 liter)

1 tablespoon (8 g) natural cocoa powder (see Note)

2 tablespoons + 1½ teaspoons (15 g) powdered freeze-dried berries (raspberry, strawberry, or a combination)

2 tablespoons (30 g) boiling water

¼ cup + 2½ teaspoons (60 g) granulated sugar

3 tablespoons + 1 teaspoon (30 g) glucose powder

½ teaspoon (2 g) tara gum (optional; see page 24)

Scant ¾ teaspoon (3 g) lecithin (optional)

1¾ cups (425 g) whole milk

3½ tablespoons (70 g) sweetened condensed milk

5½ ounces (155 g) ruby chocolate, coarsely chopped

1 cup + 1½ tablespoons (250 g) heavy cream

Citric acid

1 teaspoon (5 g) natural pink food coloring (optional)

NOTE: The bright, acidic flavor of ruby chocolate is best accented with natural cocoa powder instead of dark Dutch process. Its lighter color also helps to keep the ice cream "ruby" colored.

Ruby chocolate is made from fruity "ruby cacao beans." Unlike traditional chocolate, the process for making ruby chocolate doesn't include fermentation; instead, it's treated with citric acid to maintain its bright pink color. The result is a ruby-hued chocolate that tastes somewhere between milk and white chocolate, but with berry-like tangy notes, which are bolstered by a touch of freeze-dried berry powder in this recipe.

1. In a small bowl, combine the cocoa powder and freeze-dried berry powder. Pour the boiling water over the powders and whisk to dissolve. Set the cocoa-berry paste aside.

2. Prepare an ice bath (see page 39).

3. In a small bowl, whisk together the sugar, glucose powder, tara gum (if using), and lecithin (if using). In a tall cylindrical 1½-quart (1.5 liter) mixing vessel, blend the milk and condensed milk with a hand blender. Add the dry ingredients and blend again to dissolve all the solids.

4. Pour the mixture into a small saucepan and cook over medium-low heat, whisking constantly, until it reaches 165°F (75°C) on an instant-read thermometer. Meanwhile, place the cocoa-berry paste and ruby chocolate into the tall mixing vessel.

5. Once the base reaches 165°F (75°C), immediately remove it from the heat and pour it back into the tall mixing vessel. Blend the base to dissolve the chocolate. Add the heavy cream and blend for 2 minutes to fully homogenize.

6. Pour the base through a fine-mesh sieve into the prepared ice bath to cool. Once completely cool, taste and season with citric acid if needed. The flavor should be like milk chocolate, but with a slightly bright tangy finish. Stir in the food coloring (if using). Transfer the base to an airtight container and refrigerate for at least 12 hours and up to 3 days.

7. **Churn the ice cream:** When ready to begin, place a loaf pan in the freezer to chill. Quickly blend the ice cream base once more with a hand blender or whisk before pouring it into an ice cream machine.

Churn the ice cream until it reaches the texture of very stiff soft-serve and the surface looks dry, about 25°F (-5°C) or colder on a thermometer gun.

8. Transfer the ice cream mixture to the chilled loaf pan. Press a piece of wax paper directly on top of the ice cream and freeze for at least 4 hours before serving.

EARL GREY MILK CHOCOLATE

Makes about 1 quart (1 liter)

Immensely milky chocolate ice cream is complemented here with Earl Grey's malty notes of black tea and distinctly citrusy-floral bergamot. I like to describe the flavor as a toss-up of milk tea, chocolate milk, and "Fruity Pebbles milk."

2 tablespoons (12 g) cocoa powder

2 tablespoons (30 g) boiling water

3½ tablespoons (25 g) nonfat dry milk powder

½ cup (100 g) granulated sugar

⅓ cup + 1 teaspoon (50 g) glucose powder

½ teaspoon (2 g) tara gum (optional; see page 24)

Scant ¾ teaspoon (3 g) lecithin (optional)

3½ tablespoons (70 g) sweetened condensed milk

1½ cups + 3 tablespoons (350 g) whole milk

1½ ounces (40 g) semisweet chocolate, chopped

1¼ cups + 2½ tablespoons (325 g) heavy cream

6 tablespoons (30 g) loose Earl Grey tea leaves

1. In a small heatproof bowl, stir together the cocoa powder and boiling water to make a paste. Set aside.

2. Prepare an ice bath (see page 39).

3. In a small bowl, whisk together the milk powder, sugar, glucose powder, tara gum (if using), and lecithin (if using). In a tall cylindrical 1½-quart (1.5 liter) mixing vessel, blend the condensed milk and whole milk together with a hand blender. Add the dry ingredients and blend once more thoroughly to dissolve all the solids.

4. Pour the mixture into a small saucepan and cook over medium-low heat, whisking constantly, until it reaches 165°F (75°C) on an instant-read thermometer. Meanwhile, place the cocoa paste and chopped semisweet chocolate into the mixing vessel.

5. Once the base reaches 165°F (75°C), immediately remove it from the heat and pour it back into the tall mixing vessel. Blend to dissolve the chocolate, then add the heavy cream. Blend again for 2 minutes to fully homogenize.

6. Strain the base through a fine-mesh sieve into the prepared ice bath. Stir in the Earl Grey tea leaves. Once the base is completely cool, transfer to an airtight container and refrigerate for at least 12 hours and up to 3 days.

7. **Churn the ice cream:** When ready to begin, place a loaf pan in the freezer to chill. Quickly blend the chilled base once more with a hand blender or whisk before pouring it through a fine-mesh sieve into an ice cream machine. Churn the ice cream until it reaches the texture of very stiff soft-serve and the surface looks dry, about 25°F (−5°C) or colder on a thermometer gun.

8. Transfer the ice cream mixture to the chilled loaf pan. Press a piece of wax paper directly on top of the ice cream and freeze for at least 4 hours before serving.

CHAPTER 6

cara

mel-y

Caramel is the sweet, buttery, decadent flavor that sends our taste buds into overdrive. It's as alluring as honey, but with a flavor so much more complex. Its richness and depth of flavor are due to the interplay of various chemical reactions. Sugars and proteins in dairy undergo the Maillard reaction, resulting in an array of compounds: notes of vanilla, nuttiness, smokiness, and a subtle hint of saltiness. Caramel is a flavor phenomenon across many cuisines, used in different ways. This chapter is dedicated to exploring the flavor of caramel beyond just sugar, butter, and salt.

SALTY GULA MELAKA CARAMEL

Makes about 1 quart (1 liter)

For the caramel

¼ cup + 2 ½ teaspoons (60 g) granulated sugar

4½ ounces (130 g) gula melaka (see Note) or dark palm sugar

2 tablespoons (30 g) water

1 cup + 1½ tablespoons (250 g) heavy cream

½ cup + 2 tablespoons (135 g) coconut cream

⅛ teaspoon baking soda

For the base

1 tablespoon (15 g) granulated sugar

¼ cup + 1 tablespoon (35 g) nonfat dry milk powder

½ teaspoon (2 g) tara gum (optional; see page 24)

1¼ cups + 2 tablespoons (340 g) whole milk

50 grams egg yolks (from about 3 large eggs)

Salty element: ½ teaspoon (3 g) fine sea salt or scant ½ teaspoon (3 g) fish sauce, plus more to taste

NOTE: Real, pure gula melaka can be hard to find. Many producers dilute it with other sugars. When shopping in Southeast Asian supermarkets or online, the darker the sugar, the more authentic it is. In person, you can discern the quality by how aromatic it is (cane and palm sugar are almost scentless), and how crumbly it is (harder sugars indicate the use of palm sugar). If desperate, you can use the darkest palm sugar you can find.

In Southeast Asia, gula melaka is considered the ultimate sugar. Made from the sap of flowers from the coconut palm, it's fragrant with notes of smoke, coffee, dark dried fruit, and hints of coconut. The flavor and scent nuances can range vastly depending on the growing conditions and time of harvest. Needless to say, it makes an otherworldly caramel ice cream.

1. **Make the caramel:** In a medium saucepan, melt the granulated sugar over medium-high heat. Do not stir; pick up the pot and swirl it around occasionally as it melts. Continue heating until the sugar caramelizes, 8 to 10 minutes. Once the sugar approaches 365°F (185°C) on an instant-read thermometer, keep a very close eye on it. As soon as the temperature hits 375°F (190°C), turn off the heat and add the gula melaka, water, heavy cream, coconut cream, and baking soda; the mixture will violently bubble up and create a lot of steam. Whisk to dissolve the caramel completely. Let the caramel cool to a warm but liquid consistency before proceeding to the next step.

2. Prepare an ice bath (see page 39).

3. **Make the base:** In a small bowl, whisk together the granulated sugar, dry milk powder, and tara gum (if using). In a tall cylindrical 1½-quart (1.5 liter) mixing vessel, blend the milk and egg yolks together with a hand blender. Add the dry ingredients and blend once more to thoroughly dissolve all the solids.

4. Pour the mixture into the saucepan containing the caramel and return the pot to medium-low heat. Cook, whisking constantly, until the mixture reaches 165°F (75°C) on an instant-read thermometer.

5. Once the base reaches 165°F (75°C), immediately remove from the heat and pour it back into the tall mixing vessel. Blend the base with a hand blender for 2 minutes to fully homogenize.

6. Pour the base through a fine-mesh sieve into the prepared ice bath to cool. Season the base with a salty element of your choice. It should taste sweet and smoky, but balanced with a little salinity after seasoning.

7. Once completely cool, transfer the base to an airtight container and refrigerate for at least 12 hours and up to 3 days.

8. **Churn the ice cream:** When ready to begin, place a loaf pan in the freezer to chill. Quickly blend the chilled base once more with a hand blender or whisk before pouring it into an ice cream machine. Churn the ice cream until it reaches the texture of very stiff soft-serve and the surface looks dry, about 25°F (-5°C) or colder on a thermometer gun.

9. Transfer the ice cream mixture to the chilled loaf pan. Press a piece of wax paper directly on top of the ice cream and freeze for at least 4 hours before serving.

CARAMELIZED
HONEY HOJICHA

Makes about 1 quart (1 liter)

For the caramelized honey

¼ cup + 2 tablespoons (125 g) honey

1 tablespoon (15 g) water

1½ cups (350 g) heavy cream

¼ teaspoon (1 g) baking soda

For the base

¼ cup + 1 tablespoon (35 g) nonfat dry milk powder

2 tablespoons + ½ teaspoon (20 g) glucose powder

½ teaspoon (2 g) tara gum (optional; see page 24)

1¾ cups + 1½ tablespoons (450 g) whole milk

85 grams egg yolks (from about 5 large eggs)

½ cup (25 g) hojicha tea leaves

I bought my very first home ice cream machine just a few months before tinkering with the idea of opening an ice cream shop, and the machine was christened with this flavor. I was inspired by J. Kenji Lopez-Alt's Burnt Honey Hojicha on the Serious Eats website. Much like salted caramel, the bitterness from the burnt honey and roasted tea cuts through the richness of a high-butterfat custard base, making it an addictive flavor. We opened Wanderlust Creamery with this on the menu—and it was my personal recommendation to every single customer I served. Honey has quite a high AFP (anti-freezing power), so to maximize the burnt honey flavor without adding too much of it, I push the caramelization past a golden brown color.

1. **Make the caramelized honey:** In a medium saucepan, heat the honey over medium-high heat until it begins to boil and bubble, 3 to 4 minutes. As soon as the temperature hits 280°F (140°C) on an instant-read thermometer, remove from the heat and add the water, heavy cream, and baking soda; the mixture will violently bubble up and create a lot of steam. Whisk to dissolve the honey completely. Let the caramelized honey cool to a warm but liquid consistency before proceeding to the next step.

2. Prepare an ice bath (see page 39).

3. **Make the base:** In a small bowl, whisk together the dry milk powder, glucose powder, and tara gum (if using).

4. Whisk the milk into the caramelized honey, then pour the mixture into a tall 1½-quart (1.5 liter) mixing vessel. Add the egg yolks and blend with a hand blender. Add the dry ingredients and blend again to thoroughly dissolve all the solids.

5. Pour the mixture back into the saucepan and return to medium-low heat. Cook, whisking constantly, until the mixture reaches 165°F (75°C) on an instant-read thermometer.

6. Once the base reaches 165°F (75°C), immediately remove from the heat and pour it back into the tall mixing vessel; blend with a hand blender for 2 minutes to fully homogenize.

7. Pour the base through a fine-mesh sieve into the prepared ice bath. Stir in the hojicha tea leaves and allow the base to cool.

8. Once completely cool, transfer the base (along with the tea leaves) to an airtight container and refrigerate for at least 12 hours and up to 3 days.

9. **Churn the ice cream:** When ready to begin, place a loaf pan in the freezer to chill. Quickly blend the chilled base once more with a hand blender or whisk before straining it into an ice cream machine. Churn the ice cream until it reaches the texture of very stiff soft-serve and the surface looks dry, about 25°F (−5°C) or colder on a thermometer gun.

10. Transfer the ice cream mixture to the chilled loaf pan. Press a piece of wax paper directly on top of the ice cream and freeze for at least 4 hours before serving.

PRETZEL & RÚGBRAUÐ

Makes about 1 quart (1 liter)

This ice cream looks unassuming but will smack you with smoke, malt, toffee, and the unmistakable flavor of pretzel—all at the same time. It was a staple at Wanderlust Creamery for years, until the kitchen staff had a confession for me: They hated making it. A pretzel's distinct flavor comes from a specific Maillard reaction of lye coating on its exterior. Wash it off in a bath of hot milk, and the milk picks up the defining flavor of pretzel, which then goes into the ice cream base. The result is a salty caramel-like flavor with a cult following, but not without painstaking labor. The milk is squeezed out from the soaked pretzels through a nut milk bag. The kitchen staff would sooner volunteer to take out the trash, scrub the mop sink, or detail the walk-in fridge than be assigned to pretzel-wringing for the day. Making this at scale, forty gallons at a time, was a dreaded chore. But for a quart at home—the ~~juice~~ cream is worth the squeeze.

The other flavor component in this ice cream comes from *rúgbrauð*, an Icelandic rye bread. It's dense, hearty, and sweet with raisin-y notes of honey and molasses. Ubiquitous in Icelandic cuisine, it's also a common ice cream flavor found in Reykjavik. Because the bread is not available stateside, the ice cream below uses a crunchy mixture of pure rye flour, sugar, and butter to imitate the flavor of caramelized rúgbrauð crumbs.

For the pretzel milk

3¾ cups (205 g) mini twist pretzels

3¾ cups + 2 tablespoons (950 g) whole milk

1¼ cups (300 g) water

For the base

2½ tablespoons (20 g) nonfat dry milk powder

½ cup + 1 tablespoon (110 g) granulated sugar

¼ cup + 1½ teaspoons (40 g) glucose powder

½ teaspoon (2 g) tara gum (optional; see page 24)

3½ tablespoons (70 g) sweetened condensed milk

50 grams egg yolks (from about 3 large eggs)

1½ cups (350 g) heavy cream

For the caramelized rúgbrauð crumbs

¼ cup + 2 tablespoons (75 g) granulated sugar

½ cup + 1 tablespoon (70 g) rye flour

2 tablespoons (30 g) unsalted butter

1. **Make the pretzel milk:** Preheat the oven to 400°F (200°C).

2. Spread the pretzels on a baking sheet and toast them until they darken in color to a deep brown, 5 to 8 minutes.

3. Meanwhile, in a saucepan, combine the milk and water and bring to a simmer over medium-low heat.

4. Carefully transfer the hot toasted pretzels to a large heatproof bowl or container. Pour the hot milk and water over the pretzels. Both the toasted pretzels and milk must be hot when combined. Allow the mixture to steep for 10 minutes. Once steeped, strain the mixture through a fine-mesh sieve, pushing down on the pretzels in the sieve to fully extract all the liquid. Transfer the pretzels to a nut-milk bag or cheesecloth and squeeze as much liquid as you can from the soaked pretzels into the bowl of pretzel milk. Discard the pretzels and set the milk aside.

5. Prepare an ice bath (see page 39).

6. **Make the base:** In a small bowl, whisk together

the milk powder, sugar, glucose, and tara gum (if using). In a tall cylindrical 1½-quart (1.5 liter) mixing vessel, blend the pretzel milk, condensed milk, and egg yolks together with a hand blender. Add the dry ingredients and blend thoroughly to dissolve all the solids.

7. Pour the mixture into a small saucepan and cook over medium-low heat, whisking constantly, until it reaches 165°F (75°C) on an instant-read thermometer.

8. Once the base reaches 165°F (75°C), immediately remove from the heat and pour it back into the tall mixing vessel. Add the heavy cream and blend with a hand blender for 2 minutes to fully homogenize.

9. Pour the base through a fine-mesh sieve into the prepared ice bath to cool. Once completely cool, transfer to an airtight container and refrigerate for at least 12 hours and up to 3 days.

10. **Meanwhile, make the caramelized rúgbrauð crumbs:** Line a baking sheet with wax or parchment paper and set near the stove.

11. In a large skillet, melt the sugar over medium-high heat. When most of the

sugar has melted, about 1½ minutes, reduce the heat to low. Using a fork, gradually stir in the rye flour, adding it one-third at a time and mixing well so that it is evenly incorporated into the sugar, but forming "crumbs."

12. Once all of the mixture has combined into a loose crumble, stir in the butter, working the fork to break up the mixture into finer crumbs. The final mixture should have crumbs no larger than ⅛ inch (3 mm). Remove from the heat and continue to break up the mixture until hardened. Turn out the crumbs onto the prepared baking sheet to cool. Pulse in a food processor to break up any large pieces, if necessary. Store at room temperature in an airtight container for up to 1 week. When ready to make the ice cream, transfer the crumbs to the freezer to chill.

13. **Churn the ice cream:** When ready to begin, place a loaf pan in the freezer to chill. Quickly blend the chilled base once more with a hand blender or whisk before pouring it into an ice cream machine. Churn the ice cream until it reaches the texture of very stiff soft-serve and the surface looks dry, about 25°F (−5°C) or colder on a thermometer gun.

Add the caramelized rúg-brauð crumbs in the last few seconds of churning.

14. Transfer the ice cream to the chilled loaf pan. Press a piece of wax paper directly on top of the ice cream and freeze for at least 4 hours before serving.

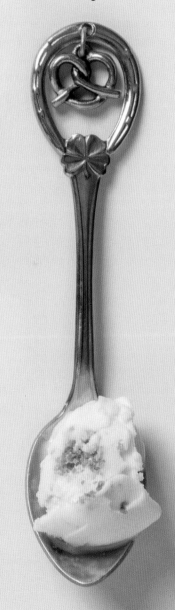

REAL DULCE DE LECHE

Unlike regular caramel, which gets its color and flavor from just burnt sugar, dulce de leche, often explained as "caramelized milk," has a more complex and buttery flavor that comes from the twofold browning: both the caramelization of sugar and Maillard reaction of proteins in the dairy. No matter what I've tried, dulce de leche ice cream recipes that utilize a can of dulce de leche itself never end up tasting as good as it does in South America. The dulce de leche gets diluted with so much white milk and cream that the notes of caramelization get watered down. Later I learned from a friend, Tyler George, a gelato master himself, how many Argentinian heladerías make the country's most beloved ice cream flavor. In large vats that continuously stir, all the dairy and sugar for an ice cream base are cooked slowly overnight until it turns a beautiful golden color. After that, any remaining ingredients (like egg yolks and stabilizer) are added. This way, every single milky molecule in the entire base that can be browned gets browned. This same process can be done at home with a pressure cooker. Bringing up the pH of the dairy via baking soda will encourage even more browning.

For the caramelized dairy

½ cup + 1½ tablespoons (120 g) granulated sugar

2 tablespoons + ½ teaspoon (15 g) nonfat dry milk powder

Scant ¾ teaspoon (3.5 g) baking soda

1¾ cups + 1½ tablespoons (450 g) whole milk

1¼ cups + 3½ tablespoons (340 g) heavy cream

¼ cup (80 g) sweetened condensed milk

For the base

¼ teaspoon (1.5 g) fine sea salt

¼ cup + 1½ teaspoons (40 g) glucose powder

½ teaspoon (2 g) tara gum (optional; see page 24)

70 grams egg yolks (from about 4 large eggs)

For the ice cream

½ cup + 2 tablespoons (200 g) dulce de leche (about ½ can)

NOTE: The sweetness of the ice cream base has been toned down a smidge to compensate for the ribbons of dulce de leche that will be swirled throughout the finished ice cream. If making this recipe without the swirl, add 1 teaspoon (5 g) of sugar to the base.

VARIATION: For cajeta ice cream, an earthy, tangier variation of dulce de leche from Mexico made with goat milk, substitute goat milk for the whole milk called for when caramelizing the dairy.

1. **Caramelize the dairy:**
In a tall cylindrical 1½-quart (1.5 liter) mixing vessel, mix the sugar, dry milk powder, and baking soda. Pour in one-quarter of the whole milk and blend with a hand blender to dissolve. Add the remaining milk, the heavy cream, and condensed milk and blend once more to combine. Split the mixture among 2 to 3 canning jars that will fit into the basket or steamer rack of your pressure cooker, lightly closing them so that the lids are just fingertip tight. Make sure the glass of the jars is not touching the walls of the pressure cooker at all. Add 1 inch (2.5 cm) of water, seal, and cook at high pressure for 2½ hours.

2. Let the pressure naturally dissipate and allow the jars to cool completely before handling, about 1 hour. The mixture should have caramelized into a dark golden brown color.

3. Prepare an ice bath (see page 39).

4. **Make the base:** In a small bowl, whisk the salt, glucose, and tara gum (if using) together. In a tall cylindrical 1½-quart (1.5 liter) mixing vessel, blend one-quarter of the caramelized dairy and egg yolks together with a hand blender. Add the dry ingredients and blend again to dissolve. Add the remaining caramelized dairy and blend once more to combine.

5. Pour the mixture into a medium saucepan and cook over medium-low heat, whisking constantly, until it reaches 165°F (75°C) on an instant-read thermometer.

6. Once the base reaches 165°F (75°C), immediately remove from the heat and pour it back into the tall mixing vessel. Blend with a hand blender for 2 minutes to fully homogenize.

7. Pour the base through a fine-mesh sieve into the prepared ice bath to cool. Once completely cool, transfer to an airtight container and refrigerate for at least 12 hours and up to 3 days.

8. **Churn the ice cream:**
When ready to make the ice cream, place a loaf pan in the freezer to chill. Quickly blend the chilled base once more with a hand blender or whisk before transferring to an ice cream machine. Churn the ice cream until it reaches the texture of very stiff soft-serve and the surface looks dry, about 25°F (−5°C) or colder on a thermometer gun.

9. Spread half of the ice cream onto the bottom of the chilled loaf pan. Spread half of the dulce de leche on top. Repeat this layering process once more. Immediately place the ice cream into the freezer for 15 minutes to firm it up.

10. Using a spatula, gently fold the ice cream and dulce de leche layers to create swirls. Three or four folds should be sufficient for visible ribbons throughout the pan; any more than that will overmix the dulce de leche into the ice cream base, which may affect freezing and final texture.

11. Press a piece of wax paper directly on top of the ice cream and freeze for at least 4 hours before serving.

ALFAJORES

Makes about 8 ice cream sandwiches

Much like the Oreo is to Americans, the alfajor is an iconic symbol of South America's culinary heritage. The cookie's origins trace back to medieval Arab cuisine: a shortbread made with honey, almonds, and spices, then filled with dates (much like modern-day ma'amoul). The Moors brought them to Spain, and the Spaniards then brought them to South America, where they would eventually be filled with dulce de leche instead of dates. Every bite reveals a symphony of textures, the tender shortbread giving way to the luscious caramelized milk jam. And each region adds its unique touch: In Argentina, the cookies are often fragrant with hints of lemon zest or coconut, or enrobed in chocolate. In Uruguay, a thinner, slightly crumblier biscuit is favored, allowing the dulce de leche to take the spotlight. In Peru, the alfajor boasts a more cake-like texture, with anise-scented shortbread and a dusting of powdered sugar. Here, an ice cream sandwich takes cues from the simpler Peruvian version.

Real Dulce de Leche (page 90)

Almond Shortbread (page 275), with changes (see step 2 below)

½ teaspoon ground anise

Powdered sugar, for dusting

1. After churning the dulce de leche ice cream, scoop it into 3-inch (7.5 cm) round silicone molds. Press a piece of wax paper directly on top of the ice cream and freeze for at least 6 hours before unmolding.

2. Meanwhile, make the shortbread dough, adding the anise to the dry ingredients. Roll out the dough between two sheets of parchment to a ½-inch (1.5 cm) thickness instead of pressing onto a sheet pan. Chill the dough in the refrigerator for 1 hour. Using a 3-inch (7.5 cm) round cookie cutter, cut the dough into rounds and bake as directed in the recipe.

3. To assemble, unmold the ice cream and place each round between 2 rounds of shortbread. Wrap each ice cream sandwich individually in plastic wrap before storing in the freezer. Allow the sandwiches to age in the freezer for at least 6 hours.

4. Temper the sandwiches at room temperature for 3 to 5 minutes before serving. Dust each sandwich with powdered sugar.

NOTE: Allowing the assembled ice cream sandwiches to age in the freezer for at least 6 hours ensures that the cookies soften by absorbing some moisture from the ice cream. Eating them freshly assembled may result in the ice cream sliding out between the hard cookies.

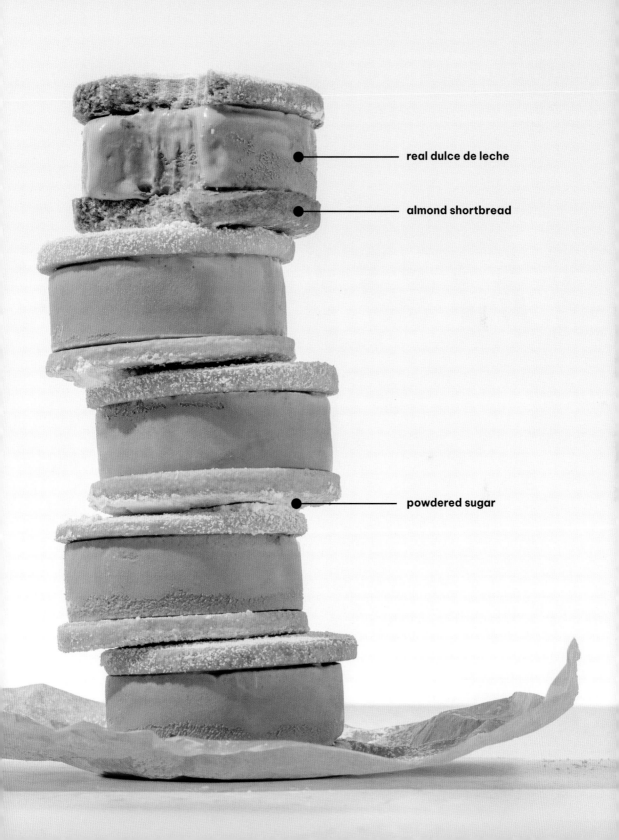

real dulce de leche

almond shortbread

powdered sugar

CHAPTER 7

berries
& tropic

At Wanderlust Creamery, the ice cream case can oftentimes lack a wide selection of fruit flavors. Maybe it's because my wanderlust has me pining for foreign or tropical fruits that aren't readily available locally. Or, perhaps, as a lover of all things creamy, I often forgo fruit-based ice creams for sorbets. When I think of what fruit ice cream should taste like, I imagine it

citrus
al fruit

bursting with brightness, acidity, and intensity of flavor—as close to eating the real thing as possible. It's not an easy feat to execute with milk and cream. And so I consider my fruit ice cream repertoire limited to a small collection of rarer fruit sorbets or ice cream recipes that allow the fruit to take the main stage.

YUZU CREAMSICLE

Makes about 2 quarts
(2 liters)

For the yuzu sorbet

¾ cup + 1 tablespoon (300 g)
Korean citron honey tea (see Tip)
or citron marmalade

2 ½ cups (600 g) water

3 ½ tablespoons (45 g) granulated
sugar, plus more to taste

¼ cup + 1 ¼ teaspoons (40 g)
glucose powder

Pinch of salt

1 teaspoon (3 g) Sorbet Stabilizer
(optional; page 33)

4 ½ tablespoons (40 g) inulin
(optional; see Note)

½ cup (120 ml) yuzu juice

⅛ teaspoon yuzu essential oil
or ¼ teaspoon fresh or dried
yuzu zest

Citric acid

For the "crème" base

Blank Base (page 48), made with
an additional 1 ¼ teaspoons (5 g)
granulated sugar

½ teaspoon (2 g) marshmallow
flavor extract or vanilla extract

NOTE: Inulin adds more body
and a creamier mouthfeel
to sorbets. If you prefer a
sorbet with a cleaner and more
refreshing meltdown, feel free to
leave it out.

TIP: Deceptively named, Korean
"citron honey tea" is made from
yuzu, not citron. It comes in jars
and looks just like marmalade,
and is sold as a concentrate
for making honey tea. As it's full
of yuzu rind, I use it to replace
most of the sugars in the recipe.
Another concentrated source
of yuzu flavor is yuzu essential
oil. Just a few drops powerfully
scent the entire base.

People go head over heels for this ice cream at Wanderlust Creamery. It's a seasonal flavor at shops because once word is out that it's in the ice cream case, people come and buy it by the pint to hoard and we can barely keep it in stock. Another reason I bring it around only occasionally is because yuzu juice is quite expensive and hard to source in the quantities needed to supply several scoop shops. But I'm about to let you in on a little secret I've discovered in my attempts to make this flavor at a food cost that won't send my business partner into panic mode. Virtually all of yuzu's defining flavor—the lovechild of a grapefruit/mandarin/lemon ménage à trois—is in its rind. Source as much flavor from its rind as you can, and the less yuzu juice you'll need. So much so that, dare I say, you can substitute lemon juice for some or all of the yuzu juice.

1. Prepare an ice bath (see page 39).

2. **Make the yuzu sorbet:** In a stand blender, process the citron honey tea and 1 cup (250 g) water into a completely smooth puree. Transfer the puree to another container and set aside.

3. In the same blender, blend the sugar, glucose powder, salt, stabilizer (if using), and inulin (if using) with the remaining 1½ cups (350 g) water on high until all the solids have completely dispersed.

4. Pour into a medium saucepan and cook over medium-high heat, whisking occasionally, until the temperature reaches 122°F (50°C) on an instant-read thermometer.

5. Remove from the heat and pour into the prepared ice bath to cool. Once the mixture has completely cooled, whisk in the yuzu juice and yuzu oil (or zest).

Using a refractometer (see page 37), measure the Brix of the base, verifying it is within the target range of 25 to 32 Brix. At this point, you can adjust the sweetness or tartness of the base with more sugar or citric acid, adding just ½ teaspoon of either at a time and rechecking the Brix after each addition to see if it's within range.

6. Transfer the sorbet to an airtight container and refrigerate for at least 12 hours and up to 2 days.

7. **Make the "crème" base:** Follow the directions for the blank base and add the extract in the last step of the recipe.

8. **Churn the "crème" base:** When ready to begin, place a loaf pan in the freezer to chill. Pour the crème base into an ice cream machine and churn until it reaches the texture of very stiff soft-serve and the surface looks dry, about

25°F (-5°C) or colder on a thermometer gun.

9. Spread the ice cream mixture into the chilled loaf pan and place in the freezer.

10. Scrape the ice cream machine clean (no need to wash it) and churn the yuzu sorbet until it reaches the texture of a stiff slushie, about 30°F (-1°C) or colder on a thermometer gun.

11. Spread the yuzu sorbet into the chilled loaf pan on top of the layer of crème ice cream. Immediately return the ice cream to the freezer for 15 minutes to firm it up.

12. Using a spatula, gently fold the ice cream layers to create visible swirls. Three or four folds should be sufficient.

13. Press a piece of wax paper directly on top of the ice cream and freeze for at least 4 hours before serving.

STRAWBERRIEST ICE CREAM

Makes about 1 quart (1 liter)

Strawberries are 92% water. Add too much to ice cream, and you'll end up with a watery base. One workaround that most recipes resort to is cooking the strawberries to reduce the water content . . . but that irks me. The taste of a cooked strawberry almost renders the idea of a peak season strawberry useless. This right here is the conundrum of strawberry ice cream. How do you get the most intense, unadulterated strawberry flavor into an ice cream without compromising the creaminess? My answers:

- Add freeze-dried strawberry. It's all fruit, no water. We replace some of the nonfat milk solids in this base with it.

- Maximize the strawberry flavor by removing some of its bland white interior.

- Last, a hack guarded by many chefs: Intensify the strawberry flavor with a dash of pink peppercorns. Yes, pink peppercorns, in an amount just barely detectable as spice but that deepens the strawberry's essence.

This is my cheat sheet to a strawberry ice cream with the highest concentration of strawberry flavor but with all the creaminess of 14% butterfat—the "strawberriest" ice cream.

10½ ounces (300 g) extra-ripe hulled strawberries (from about 15 ounces/365 g strawberries; see Notes), fresh or frozen and partially thawed

7½ tablespoons (45 g) freeze-dried strawberry powder (see Notes)

Heaping ¼ teaspoon (1 g) ground pink peppercorns

1 tablespoon + ½ teaspoon (8 g) nonfat dry milk powder

½ cup + 1½ tablespoons (120 g) granulated sugar

Scant ¾ teaspoon (3 g) lecithin (optional)

5 tablespoons (80 g) whole milk

3½ tablespoons (70 g) sweetened condensed milk

1½ cups + 2 teaspoons (355 g) heavy cream

1. In a blender, blend the strawberries with the freeze-dried strawberry powder and ground peppercorns until completely smooth. Leave the puree in the blender and set aside.

2. Prepare an ice bath (see page 39).

3. In a small bowl, whisk together the milk powder, sugar, and lecithin (if using). In a tall cylindrical 1½-quart (1.5 liter) mixing vessel, blend the whole milk, condensed milk, and heavy cream with a hand blender. Add the dry ingredients and blend again to dissolve all the solids.

4. Pour the mixture into a small saucepan and cook over medium-low heat, whisking constantly, until it reaches 165°F (75°C) on an instant-read thermometer.

NOTES:
Whether you're using fresh or frozen strawberries, just be sure to hull them, which includes taking out the hard white core, not just the green leaves.

If you can't find freeze-dried strawberry powder, pulverize freeze-dried whole or sliced strawberries into a fine powder in a spice grinder.

All the natural soluble fiber in the fresh and freeze-dried strawberries provides enough thickening to forgo tara gum in this recipe.

5. Once the base reaches 165°F (75°C), immediately remove it from the heat and pour it through a fine-mesh sieve into the stand blender with the strawberry puree. Process the base for 2 minutes to fully homogenize.

6. Pour the base into the prepared ice bath to cool. Once completely cooled, transfer it to an airtight container and refrigerate for at least 12 hours and up to 24 hours.

7. **Make the ice cream:** When ready to begin, place a loaf pan in the freezer to chill. Quickly blend the ice cream base once more with a hand blender or whisk before processing it in an ice cream machine according to the manufacturer's instructions.

8. Churn the ice cream until it reaches the texture of very stiff soft-serve and the surface looks dry, about 25°F (-5°C) or colder on a thermometer gun.

9. Transfer the ice cream mixture to the chilled loaf pan. Press a piece of wax paper directly on top of the ice cream and freeze for at least 4 hours before serving.

TIP: There's no need for picture-perfect strawberries here—just the reddest ultraripe strawberries you can find. In fact, you'll get extra flavor points for using strawberries ripened to the point of being blemished and bruised. Using store-bought frozen strawberries works, too, because they're usually picked at peak season. Fellow ice cream expert Dana Cree even contends that a special enzymatic process takes place when strawberries are frozen and then partially thawed that intensifies their flavor.

PASSION FRUIT CACAO

Makes about 1 quart (1 liter)

What makes puckery, tropical passion fruit pair so perfectly with the baritone notes of cacao? Perhaps it's their common tropical origins. Or maybe, as science suggests, their common aromatic flavor compounds. Whatever the answer, they find each other in this Wanderlust Creamery signature vegan ice cream that customers often find "too good to be true."

The form of chocolate you add will determine how "dark" the chocolate flavor is. Using cocoa liquor, which is pure cocoa solids (think 100% chocolate), will yield a strong chocolate flavor. For a white chocolate/passion fruit flavor, use cocoa butter. If you prefer a passion fruit ice cream with a back note of milk chocolate, use a solid chocolate with a cacao percentage of around 65%.

For the base

¾ cup + 1 tablespoon (160 g) granulated sugar

½ cup + 1½ teaspoons (75 g) glucose powder

1 teaspoon (4 g) Nondairy Stabilizer (optional; page 33)

2 cups (425 g) coconut cream

4½ teaspoons (20 g) refined coconut oil

⅓ ounce (10 g) cocoa liquor, cocoa butter, or dark chocolate (65% cacao or greater)

1⅓ cups (260 g) seedless passion fruit puree

1 teaspoon (4 g) vanilla extract

1 teaspoon (5 g) natural yellow food coloring

For the ice cream

⅓ cup (45 g) cacao nibs

1. Prepare an ice bath (see page 39).

2. **Make the base:** In a small bowl, whisk together the sugar, glucose powder, and stabilizer (if using). In a tall cylindrical 1½-quart (1.5 liter) mixing vessel, blend the coconut cream and dry ingredients with a hand blender thoroughly to dissolve all the solids.

3. Pour the mixture into a small saucepan and cook over medium-low heat, whisking constantly, until it reaches 165°F (75°C) on an instant-read thermometer.

4. Once the base reaches 165°F (75°C), immediately remove from the heat and pour it back into the tall mixing vessel. Add the coconut oil and cocoa liquor and blend with a hand blender for 2 minutes to fully homogenize.

5. Pour the base through a fine-mesh sieve into the prepared ice bath to cool. Once completely cool, stir in the passion fruit puree, vanilla, and food coloring. Transfer the base to an airtight container and refrigerate for at least 12 hours and up to 3 days.

6. **Churn the ice cream:** When ready to begin, place a loaf pan and the cacao nibs in the freezer to chill. Quickly blend the ice cream base once more with a hand blender or whisk before pouring into an ice cream machine. Churn the ice cream until it reaches the texture of very stiff soft-serve and the surface looks dry, about 25°F (−5°C) or colder on a thermometer gun. Add the cacao nibs in the last few seconds of churning.

7. Transfer the ice cream to the chilled loaf pan. Press a piece of wax paper directly on top of the ice cream and freeze for at least 3 hours before serving.

CHÈ THÁI

I grew up with a Vietnamese best friend. As soon as she got a car in high school, we'd pass the weekends adventuring an hour south of Los Angeles to Orange County, where we'd spend the entire day eating around the sprawling unassuming suburbs of Westminster and Garden Grove, aka Little Saigon. The day would look something like the following: an appetizer of translucent spring rolls at a hole in the wall, followed by a second course of crispy bite-sized savory crepes at another mom-and-pop. The main course varied, depending on whether we felt like waiting in line for oxtail pho, unwrapping rice specialties from Huế, or slurping rice sheets slippery in nuoc mam, piled high with crunchy fried toppings and a garden of Vietnamese herbs. But no matter what, every trip to Little Saigon ended with a stop at a banh mi shop for sandwiches to take home. And while waiting for our number to be called up to the counter, we'd peruse the aisle of colorful cups of parfait called chè (see Note) and pick one for the long ride home. Sitting in 405 Freeway traffic in a used Honda Civic with defunct air conditioning, we'd take turns spooning tropical fruits, mung bean custard, and chewy thingamabobs from a plastic cup of icy coconut milk. This ice cream version buries jewels of tropical jellies like hidden treasure—pandan "noodles" and toothsome red rubies in jackfruit-kissed coconut cream.

For the base
5½ ounces (160 g) very ripe jackfruit, canned or fresh

1¾ cups (420 g) coconut cream

⅓ cup (70 g) granulated sugar

¾ cup + 3½ tablespoons (140 g) glucose powder

¼ teaspoon salt

¾ teaspoon (3 g) Nondairy Stabilizer (optional; page 33)

½ cup (125 g) water

2 tablespoons (25 g) virgin coconut oil

For the mix-ins
5 tablespoons Pandan Jellies (page 281), cut into "noodles"

5 tablespoons Lychee or Rambutan Jellies (page 281) or lychee popping boba

5 tablespoons canned toddy palm seeds, quartered

5 tablespoons "Red Rubies" (page 281)

NOTE: Chè refers to an assortment of coconut milk parfaits made with varying ingredients. Chè Thái (meaning "Thai-style chè") is based on a Thai dessert called tub tim krob, which is made with red-dyed bits of water chestnuts, referred to as "red rubies." Water chestnuts? Yes, but not the kind you may know only from a can. Fresh water chestnuts taste like the offspring of a coconut and an apple. To imitate these little crunchy things, this recipe calls for a firm jelly made from coconut and green apple.

TIP: It might be tempting to try putting in actual rambutan or lychee pieces, but they do not work in ice cream because their water content will render them flavorless and icy once frozen. Instead, we make the fruit into soft jellies. Alternatively, you can use popping boba, which will freeze into little spheres of lychee sorbet within the ice cream!

1. **Make the base:** In a stand blender, puree the jackfruit with 1 cup (240 g) of the coconut cream until completely smooth. Set aside.

2. In a small bowl, whisk together the sugar, glucose powder, salt, and stabilizer (if using). In a tall cylindrical 1½-quart (1.5 liter) mixing vessel, blend the water and remaining coconut cream with a hand blender. Add the dry ingredients and blend again to dissolve all the solids.

3. Pour the mixture into a medium saucepan and cook over medium-low heat, whisking constantly, until it reaches 165°F (75°C) on an instant-read thermometer.

4. Once the base reaches 165°F (75°C), immediately remove it from the heat and pour it back into the tall mixing vessel. Add the coconut oil and blend with a hand blender for 2 minutes to fully homogenize.

5. Pour the base through a fine-mesh sieve into the prepared ice bath to cool. Once completely cool, whisk in the jackfruit puree. Transfer the base to an airtight container and refrigerate for at least 12 hours and up to 3 days.

6. **Churn the ice cream:** When ready to begin, place a loaf pan and all the mix-ins in the freezer to chill. Quickly blend the ice cream base once more with a hand blender or whisk before pouring it through a fine-mesh sieve into an ice cream machine. Churn the ice cream until it reaches the texture of very stiff soft-serve and the surface looks dry, about 25°F (-5°C) or colder on a thermometer gun.

7. Spread half of the ice cream in the chilled loaf pan, then evenly sprinkle with half of each mix-in. Repeat the layering process once more. Immediately place the ice cream into the freezer for 15 minutes to firm it up.

8. Using a spatula, gently fold the ice cream to evenly distribute the mix-ins throughout the pan. Press a piece of wax paper directly on top of the ice cream and freeze for at least 4 hours before serving.

LILIKOI LI HING PINEAPPLE

Makes about 1 quart (1 liter)

As a child, I remember thinking (naively) that my mom had such an odd taste in snacks. Most notably, she always kept a bag of giant wrinkly salted dried plums in the pantry. Sometimes they'd even be deceptively wrapped individually like candies. What they tasted like were the antithesis of candy: electrically salty, a little sour, with a bittersweet ending that reminded me of Sweet'n Low. But this exact same salted dried plum (li hing mui) hit differently later in life, thanks to Hawaiians, who reintroduced me to it as a powder sprinkled on gummy bears, on pineapples, shaved ice, and popcorn. On its own I personally find it inedible, but salted dried plum can make everything it touches addictive. The Hawaiian name for the dried plums is "crack seed," which may seem indicative of its crack-like addictiveness but is actually a reference to the preservation process that cracks the plum pits open.

½ cup + 2 tablespoons (125 g) passion fruit puree, fresh or frozen

12 ounces (350 g) extra-ripe fresh pineapple, peeled, cored, and cut into 1-inch (2.5 cm) chunks

¾ cup + 1 tablespoon (165 g) granulated sugar, plus more to taste

⅓ cup + 1 teaspoon (50 g) glucose powder

¾ teaspoon (3 g) Sorbet Stabilizer (optional; page 33)

3½ tablespoons (30 g) inulin (optional)

1½ cups (325 g) water

¾ teaspoon (4 g) li hing mui powder (salted dried plum powder; see Tip)

Citric acid

NOTE: Inulin adds more body and a creamier mouthfeel to sorbets. If you prefer a sorbet with a cleaner and more refreshing meltdown, feel free to leave it out.

TIP: Salted dried plum powder is available widely online. Many Asian cultures have their own version (Vietnamese xi-moi, Japanese ume, Mei zi fen in Taiwan [China]). For this recipe, look for one with four main ingredients: plum, salt, sugar, and licorice. Some may contain a minuscule percentage of aspartame or saccharin, but don't worry, the amount won't add an off-putting taste to the final sorbet.

1. In a stand blender, process the passion fruit puree and pineapple into a completely smooth puree. Transfer the puree to another container and set aside.

2. In the same blender, blend the sugar, glucose, sorbet stabilizer (if using), and inulin (if using) with half of the water on high speed until all the solids have completely dispersed.

3. Pour into a small saucepan, add the remaining water, and cook over medium-high heat, whisking occasionally, until the temperature reaches 122°F (50°C) on an instant-read thermometer.

4. Pour the base through a fine-mesh sieve into the prepared ice bath to cool. Once the mixture has completely cooled, whisk in the fruit puree and li hing mui powder.

5. Using a refractometer (see page 37), measure the Brix of the base, verifying it is within the target range of 25 to 32 Brix. At this point, you can adjust the sweetness or tartness of the base with more sugar or citric acid, adding just ½ teaspoon at a time and rechecking the Brix after each addition.

6. Transfer the base to an airtight container and refrigerate for at least 12 hours and up to 2 days.

7. **Churn the sorbet:** When ready to begin, place a loaf pan in the freezer to chill. Quickly blend the base once more with a hand blender or whisk and pour into an ice cream machine. Churn the sorbet until it reaches the texture of a stiff slushie, about 30°F (−1°C) or colder on a thermometer gun.

8. Spread the sorbet into the chilled loaf pan. Press a piece of wax paper directly on top of the sorbet and freeze for at least 4 hours before serving.

GREEN MANGO SORBET

Makes about 1 quart (1 liter)

Growing up Southeast Asian, I learned that some fruits are more prized when unripened. Many times I've heard older relatives lament that they'd waited too long to harvest their backyard guavas, which were now pink and "inedible" to them. When it came to mangoes, the green, sour, and hard ones were often prized over sweet, juicy, and ripe ones. This sorbet is the antithesis of Western standards for fruit sorbet (which is sweet, made with height-of-season fruit). Instead, it's delightfully tangy and perfectly paired with a sprinkling of chamoy, chile, or even a drizzle of sambal rojak (a sweet and spicy palm sugar sauce).

1 pound 3 ounces (550 g) peeled and cubed green mango

1½ cups (360 g) water

¾ cup + 2½ tablespoons (180 g) sugar, plus more to taste

½ cup + 1½ tablespoons (85 g) glucose powder

1 teaspoon (3 g) Sorbet Stabilizer (optional; page 33)

3½ tablespoons (30 g) inulin (optional; see Note)

¼ teaspoon (1 g) salt, plus more to taste

Malic acid

1. Prepare an ice bath (see page 39).

2. In a stand blender, process the green mango and ¼ cup (60 g) of the water into a completely smooth puree. Transfer the puree to another container and set aside.

3. In the same blender, blend the remaining 1¼ cups (300 g) water, the sugar, glucose, stabilizer (if using), inulin (if using), and salt on high speed until all the solids have completely dissolved.

4. Transfer to a medium saucepan and cook over medium-high heat, whisking occasionally, until the temperature reaches 120°F (50°C) on an instant-read thermometer.

5. Pour the base through a fine-mesh sieve into the prepared ice bath to cool. Once the mixture has completely cooled, whisk in the green mango puree.

6. Using a refractometer (see page 37), measure the Brix of the base, verifying it is within the target range of 25 to 32 Brix. At this point, you can adjust the sweetness, saltiness, and tartness of the base with more sugar, salt, and malic acid, adding each in increments of ½ teaspoon at a time and rechecking the Brix after each addition to verify it is within the target range.

7. Transfer the base to an airtight container and refrigerate for at least 12 hours and up to 2 days.

NOTE: Inulin adds more body and a creamier mouthfeel to sorbets. If you prefer a sorbet with a cleaner and more refreshing meltdown, feel free to leave it out.

8. **Churn the sorbet:** When ready to begin, place a loaf pan in the freezer to chill. Quickly blend the base once more with a hand blender or whisk. Pour the sorbet base into an ice cream machine and churn until it reaches the texture of a very stiff slushie, about 30°F (–1°C) or colder on a thermometer gun.

9. Spread the sorbet in the chilled loaf pan. Press a piece of wax paper directly on top of the sorbet and freeze for at least 4 hours before serving.

KALAMANSI MIGNONETTE SORBET

Makes about 1 quart (1 liter)

4 ½ teaspoons (20 g) granulated sugar, plus more to taste

1 ¾ cups + 1 tablespoon (260 g) glucose powder, or to taste

1 teaspoon (3 g) Sorbet Stabilizer (optional; page 33)

½ cup (119 g) water

2 cups + scant 2 tablespoons (500 g) kalamansi juice (see Notes)

¼ shallot, finely minced

⅓ cup + ½ tablespoon (85 g) champagne vinegar, or to taste

1 tablespoon (15 g) patis or nuoc mam (Asian fish sauce), or to taste

Ground black or pink peppercorns

NOTES:

Kalamansi, a Philippine lime, is a very sour citrus. You can substitute with something equally sour like yuzu, sour orange, sudachi, or makrut lime. Do not substitute with any regular citrus, as that will yield a sweet sorbet.

Add any other herbs or spices to your liking as well, such as fresh chile, chive, etc.

This sorbet recipe leaves out inulin for a more refreshing finish to complement the oysters.

A family friend and well-respected chef, Maynard Llera (known endearingly in the Los Angeles culinary scene as Kuya Lord), once asked me for a custom batch of kalamansi sorbet, but with an odd request. "Can you make it really sour?" he asked. "I'm going to put them on oysters." Not at all surprised by his culinary genius (he's full of these kinds of innovations), I ran him a custom batch of extra zesty and sour kalamansi sorbet. But I saved myself a pint. I busted it out for my next dinner party—on a platter nestled in crushed ice and surrounded by oysters—instead of mignonette, the zingy sauce of vinegar and shallots usually served with oysters. The pairing was not only fun and unexpected, but it actually worked really well. Future iterations of this sorbet would eventually evolve into various types of citrus mignonette in ice cream form.

To serve this sorbet with oysters, nestle a bowl in a mound of ice with a melon baller beside it in the center of your oyster platter. Have your guests scoop a pearl of cold icy sorbet onto each briny oyster.

1. Prepare an ice bath (see page 39).

2. In a small bowl, whisk together the sugar, glucose powder, and stabilizer (if using). In a tall cylindrical 1½-quart (1.5 liter) mixing vessel, blend together the water and dry ingredients until dissolved.

3. Pour the mixture into a small saucepan and cook over medium-high heat, whisking occasionally, until the temperature reaches 120°F (50°C) on an instant-read thermometer.

4. Pour the liquid through a fine-mesh sieve back into the tall mixing vessel. Add the kalamansi juice, minced shallot, champagne vinegar, and fish sauce and blend until thoroughly combined and the shallots are partially pureed (they do not need to be completely pureed).

5. Pour the sorbet base into the prepared ice bath to cool.

6. Using a refractometer (see page 37), measure the Brix of the base, verifying it is within the target range of 25 to 32 Brix. At this point, you can adjust the base with more glucose, vinegar, and fish sauce to taste, adding just ½ teaspoon at a time and rechecking the Brix after each addition. Season the base with ground pepper.

7. Transfer the base to an airtight container and refrigerate for at least 12 hours and up to 2 days.

8. **Churn the sorbet:** When ready to begin, place four small metal bowls in the freezer to chill. Quickly blend the base once more with a hand blender or whisk. Pour the base into an ice cream machine and churn until it reaches the texture of a stiff slushie, about 30°F (-1°C) or colder on a thermometer gun.

9. Spread the sorbet into the chilled metal bowls, press a piece of wax paper directly on top of the sorbet, and freeze for at least 4 hours before serving.

CHAPTER 8

nu

As someone who makes ice cream for a living, I often get asked what my favorite ice cream flavor is. When I tell them it's pistachio, they impulsively reply that Wanderlust's version must then be the best. But gut-wrenchingly, I'm left to explain that we don't make one.

When I think back to all the ice cream moments of my youth, the one that shook me to the core was when I, as an eleven-year-old, had my first taste of pistachio gelato in Rome. It was brown, not green. It tasted of earth and sweet butter, not like the almond extract-doused fluff we had back home at Thrifty's. That olive-hued dollop of gelato smeared around a cone forever shaped my palate into a nutty-dessert lover. And so when I opened an ice cream shop, I gushed over the possibilities of what the pistachio option in the ice cream case might be. Sicilian, untoasted, and emerald green. Or *tty'*

roasted and salty. Or maybe Turkish-style, made with Anatolian pistachios and lightly scented with orange flower and piney mastic gum. My imagination ran wild until I sat down with a pastry vendor who showed me the prices for pistachio paste. Let's just say that this stuff is so pricey, that hijacking cargo trucks carrying pistachios is one of the more lucrative and preferred crimes of the Sicilian mafia. My boyfriend, JP, often jokes that selling a scoop of pistachio ice cream (the way I want to make it) would be the financial equivalent of wrapping the cone with a few dollar bills before handing it off to the customer. In my grief over a pistachio-less menu throughout the years, I've been forced to find other nutty alternatives to ice cream that don't involve us going bankrupt, or the expected usuals like butter pecan or peanut butter fudge.

NOYAUX & PINK PRALINES

Makes about 1 quart (1 liter)

In studying food science, one concept I found most interesting was aromatic compounds: chemical compounds whose atoms are joined in the shape of a ring. These compounds are highly volatile, resulting in them being odorant, or aromatic. Every aroma or flavor you perceive is made up of several aromatic compounds, and things that smell or taste alike do so because they share common aromatic compounds. Benzaldehyde is the aromatic compound responsible for the defining characteristic aroma and flavor of marzipan, or almond extract. But interestingly, it's also found in the pits of stone fruits and mamey—a tropical fruit found in Central and South America and the Caribbean. The French refer to the aroma and flavor as noyaux (see Note), the Mediterranean and Middle East call it mahleb (from the pits of St Lucie cherries), and in Mexico it's known as pixtle (from the mamet pit)—where it flavors ice cream and a Oaxacan drink called tejate. Its scent is an intoxicating mix of marzipan, rose, and faint peaches-and-cream. It delicately scents this ice cream dotted with rose-pralined almonds (a literal riff off Lyonnaise "pralines roses").

For the noyaux-infused milk
15 grams noyaux (see Notes)

1¾ cups + 1½ tablespoons (450 g) whole milk

For the base
2 tablespoons + 2½ teaspoons (20 g) nonfat dry milk powder

⅔ cup (135 g) granulated sugar

¾ teaspoon (3 g) tara gum (optional; see page 24)

⅓ cup + 1 teaspoon (50 g) glucose powder

¼ cup (80 g) sweetened condensed milk

70 grams egg yolks (from about 4 large eggs)

1¾ cups (400 g) heavy cream

For the ice cream
1 cup (165 g) Pink Pralines (recipe follows)

1. **Make the noyaux-infused milk:** In a spice grinder, pulverize the noyaux into a coarse powder.

2. In a small saucepan, scald the milk. Stir in the ground noyaux and remove from the heat. Allow the mixture to cool to at least 120°F (50°C).

3. Prepare an ice bath (see page 39).

4. **Make the base:** In a small bowl, whisk together the milk powder, sugar, tara gum (if using), and glucose. In a tall cylindrical 1½-quart (1.5 liter) mixing vessel, blend the infused milk, condensed milk, and egg yolks with a hand blender. Slowly add the dry ingredients while blending and blend thoroughly to dissolve all the solids.

5. Pour the mixture into a medium saucepan and cook over medium-low heat, whisking constantly, until it reaches 165°F (75°C) on an instant-read thermometer.

6. Once the base reaches 165°F (75°C), immediately remove from the heat and pour it back into the tall mixing vessel. Add the heavy cream and blend with a hand blender for 2 minutes to fully homogenize.

7. Pour the base into the prepared ice bath to cool. Once completely cool, transfer to an airtight container. Cover and refrigerate for at least 18 hours and up to 2 days.

8. **Churn the ice cream:** When ready to begin, place a loaf pan and the pink pralines in the freezer to chill. Quickly loosen the base with a hand blender or whisk before pouring it through a fine-mesh sieve into an ice cream machine. Churn the ice cream until it reaches the texture of very stiff soft-serve and the surface looks dry, about 25°F (-5°C) or colder on a thermometer gun. Add the pink pralines in the last few seconds of churning.

9. Transfer the ice cream to the chilled loaf pan. Press a piece of wax paper onto the top of the ice cream and freeze for at least 3 hours before serving.

NOTES:

Noyaux can be retrieved from any stone fruit: Take the pit of the fruit and lightly wrap it in a kitchen towel. Using a mallet or rolling pin, firmly crack the pit open to reveal the inner kernel. The 15 grams of noyaux needed for this recipe roughly equals 24 apricot, peach, or plum kernels, or seeds from the pits of 1 pound (453 g) of cherries.

If stone fruits aren't in season, you can also buy packaged raw and "bitter" apricot kernels on Amazon, where they're sold as a health food.

Alternatively, there's an aromatic Middle Eastern and Mediterranean spice called mahleb, made from the seeds inside the pits of St Lucie cherries. You can find mahleb, ground or whole, at Middle Eastern supermarkets or spice shops.

Another option is to omit the fruit kernels and use 1 tablespoon of crème de noyaux liqueur, added to the base after cooling, which will color the ice cream a light pink to match the pralines.

PINK PRALINES

Makes about 2⅓ cups (380 g)

2 cups (280 g) whole almonds

½ cup (100 g) granulated sugar

2 tablespoons (30 g) water

2 tablespoons (30 g) rose water

All-natural pink food coloring

1. Place the almonds in the bowl of a stand mixer and snap on the paddle. (Alternatively, place the almonds in a very large glass or metal bowl, about four times the volume of the almonds.)

2. In a small saucepan, cook the sugar, water, rose water, and pink food coloring over medium-high heat. Do not stir the mixture; pick up the pot and swirl it around occasionally as the sugar melts. The mixture should begin to boil and thicken. Continue cooking until the syrup reaches 240°F (115°C) on an instant-read thermometer.

3. When the syrup reaches 240°F (115°C), remove from the heat and immediately turn the mixer on the lowest speed setting. Moving quickly from the stove to the mixer, slowly drizzle in about half of the hot syrup. The syrup should begin to coat the nuts with a thin, powdery rose-colored coating. Once all the nuts have been lightly coated and are somewhat dry, stop the mixer. (Alternatively, drizzle the hot syrup over the almonds in a bowl and use a heatproof spatula or wooden spoon to stir and coat all the almonds until the syrup forms a thin crust around each nut.)

4. Return the saucepan of syrup to medium-high heat and cook until it comes back to 240°F (115°C). Remove the syrup from the heat and immediately turn the mixer back on the lowest speed setting. Drizzle in the remaining hot syrup to coat the almonds for a second time. (If mixing by hand, drizzle the hot syrup over the almonds in a bowl and stir to coat all the almonds until the syrup forms a second coating around each nut.) Continue mixing until all the nuts are evenly coated and dry. Spread out the nuts on a sheet pan lined with parchment or wax paper to cool. Once completely cooled, transfer to an airtight container and store at room temperature until ready to use, up to 1 week.

KINAKO & KYOHO GRAPE JELLY

Makes about 1 quart (1 liter)

This confession might get me disowned, but I loathe peanut butter desserts. While peanut butter cups, PB&J's, and Elvis-inspired peanut butter/honey/banana sandwiches might not be to my personal taste, I understand their broad appeal to the American palate for sweeter flavors. A flavor I can do, however, is roasted soybean flour. Known as kinako in Japan and injeolmi in Korea, it has a richness that reminds people of peanut butter—a nutty and slightly sweet taste, with a toasty and earthy aroma reminiscent of roasted barley or wheat. Blended into an ice cream base, the result is a toasted nutty flavor like a milky subdued peanut butter. Swirled with a jelly of floral and musky Kyoho grapes, this ice cream is the Asian "not-too-sweet" answer to American PB&J.

TIP: Kyoho grapes are a popular variety of grape that is grown in Japan and Korea. They are known for their large size, deep purple skins, and juicy flesh. In terms of flavor, Kyoho grapes are generally quite sweet and have a specific candy-like taste. If you've ever had an artificially flavored muscat Hi-Chew, it accurately captures the too-good-to-be-true flavor of a Kyoho grape. Their thick skins are peeled to reveal texture that is often described as "bursting" in the mouth. In the United States, you can find them and similar varieties (Black Muscat, Thomcord) in Asian supermarkets and farmers' markets beginning in late August or early September. Thomcord grapes make an acceptable albeit paler-in-flavor substitution. If Kyoho or Thomcord grapes are out of season, popular jam brand Bonne Maman makes a muscat grape jelly that will work as a substitute for the Kyoho grape jelly swirl.

For the base

1 tablespoon (15 g) kinako (roasted soybean flour)

2 tablespoons + ½ teaspoon (15 g) nonfat dry milk powder

½ cup + 2 tablespoons (125 g) granulated sugar

½ teaspoon (2 g) tara gum (optional; see page 24)

¼ cup + 2 tablespoons + ½ teaspoon (55 g) glucose powder

1¾ cups + 1½ tablespoons (450 g) whole milk

3½ tablespoons (70 g) sweetened condensed milk

70 grams egg yolks (from about 4 large eggs)

1½ cups + 2 tablespoons (375 g) heavy cream

For the Kyoho grape jelly swirl

15 ounces (400 g) Kyoho grapes (see Tip), stemmed and washed

1¾ cups (350 g) granulated sugar

2½ cups (350 g) glucose powder

¼ cup (60 g) water

¼ teaspoon (1 g) Sorbet Stabilizer (page 33) or 2½ tablespoons (30 g) instant pectin

Citric acid

1. Prepare an ice bath (see page 39).

2. **Make the base:** In a small bowl, whisk together the kinako, milk powder, sugar, tara gum (if using), and glucose. In a tall cylindrical 1½-quart (1.5 liter) mixing vessel, blend the whole milk, condensed milk, and egg yolks with a hand blender. Slowly add the dry ingredients while blending and blend thoroughly to dissolve all the solids.

3. Pour the mixture into a small saucepan and cook over medium-low heat, whisking constantly, until it reaches 165°F (75°C) on an instant-read thermometer.

4. Once the base reaches 165°F (75°C), immediately remove from the heat and pour it back into the tall mixing vessel. Add the heavy cream and blend with a hand blender for 2 minutes to fully homogenize.

5. Pour the base through a fine-mesh sieve into the prepared ice bath to cool. Once completely cool, transfer to an airtight container, cover, and refrigerate for at least 12 hours and up to 3 days.

6. **Meanwhile, make the Kyoho grape jelly swirl:** Prepare an ice bath (see page 39).

7. Juice the grapes with a juicer. (Alternatively, pulse them in a food processor until crushed, and pass through a fine-mesh sieve to remove the skins and seeds.)

8. In a small saucepan, whisk together the sugar, glucose, water, and sorbet stabilizer or pectin. Add half of the grape juice and heat over low heat, whisking frequently, until the mixture registers 122°F (50°C) on an instant-read thermometer. Remove from the heat and pour into the ice bath, along with the remaining grape juice.

9. Once completely cooled, season with citric acid to taste. Transfer the jelly to an airtight container. Keep refrigerated until ready to use, for up to 1 week.

10. **Churn the ice cream:** When ready to begin, place a loaf pan and the Kyoho grape jelly in the freezer to chill. Quickly blend the ice cream base once more with a hand blender or whisk before pouring it into an ice cream machine. Churn the ice cream until it reaches the texture of very stiff soft-serve and the surface looks dry, about 25°F (−5°C) or colder on a thermometer gun.

11. Spread half of the ice cream into the bottom of the chilled loaf pan. Pour half of the jelly on top of the ice cream. Repeat this layering process once more. Immediately place the ice cream into the freezer for 15 minutes to firm it up.

12. Using a spatula, gently fold the ice cream and jam layers to create visible swirls. Three or four folds should be sufficient.

13. Press a piece of wax paper directly on top of the ice cream and freeze for at least 4 hours before serving.

NOUGAT DE MONTÉLIMAR

When we first opened, honey lavender ice cream was all the rage. Just about every "artisanal" ice cream maker worth their cream had a version in their case. The taste reminded me so much of Provence—not only because of lavender's association to the region, but its flavor was evocative of something I'd tasted there before. Take a walk around the unassuming town of Montélimar (dubbed "the gateway to Provence") and you'll find it isn't necessarily a tourist destination. Yet among the almond-colored stone buildings with rooftops in varying shades of toast, you'll find random curiosities. A twelfth-century castle, cobblestone streets that taper into quaint alleyways of pastel-hued townhouses, and an entire avenue of ateliers selling the city's most cherished tradition: airy almond-studded nougat sweetened with honey from local lavender fields. To me, honey lavender ice cream was reminiscent of nougat de Montélimar.

For the base

¼ cup + 2 teaspoons (100 g) honey

1 tablespoon dried lavender

⅛ teaspoon salt

4½ teaspoons (20 g) granulated sugar

⅓ cup + 1 teaspoon (50 g) glucose powder

2 tablespoons + ½ teaspoon (15 g) nonfat dry milk powder

½ teaspoon (2 g) tara gum (optional; see page 24)

2⅓ cups (560 g) whole milk

2½ tablespoons (50 g) sweetened condensed milk

70 grams egg yolks (from about 4 large eggs)

¾ cup + 2½ tablespoons (210 g) heavy cream

7 tablespoons (115 g) pure toasted almond paste or pure roasted almond butter

¼ teaspoon (1 g) marshmallow flavor extract

For the ice cream

½ cup (55 g) roughly chopped roasted almonds and/or pistachios

1. Prepare an ice bath (see page 39).

2. **Make the base:** In a small saucepan, heat the honey and dried lavender over medium heat until the honey begins to bubble. Remove from the heat and allow to cool.

3. In a small bowl, whisk together the salt, sugar, glucose, milk powder, and tara gum (if using). In a tall cylindrical 1½-quart (1.5 liter) mixing vessel, blend the whole milk, condensed milk, and egg yolks with a hand blender. Slowly add the dry ingredients while blending and blend thoroughly to dissolve all the solids.

4. Pour the mixture into the saucepan containing the honey and lavender and cook over medium-low heat, whisking constantly, until it reaches 165°F (75°C) on an instant-read thermometer. Add the heavy cream and almond paste to the mixing vessel.

5. Once the base reaches 165°F (75°C), immediately remove from the heat and pour into the mixing vessel and blend with a hand blender for 2 minutes to fully homogenize.

6. Transfer the base to the prepared ice bath to cool. Once completely cool, add the marshmallow flavor extract and pour through a fine-mesh sieve into an airtight container. Cover and refrigerate for at least 12 hours and up to 3 days.

7. **Churn the ice cream:** When you are ready to begin, place a loaf pan and the chopped roasted nuts in the freezer to chill. Quickly blend the ice cream base once more with a hand blender or whisk before pouring it into an ice cream machine. Churn the ice cream until it reaches the texture of very stiff soft-serve and the surface looks dry, about 25°F (-5°C) or colder on a thermometer gun. Add the nuts in the last few seconds of churning.

8. Transfer the ice cream to the chilled loaf pan and press a piece of wax paper directly on top of the ice cream and freeze for at least 3 hours before serving.

BROWN BUTTER HALVA

Makes about 1 quart (1 liter)

Tarzana, where our first store opened, is home to one of LA's biggest Israeli communities. Up and down Ventura Boulevard, Israeli restaurants, hookah bars, and cafes dot the sidewalk. You can see locals congregate for hours on end over continuous cups of coffee, cigarettes, banter, and debate. And all around, kosher delis and markets offer inspiration for ice cream flavors. A common sight in the deli cases are blocks of tahini halva, a dense fudge made of sesame and honey, in an array of flavors. This recipe adds brown butter to play up the nuttiness of halva.

For the base

3½ tablespoons (25 g) nonfat dry milk powder

4½ tablespoons (65 g) unsalted butter

3 tablespoons + 2 teaspoons (45 g) granulated sugar

¼ cup + 1½ teaspoons (40 g) glucose powder

½ teaspoon (2 g) tara gum (optional; see page 24)

2 cups + 3 tablespoons (530 g) whole milk

¼ cup (85 g) honey

70 grams egg yolks (from about 4 large eggs)

¾ cup + 2 tablespoons (200 g) heavy cream

1 tablespoon + 2 teaspoons (25 g) white tahini

For the brown butter halva fudge swirl

1 tablespoon + 2 teaspoons (12 g) nonfat dry milk powder

6 tablespoons (85 g) butter

Scant ½ cup (155 g) sweetened condensed milk

2 tablespoons (40 g) honey

Pinch of salt

½ teaspoon (2 g) vanilla extract

1½ tablespoons (20 g) white tahini

1. **Make the base:** In a spice grinder, process the nonfat dry milk powder into a fine powder.

2. In a small saucepan, melt the butter over medium heat until it begins to bubble and the milk solids begin to separate from the fat, about 5 minutes. Whisk in the dry milk powder and continue to cook, whisking frequently, until the milk solids begin to turn color. Remove from the heat, and let it cool in the saucepan; the milk solids will continue to darken and brown. Set aside.

3. Prepare an ice bath (see page 39).

4. In a small bowl, whisk together the sugar, glucose, and tara gum (if using). In a tall cylindrical 1½-quart (1.5 liter) mixing vessel, blend the milk, honey, and egg yolks with a hand blender. Add the dry ingredients, then blend again thoroughly to dissolve all the solids.

5. Pour the mixture into a small saucepan and cook over medium-low heat, whisking constantly, until it reaches 165°F (75°C) on an instant-read thermometer.

6. Once the base reaches 165°F (75°C), immediately remove from the heat and pour it through a fine-mesh sieve back into the tall mixing vessel. Add the heavy cream, white tahini, and browned butter (make sure to include all the browned milk solids, scraped from the bottom of the pan). Blend the mixture with a hand blender for 2 minutes to fully homogenize it.

7. Pour the mixture into the prepared ice bath to cool. Once completely cool, transfer the ice cream base to an airtight container. Cover and refrigerate for at least 12 hours and up to 3 days.

8. **Make the brown butter halva fudge swirl:** In a spice grinder, process the milk powder into a fine powder. Prepare the brown butter as in step 2 above. Let cool for a few minutes.

9. Add the condensed milk, honey, salt, vanilla, and tahini and whisk to combine. Transfer the fudge to an airtight container and store refrigerated for up to 1 week.

10. **Churn the ice cream:** When ready to begin, place a loaf pan and the halva fudge in the freezer to chill. Quickly blend the ice cream base once more with a hand blender or whisk before pouring it into an ice cream machine. Churn the ice cream until it reaches the texture of very stiff soft-serve and the surface looks dry, about 25°F (−5°C) or colder on a thermometer gun.

11. Spread half of the ice cream mixture into the chilled loaf pan. Spread half of the halva fudge on top. Repeat the layering process once more. Immediately place the ice cream into the freezer for 15 minutes to firm it up.

12. Using a spatula, gently fold the ice cream and halva fudge layers to create swirls. Three or four folds should be sufficient for visible ribbons throughout the pan.

13. Press a piece of wax paper directly on top of the ice cream and freeze for at least 4 hours before serving.

CHAPTER 9

rm

In a Facebook group page for ice cream business owners, someone asked if anyone was willing to share a recipe for corn ice cream. The post's comments reflected a consensus from the group: "Don't." One comment read, "Some things are not meant to be in ice cream and corn is one! Stick to basic flavors, the best ingredients, you can't go wrong!" Cringe. In Brazil and Latin America, the Philippines, Korea, and beyond, sweet corn *is* a basic ice cream flavor. And in other parts of the world, corn is considered dessert before anything else. So to whoever asked for a corn ice cream recipe: Here are a few of mine.

COCONUT & CORN

Makes about 1 quart (1 liter)

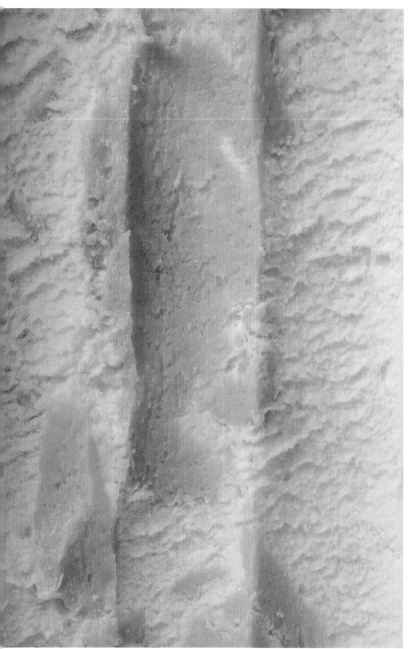

For the base

¾ cup (150 g) granulated sugar

1¼ cups + 2½ tablespoons (200 g) glucose powder

⅛ teaspoon salt

¾ teaspoon (2 g) Nondairy Stabilizer (optional; page 33)

1⅓ cups (325 g) water

2 cups (426 g) coconut cream

6 tablespoons (80 g) virgin coconut oil

For the ice cream
Corn Jam (recipe follows)

CORN JAM

Makes about 1 cup (315 g)

2 tablespoons (30 g) unsalted butter

6 tablespoons (75 g) granulated sugar

¼ cup + ¾ teaspoon (40 g) glucose powder

1¼ cups (6 ounces/175 g) cooked corn kernels

In a small saucepan, melt the butter with the sugar and glucose. Pour the mixture into a stand blender along with the corn and process until completely smooth. Store in an airtight container in the refrigerator until ready to use, for up to 3 days.

One of the main reasons I started Wanderlust Creamery was to celebrate different cultures through their cuisines. In learning about what's eaten around the world, I've found that many cultures, though geographically far apart, cherish the same dishes. It makes one realize that no matter how vast the world might seem, we are in many ways more alike than different. A flavor that exemplifies this is coconut and corn. I grew up thinking this was an odd flavor pairing found only in Filipino desserts but later learned that corn and coconut are a common duo in Nigerian cuisine. In the Philippines, street vendors offer cups of binatog—boiled corn topped with freshly shaved coconut, seasoned sugar, and salt—exactly as they do in Nigeria, where it's called agbado ati agbon.

1. Prepare an ice bath (see page 39).

2. **Make the base:** In a small bowl, whisk together the sugar, glucose, salt, and stabilizer (if using). In a tall cylindrical 1½-quart (1.5 liter) mixing vessel, blend the water and half of the coconut cream with a hand blender. Slowly add the dry ingredients while blending and blend thoroughly to dissolve all the solids.

3. Pour the mixture into a medium saucepan and cook over medium-low heat, whisking constantly, until it reaches 165°F (75°C) on an instant-read thermometer.

4. Once the base reaches 165°F (75°C), immediately remove from the heat and pour it back into the tall mixing vessel. Add the remaining coconut cream and the coconut oil and blend with a hand blender for 2 minutes to fully homogenize.

5. Transfer the base to the prepared ice bath to cool. Once completely cool, pour through a fine-mesh sieve into an airtight container. Cover and refrigerate for at least 12 hours and up to 3 days.

6. **Churn the ice cream:** When ready to begin, place a loaf pan and the corn jam in the freezer to chill. Quickly blend the ice cream base once more with a hand blender or whisk before pouring it into an ice cream machine. Churn the ice cream until it reaches the texture of very stiff soft-serve and the surface looks dry, about 25°F (-5°C) or colder on a thermometer gun.

7. Transfer half the ice cream to the chilled loaf pan, then top with half of the corn jam. Repeat the layer process once more. Immediately place the ice cream into the freezer for 15 minutes to firm it up.

8. Using a spatula, gently fold the ice cream to create swirls of corn throughout. Three or four folds should be sufficient.

9. Press a piece of wax paper directly on top of the ice cream and freeze for at least 3 hours before serving.

HONEY-BUTTER CORN DALGONA

Makes about 1 quart (1 liter)

In the multicultural landscape of Los Angeles, inspiration can be found everywhere. My favorite pastime is wandering the aisles of Middle Eastern, El Salvadorean, or Asian supermarkets to imagine what interesting ingredients and flavors could be translated into ice cream flavors. Strolling the snack aisle of any Korean supermarket, you're likely to notice recurring flavors: honey, butter, and corn. This ice cream combines all three, studded with bits of honeycomb candy—also cherished in South Korea, famously known as dalgona. Some of the candy stays crunchy, while other bits of it melt into mini pools of honey within the buttery corn ice cream.

For the corn base

2¼ cups (11 ounces/305 g) cooked corn kernels (canned, or fresh from 3 ears)

¾ cup + 1 tablespoon (200 g) whole milk

½ cup plus 1 tablespoon (110 g) granulated sugar

2½ tablespoons (18 g) nonfat dry milk powder

½ teaspoon (2 g) tara gum (optional; see page 24)

¼ cup (36 g) glucose powder

3½ tablespoons (70 g) sweetened condensed milk

70 grams egg yolks (from about 4 large eggs)

1¼ cups (290 g) heavy cream

2 tablespoons (30 g) unsalted butter

For the dalgona
Honeycomb Candy (page 287)

1. **Make the corn base:** In a stand blender, puree the corn with the milk into a completely smooth puree. Transfer to a tall 1½-quart (1.5 liter) mixing vessel.

2. Prepare an ice bath (see page 39).

3. In a small bowl, whisk together the sugar, milk powder, tara gum (if using), and glucose powder. Add the condensed milk and egg yolks to the mixing vessel with the corn puree. Blend with a hand blender, slowly adding the dry ingredients while blending and blend thoroughly to dissolve all the solids. Pour the mixture into a medium saucepan and cook over medium-low heat, whisking constantly, until it reaches 165°F (75°C) on an instant-read thermometer.

4. Once the base reaches 165°F (75°C), immediately remove from the heat and pour it back into the tall mixing vessel. Add the heavy cream and butter and blend with a hand blender for 2 minutes to fully homogenize.

5. Transfer the base to the prepared ice bath to cool. Once completely cool, pour through a fine-mesh sieve into an airtight container. Cover and refrigerate for at least 12 hours and up to 3 days.

6. **Churn the ice cream:** When ready to begin, place a loaf pan in the freezer to chill. Quickly blend the ice cream base once more with a hand blender or whisk before pouring it into an ice cream machine. Churn the ice cream until it reaches the texture of very stiff soft-serve and the surface looks dry, about 25°F (−5°C) or colder on a thermometer gun. Add the honeycomb candy in the last few seconds of churning.

7. Transfer the ice cream to the chilled loaf pan. Press a piece of wax paper directly on top of the ice cream and freeze for at least 3 hours before serving.

CHICHA MORADA

3¼ cups (770 g) water

3 ounces (85 g) dried purple corn (about 1 large ear or 1 heaping cup dried kernels; see Notes)

1 cinnamon stick, about 4 to 5 inches long

1 clove

1 medium (100 g) green apple, peeled, cored, and quartered, skins reserved

7 ounces (200 g) cored and peeled pineapple, cut into chunks

⅓ cup (80 ml) freshly squeezed lime juice

⅛ teaspoon ground cinnamon

1⅓ cups (260 g) granulated sugar

100 g glucose

½ teaspoon (1 g) salt

1 teaspoon (3 g) Sorbet Stabilizer (optional; page 33)

2 tablespoons (17 g) inulin (optional; see Notes)

1 tablespoon (15 ml) citric acid, plus more to taste

NOTES: Andean dried purple corn is sold as ears or loose kernels in many Latin supermarkets.

Inulin adds more body and a creamier mouthfeel to sorbets. If you prefer a sorbet with a cleaner and more refreshing meltdown, feel free to leave it out.

An Andean punch made with purple corn, tart fruit, and warm spices stewed for hours, chicha morada is a refreshing drink consumed on the same scale as Coca-Cola in its native Peru. Imagine the aroma of a fall candle, yet bright with lime, juicy pineapple, and green apple. It's the opposite of what one would expect from a beverage mainly made of corn. Spun into a sorbet, chicha morada is a paradox—the flavor of a comforting hug delivered in an icy, refreshing medium. Whenever this ruby-hued ice cream makes a cameo in the dipping cases in stores, the staff pack themselves pints to make foamy pisco sour floats at home.

1. Pour ⅔ cup (150 g) of the water into a glass and set aside. In a large pot, bring the remaining water, along with the purple corn, cinnamon stick, clove, and reserved apple skins to a boil.

2. Lower the heat to medium-low, and allow the mixture to gently simmer for 1 hour, until aromatic and the flavors have blended together.

3. Meanwhile, in a countertop blender, process the green apple, pineapple, lime juice, and ground cinnamon into a completely smooth puree. Transfer the puree to another container and set aside.

4. In the same blender, blend the sugar, glucose salt, stabilizer (if using), and inulin (if using) with the reserved ⅔ cup (150 g) of water on high until all the solids have completely dispersed. Set aside.

5. Once the chicha morada has finished stewing, remove from the heat, and allow it to cool to warm. Strain half the chicha morada into the blender containing the sugars and stabilizers; blend once more.

6. Pour the mixture from the blender along with the rest of the chicha morada through a fine mesh strainer into the prepared ice bath to cool completely. Once cooled, whisk in the fruit puree.

7. Using a refractometer, measure the Brix of the base, verifying it is within the target range of 25 to 32 Brix. At this point, you can adjust the sweetness or tartness of the base with more sugar or citric acid, adding just a teaspoon at a time and re-reading the Brix after each addition.

8. Transfer the sorbet base to an airtight container and refrigerate for at least 12 hours and up to 2 days.

9. **Churn the sorbet:** When ready to begin, place a loaf pan in the freezer to chill. Quickly blend the sorbet base with a hand blender or whisk before pouring it into an ice cream machine. Churn the sorbet until it reaches the texture of a stiff slushie, about 30°F (-1°C) or colder on a thermometer gun.

10. Transfer the sorbet to the chilled loaf pan. Press a piece of wax paper directly on top of the sorbet and freeze for at least 3 hours before serving.

THAI CANDY CORN

Makes almost 2 quarts
(1.8 liters)

A fun ice cream we make for Halloween is this "candy corn" reimagined with classic Thai ice cream flavors. The three-layered look is familiar and nostalgic, but the taste is unexpected, with buttery notes of original candy corn translated through coconut and corn ice creams, touched with warm spiced vanilla via Thai tea.

For the Thai tea base

1 tablespoon + ½ teaspoon (8 g) dry milk powder

⅓ cup + 1½ tablespoons (85 g) granulated sugar

¼ teaspoon (1 g) tara gum (optional; see page 24)

2 tablespoons + 2½ teaspoons (25 g) glucose powder

1¾ cups (425 g) whole milk

2 tablespoons (40 g) sweetened condensed milk

35 grams egg yolks (from about 2 large eggs)

¾ cup + 2 tablespoons (200 g) heavy cream

Scant ½ cup (20 g) Thai tea leaves

For the ice creams

½ recipe ice cream base from Coconut & Corn (page 128)

½ recipe corn base from Honey-Butter Corn Dalgona (page 130)

TIPS:

If you have a large-capacity ice cream machine (bigger than 1.6 quarts/1.6 liters), I would suggest doubling the recipes to meet the volume requirements for proper churning.

The ice cream must be extremely cold and hardened when slicing, which may be difficult to achieve with a home freezer. The quick-freezing method using dry ice (see Blast Freezing, page 45) is very useful for this recipe.

If you prefer a scooped ice cream instead of a sliced terrine, fold the ice cream layers at the end of assembly, before freezing the finished pan.

1. Prepare an ice bath (see page 39).

2. **Make the Thai tea base:** In a small bowl, whisk together the milk powder, sugar, tara gum (if using), and glucose. In a tall cylindrical 1½-quart (1.5 liter) mixing vessel, blend the whole milk, condensed milk, and egg yolks with a hand blender. Slowly add the dry ingredients while blending and blend thoroughly to dissolve all the solids.

3. Pour the mixture into a medium saucepan and cook over medium-low heat, whisking constantly, until it reaches 165°F (75°C) on an instant-read thermometer.

4. Once the base reaches 165°F (75°C), immediately remove from the heat and pour the mixture back into the mixing vessel. Add the heavy cream and blend with a hand blender for 2 minutes to fully homogenize. Stir in the Thai tea leaves.

5. Pour the base into the prepared ice bath to cool. Once completely cool, transfer the base to an airtight container. Cover and refrigerate for at least 12 hours and up to 3 days.

6. **Make the ice creams:** Make the two other ice cream bases and chill as directed in the recipes. Once all three of the ice cream bases are completely chilled, line a metal loaf pan with wax or parchment paper (see page 45). (Alternatively, you can use a silicone loaf pan.) Place the loaf pan in the freezer to chill.

7. Starting with the coconut and corn cream base, blend it with a whisk or hand blender before churning in an ice cream machine until it reaches the texture of very stiff soft-serve and the surface looks dry, about 25°F (-5°C) or colder on a thermometer gun. Spread the ice cream into the chilled loaf pan and place in the freezer.

8. Scrape the ice cream machine clean (no need to wash it) and pour the Thai tea base through a fine-mesh sieve into the machine. Churn the ice cream until it reaches the texture of very stiff soft-serve and the surface looks dry, about 25°F (-5°C) or colder on a thermometer gun.

9. Spread the Thai tea ice cream mixture into the chilled loaf pan, on top of the layer of coconut and corn ice cream and return to the freezer.

10. Clean and dry the ice cream machine completely, pour in the butter corn dalgona ice cream base and churn until it reaches the textureof very stiff soft-serve and the surface looks dry, about 25°F (-5°C) or colder on a thermometer gun.

11. Spread the second butter corn dalgona ice cream mixture into the chilled loaf pan on top of the layer of Thai tea ice cream. Press a piece of wax paper directly on top of the ice cream and freeze for at least 8 hours before unmolding. (Alternatively, use the dry ice to quick-freeze the ice cream; see Blast Freezing, page 45.)

12. When the ice cream has completely hardened, unmold the ice cream onto a piece of parchment or wax paper. Working quickly with a wet chef's knife, slice the ice cream into slices 1½ inches (4 cm) thick. Cut each slice diagonally into 2 triangles and serve.

ELOTE ICE CREAM BARS

Makes about 10 ice cream bars

In the 1990s in the San Fernando Valley, the elote man was elusive. In Canoga Park, you could find a fruit stand on almost every other corner . . . a paleta man waiting outside the Catholic kindergarten I went to . . . but when we saw the elote man, we ran. Because better than ice cream on a stick, to me, was corn on a stick—dripping in cream, with salty granules of cheese, chile, and lime. With this recipe, you can have both!

Corn base from Honey-Butter Corn Dalgona (page 130)

About 10 ice pop sticks

For the lime-butter coating

5 tablespoons + 1 teaspoon (71 g) ghee

5 tablespoons + 1 teaspoon (71 g) refined coconut oil

2½ teaspoons (3 g) salt

16 ounces (453 g) white chocolate

2 teaspoons grated lime zest

For the "cheese" chocolate flakes

2 tablespoons + 1 teaspoon (32 g) refined coconut oil

2½ teaspoons (3 g) salt

4 ounces (113 g) white chocolate, chopped

3¾ teaspoons (10 g) dried Parmesan powder or white cheddar powder

For assembly

3 tablespoons grated lime zest

3 tablespoons habanero sugar (see Note)

NOTE: Habanero sugar is available online or in specialty food shops. Alternatively, chili powder or Tajín seasoning can be used.

1. Make the corn ice cream base and chill as directed in step 7 for at least 12 hours.

2. Set out two silicone corn-cob molds, with a total of 10 cavities, each holding 3 ounces (90 ml). (You'll have a scoop of ice cream left over to enjoy while the ice cream bars freeze.) Using a paring knife or a pair of scissors, cut or snip a slit at the bottom end of each "ear of corn," where the ice pop stick will be inserted. The slit should be just as wide as the stick. Too wide of a slit may cause the mold to leak ice cream; too narrow will make the insertion of the stick difficult.

3. **Churn the ice cream:** When ready to begin, place the silicone corn molds in the freezer to chill. Pour the ice cream base into an ice cream machine and churn the ice cream until it reaches the texture of very stiff soft-serve and the surface looks dry, about 25°F (−5°C) or colder on a thermometer gun.

4. Fill the silicone corn molds with the ice cream, pressing down and smoothing the top of each cavity with an offset spatula to ensure each mold is completely filled. Press a piece of wax paper directly on top of the ice cream in the mold, then (wearing oven mitts) place a block of dry ice on top of the mold to flash-freeze it for 5 to 8 minutes. (Alternatively, place the mold in the coldest part of your freezer for at least 1 hour.)

Method continued on next page

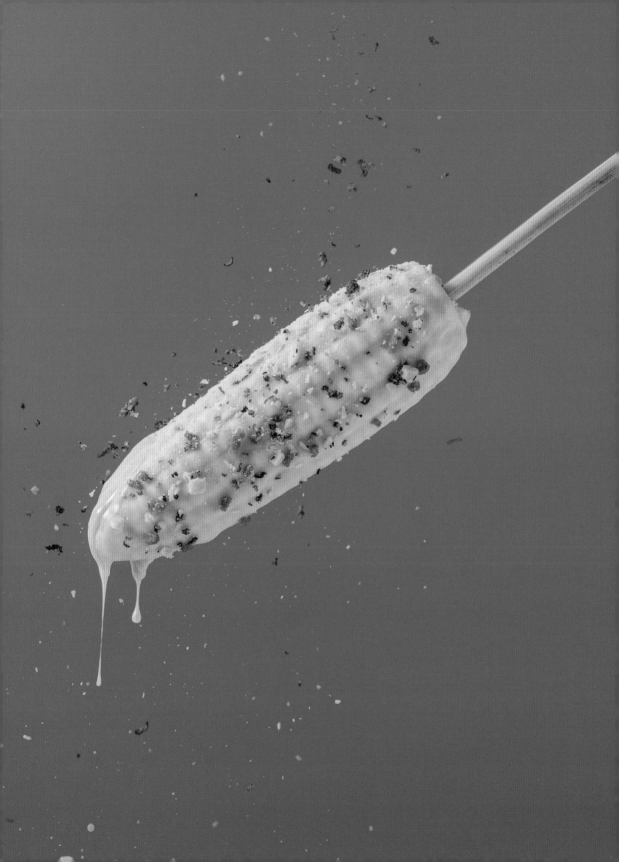

5. Once the ice cream is firm yet soft enough to pierce, slide the ice pop sticks into the slits in the mold. At least one-third of the length of the stick should be inside the ice cream. Return the ice cream to freeze for 30 to 45 minutes beneath the block of dry ice, or in the freezer for a minimum of 8 hours.

6. Once the ice cream bars have completely hardened, carefully unmold them and return them to beneath the block of dry ice, or in the coldest part of your freezer.

7. **Meanwhile, make the lime-butter coating:** In a glass bowl, microwave the ghee and coconut oil until it registers 130°F (55°C) or higher on an instant-read thermometer.

8. Add the salt and chocolate and use a whisk or silicone spatula to stir the mixture until all the chocolate has melted. Let the chocolate cool to 80°F (25°C), then stir in the lime zest. Keep in an airtight container at room temperature until ready to use, for up to 1 week.

9. **Make the "cheese" chocolate flakes:** Line a baking sheet with wax or parchment paper.

10. In a glass bowl, microwave the coconut oil until it registers 130°F (55°C) or higher on an instant-read thermometer.

11. Add the salt, chocolate, and cheese powder and use a whisk or silicone spatula to stir the mixture until all the chocolate has melted.

12. Pour the chocolate onto the prepared baking sheet. Using an offset spatula, spread the chocolate out onto the parchment or wax paper as thinly as possible. Place another piece of wax or parchment paper over the chocolate and place the dry ice on top for a few minutes to blast-freeze. (Alternatively, place the pan in the freezer, uncovered, until the chocolate has hardened, about 20 minutes.)

13. Once the chocolate has hardened, working as quickly as possible, lift the wax or parchment and crumple up the paper to break the chocolate into small flakes. Quickly transfer the flakes to a small bowl or airtight container and keep frozen until use. They will keep indefinitely.

14. **Assemble the ice cream bars:** Line a quarter-sheet or half-sheet pan with wax or parchment paper. Set aside.

15. Transfer lime-butter coating to a microwave-safe bowl and microwave to brings its temperature to 80°F (25°C). Transfer it to a tall and narrow vessel like a Collins glass or immersion blender container.

16. Line a work surface on your counter with a large baking sheet or sheet of parchment. Working with one ice cream bar out at a time, dip the bar into the lime-butter coating to coat it completely: pick up the container of lime-butter coating with one hand and tilt it at a 45-degree angle to get more depth for the coating. With the other hand, dip and rotate the ice cream bar in the coating to fully cover it. Working quickly before the coating hardens, sprinkle the top of the ice cream bar with the "cheese" chocolate flakes, lime zest, and a pinch of habanero sugar. Place the bar on the prepared baking sheet and place in the freezer.

17. Repeat the process for all the remaining bars, placing them on the baking sheet in the freezer as you work.

18. Individually wrap each elote ice cream bar in plastic wrap until ready to serve.

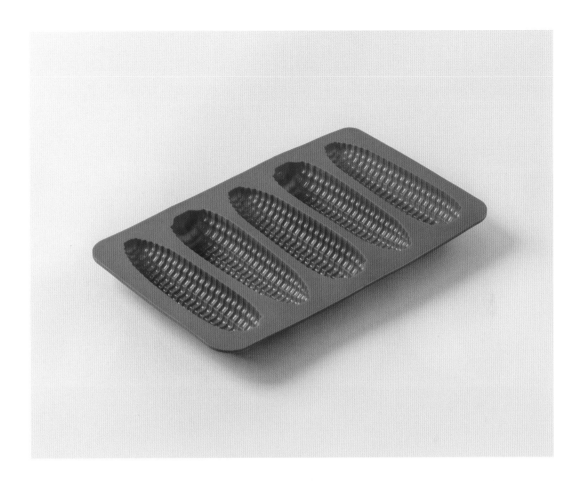

TIPS:

Silicone corn cob shaped molds (originally meant for cornbread) are available online or on Amazon. Alternatively, you can use any silicone ice cream novelty mold.

Dried Parmesan powder, which is dehydrated cheese used to season popcorn, snacks, or emergency food, can also be found online or on Amazon.

The ice cream bars must be extremely cold and hardened when unmolding and dipping. If not hard enough during unmolding, they can break. If not cold enough during dipping, any melting ice cream can break the emulsion of the liquid chocolate. This may be very difficult to achieve with a home freezer if you live in a warmer climate. Instead, I urge you to use the quick-freezing method using dry ice (see Blast Freezing, page 45).

Important: If using the dry ice blast-freezing method, which takes only minutes, be sure to prepare the lime butter coating, "cheese" chocolate flakes, and mise en place for assembly ahead of churning the ice cream.

baka

er's

ack

There's no denying the proximity of ice cream making to the art of baking. Both are exact sciences. I find inspiration in the pasty and bread case and often translate it into my ice cream case.

AMALFI PEAR TORTE

Makes about 1 quart (1 liter)

In the late nineties, pastry chef Salvatore De Riso invented the torta di pere e ricotta—two hazelnut sponge cakes sandwiching a ricotta cream bejeweled with poached pears. His pastry shop, Minori, became famous for this cake, which can now be found at every pasticceria along the Amalfi Coast.

This ice cream is made with a hazelnut meringue cake instead of sponge and replaces fat from egg yolks with brown butter. The result is an intensely flavored hazelnut cake with nuttiness oomph-ed to the nth degree.

For the base

Mascarpone Base (page 51), with changes (see step 1 below)

1 vanilla bean, split lengthwise, or 1 teaspoon (4 g) vanilla extract

2 tablespoons (30 ml) pear liqueur

For the ice cream

1 cup (72 g) crumbled Brown Butter Nut Cake (page 274), made with toasted hazelnuts

1. **Make the base:** Follow the recipe for the Mascarpone Base, scraping the vanilla seeds and adding the vanilla pod to the mixture in the saucepan in step 3. Remove the vanilla pod just after the ice cream base reaches temperature and you pour it back into the mixing vessel. When you add the heavy cream and mascarpone, add the pear liqueur. If using vanilla extract, add it to the base after cooling in the ice bath. Refrigerate the base as directed.

2. **Churn the ice cream:** When ready to begin, place a loaf pan and the cake crumbles in the freezer to chill. Quickly blend the ice cream base once more with a hand blender or whisk before pouring it into an ice cream machine. Churn the ice cream until it reaches the texture of very stiff soft-serve and the surface looks dry, about 25°F (-5°C) or colder on a thermometer gun. Add the cake crumbles in the last few seconds of churning.

3. Transfer the ice cream to the chilled loaf pan. Press a piece of wax paper directly on top of the ice cream and freeze for at least 4 hours before serving.

TIP: The pear liqueur acts as a pear extract or flavoring, allowing you to make this recipe even when pears aren't in season. You don't need a fancy one; a $12 bottle (like Mathilde or Drillaud) will do.

CREOLE COFFEE & DONUTS

Makes about 1 quart (1 liter)

This fan-favorite flavor at Wanderlust Creamery is inspired by the archetypical tourist's breakfast at the famous Café Du Monde in New Orleans: a plate of pillowy fried beignets next to a piping hot Creole café au lait. The ice cream base is steeped with earthy and bitter chicory coffee and dark French roast—unmistakably "Creole style"—then churned with fried beignet crumbs.

For the base

2 tablespoons + 2½ teaspoons (20 g) nonfat dry milk powder

¾ cup + 1 tablespoon (165 g) granulated sugar

½ teaspoon (2 g) tara gum (optional; see page 24)

3 tablespoons + 1 teaspoon (30 g) glucose powder

1¾ cups + 1½ tablespoons (450 g) whole milk

¼ cup + 1 teaspoon (85 g) sweetened condensed milk

70 grams egg yolks (from about 4 large eggs)

1¾ cups (400 g) heavy cream

3 tablespoons (20 g) ground dark French roast coffee

2 tablespoons (12 g) ground Creole-style coffee, such as Café Du Monde coffee

For the fried donut crumbs

4 beignets, 1 Chinese cruller, or 2 plain French crullers, crumbled or cut into ¼-inch (6 mm) pieces (see Note)

Vegetable oil, for deep-frying

1. Prepare an ice bath (see page 39).

2. **Make the base:** In a small bowl, whisk together the milk powder, sugar, tara gum (if using), and glucose. In a tall cylindrical 1½-quart (1.5 liter) mixing vessel, blend the whole milk, condensed milk, and egg yolks with a hand blender to combine. Slowly add the dry ingredients while blending and blend thoroughly to dissolve all the solids.

3. Pour the mixture into a medium saucepan and cook over medium-low heat, whisking constantly, until it reaches 165°F (75°C) on an instant-read thermometer.

4. Once the base reaches 165°F (75°C), immediately remove from the heat and pour it back into the tall mixing vessel. Add the heavy cream and ground coffees and blend with a hand blender for 2 minutes to fully homogenize.

5. Transfer the base to the prepared ice bath to cool. Once completely cool, transfer the base to an airtight container and refrigerate for at least 12 hours and up to 3 days.

6. **Meanwhile, make the fried donut crumbs:** Pour 3 inches (7½ cm) oil into a medium pot and heat the oil over medium-high heat to 350°F (175°C).

NOTE: Beignets are essentially fried choux pastry, which is different from typical American donuts. You can make your own beignets from scratch or from a packaged mix (Café Du Monde sells a mix available online) or—use ready-made Chinese crullers, which will yield a fairly similar result. Lastly, a plain French cruller from your local donut shop can work, albeit with a slight flavor difference.

7. Line a plate with paper towels. Fry the crumbs in the hot oil until crispy and golden brown. Scoop out with a slotted spoon or spider and drain on the paper towels. Let cool completely before transferring to an airtight container. Store at room temperature for up to 3 days.

8. **Churn the ice cream:** Once the ice cream base is completely chilled, place a loaf pan and the crumbs in the freezer to chill. Quickly blend the base with a whisk or hand blender before pouring through a fine-mesh sieve into an ice cream machine. Churn the ice cream until it reaches the texture of very stiff soft-serve and the surface looks dry, about 25°F (−5°C) or colder on a thermometer gun. Add the fried donut crumbs in the last few seconds of churning.

9. Transfer the ice cream to the chilled loaf pan. Press a piece of wax paper directly on top of the ice cream and freeze for at least 4 hours before serving.

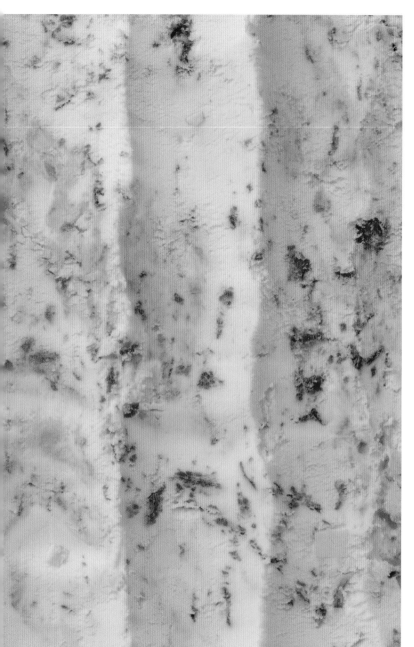

AUSTRALIAN PAVLOVA

Makes about 1 quart (1 liter)

For the "meringue" base
Blank Base (page 48)
½ teaspoon (2 g) marshmallow flavor extract

For the ice cream
Raspberry Stracciatella (page 279), tempered to 80°F (25°C)
1 cup (120 g) crumbled store-bought meringues
Passion Fruit Ripple (recipe follows)

TIP: Marshmallow flavor extract adds an airy flavor note to the eggless ice cream base, which results in a meringue-flavored ice cream.

Whenever this flavor comes around at Wanderlust Creamery, debate ensues. "Pavlova is Kiwi, not Australian," a New Zealander will comment. "Only because you got it from us," an Australian will reply. A quick Google search tells me it's named after a Russian ballerina, only adding to the confusion. Whatever the origin, I consider this ice cream Australian because of the flavors: white chocolate, raspberry, and passion fruit—a trio I commonly see in Australian desserts.

1. **Make the "meringue" base:** Make the blank base as directed and add the marshmallow flavoring extract once the base has completely cooled in the ice bath.

2. **Churn the ice cream:** When ready to begin, place a loaf pan in the freezer to chill. Quickly blend the ice cream base once more with a hand blender or whisk before pouring it into an ice cream machine. Churn the ice cream until it reaches the texture of very stiff soft-serve and the surface looks dry, about 25°F (-5°C) or colder on a thermometer gun.

3. While the ice cream is churning, pour one-quarter of the raspberry stracciatella into a separate bowl. Add the meringue crumble and stir lightly to coat the crumbs.

4. Once the ice cream reaches the texture of very stiff soft-serve and the surface looks dry,

about 25°F (-5°C), pour in the remaining raspberry stracciatella in the last few seconds of churning to create freckles. Quickly follow with the chocolate-coated meringue crumble.

5. Spread half of the ice cream into the chilled loaf pan. Pour half of the passion fruit ripple on top. Repeat the layering process once more. Immediately place the ice cream into the freezer for 15 minutes to firm it up.

6. Using a spatula, gently fold the ice cream and jam layers to create swirls. Three or four folds should be sufficient for visible ribbons throughout the pan; any more than that will overmix the jam into the ice cream base, which may affect freezing and final texture.

7. Press a piece of wax paper directly on top of the ice cream and freeze for at least 4 hours before serving.

PASSION FRUIT RIPPLE

Makes 1 cup (360 g)

1 cup (195 g) unsweetened passion fruit puree

½ cup (100 g) granulated sugar

3 tablespoons (65 g) glucose syrup or corn syrup

¼ teaspoon agar-agar powder

1. Combine all the ingredients in a small saucepan over medium heat, whisking until all solids are dissolved.

2. Continue cooking until the mixture comes to a boil and continue boiling for 30 seconds.

3. Remove the mixture from the heat and allow it to cool completely. Transfer to an airtight container and keep refrigerated until ready to use, up to 3 days.

OKINAWAN MONT BLANC

Makes about 1 quart (1 liter)

I had my first bite of a Mont Blanc at the famous Angelina in Paris—an airy cloud of meringue and whipped cream topped with the thinnest strands of chestnut cream that epitomized the flavor of autumn. I didn't think that experience could be topped, until I tried an Okinawan Mont Blanc. Made with Okinawan purple sweet potatoes (beni imo) instead of chestnuts, it has the same earthiness and nuttiness, but somehow it's more buttery yet slightly less sweet, with a vibrant purple hue instead of chestnut's dull brown.

For the base
Mascarpone Base (page 51), with changes (see step 1)

1 vanilla bean, split lengthwise

For the beni imo variegate
8 ounces (225 g) purple sweet potato, peeled and cubed

¼ cup (50 g) granulated sugar

½ cup + 2 tablespoons (200 g) sweetened condensed milk

3½ tablespoons (50 g) unsalted butter, at room temperature

2½ teaspoons dark rum

For the ice cream
1⅓ cups (200 g) crumbled Almond Shortbread (page 275)

1. **Make the base:** Make the mascarpone base as directed, scraping the vanilla seeds into the base after straining it into the ice bath (step 5).

2. **Make the beni imo variegate:** Bring a medium pot of water to a boil and add the sweet potatoes. Boil until fork-tender, 8 to 10 minutes.

3. Drain and transfer the hot sweet potatoes to a food processor. Add the sugar, condensed milk, butter, and rum and process until smooth. Transfer the mixture to an airtight container and refrigerate until ready to use or up to 3 days.

4. **Churn the ice cream:** When ready to begin, place a loaf pan and the almond shortbread crumble in the freezer to chill. Quickly blend the ice cream base once more with a hand blender or whisk before pouring it into an ice cream machine. Churn the ice cream until it reaches the texture of very stiff soft-serve and the surface looks dry, about 25°F (−5°C) or colder on a thermometer gun. Add the almond shortbread crumble in the last few seconds of churning.

5. Spread half of the ice cream mixture into the chilled loaf pan. Spread half of the sweet potato puree on top. Repeat the layering process once more. Immediately place the ice cream into the freezer for 15 minutes to firm it up.

6. Using a spatula, gently fold the ice cream and sweet potato layers to create swirls. Three or four folds should be sufficient for visible ribbons throughout the pan; any more than that will overmix the variegate into the ice cream base, which may affect freezing and final texture.

7. Press a piece of wax paper directly on top of the ice cream and freeze for at least 3 hours before serving.

PA AMB XOCOLATA

For the olive oil base

⅔ cup (130 g) granulated sugar

½ cup + 3 tablespoons (100 g) glucose powder

3 tablespoons + ½ teaspoon (22 g) nonfat dry milk powder

½ teaspoon (2 g) tara gum (optional; see page 24)

Scant ¾ teaspoon (3 g) lecithin (optional)

2⅓ cups + 1 tablespoon (575 g) whole milk

3½ tablespoons (70 g) sweetened condensed milk

¾ cup + 2 tablespoons (200 g) heavy cream

¼ cup + 3 tablespoons (90 g) Arbequina olive oil

Grated zest of ¼ lemon or ⅛ orange

For the ice cream

½ recipe Dark Chocolate Freckles (page 279), tempered to 78°F (25°C)

½ cup (70 g) crumbs from day-old pain au levain or sourdough

1 teaspoon flaky sea salt or finishing salt

In the winter of 2009, I spent some time exploring several cities along the Mediterranean coastline. My first destination was Barcelona. Night after night of my visit, I became familiar with the budget-friendly menus of tapas bars, knowing full well that I was saving to splurge on a final dinner at a renowned restaurant in the Gothic quarter known for its exceptional prix-fixe Catalonian menu. Finally, the highly anticipated grand finale night arrived. The mere presence of three distinct varieties of olive oil on the table, each with a different color, aroma, and viscosity, hinted at the culinary masterpiece that I was about to experience. But the vibe was killed when I read the underwhelming description of the dessert course: "Day-old toast, chocolate, olive oil, sea salt." Curious, I asked the waiter to elaborate. He explained that it was pa amb xocolata, a traditional after-school snack enjoyed by Spanish children for generations. What seemed like a humble dessert actually turned out to be the highlight of the entire meal. The combination of crusty bread and melted milky chocolate, complemented by the verdant grassy notes of the Arbequina olive oil, the crunchy flaky sea salt, and the simple yet sublime melding of it all together reaffirmed my fascination with Catalonian cuisine.

1. Prepare an ice bath (see page 39).

2. **Make the olive oil base:** In a small bowl, whisk together the sugar, glucose, milk powder, tara gum (if using), and lecithin (if using). In a tall cylindrical 1½-quart (1.5 liter) mixing vessel, blend the whole milk and condensed milk together with a hand blender. Slowly add the dry ingredients while blending and blend thoroughly to dissolve all the solids.

3. Pour the mixture into a small saucepan and cook over medium-low heat, whisking constantly, until it reaches 165°F (75°C) on an instant-read thermometer.

4. Once the base reaches 165°F (75°C), immediately remove from the heat and pour it back into the tall mixing vessel along with the heavy cream; blend with a hand blender for 2 minutes to fully homogenize. Slowly drizzle in the olive oil in the last 30 seconds of blending.

5. Pour the ice cream base through a fine-mesh sieve into the prepared ice bath to cool. Once completely cool, add the citrus zest and transfer to an airtight container. Cover and refrigerate for at least 12 hours and up to 3 days.

6. **Churn the ice cream:** When ready to begin, place a loaf pan in the freezer to chill. Quickly blend the ice cream base once more with a hand blender or whisk before pouring it into an ice cream machine. Churn the ice cream until it reaches the texture of very stiff soft-serve and the surface looks dry, about 25°F (-5°C) or colder on a thermometer gun.

7. Meanwhile, in a small bowl, stir the dark chocolate into the bread crumbs. Add the flaky salt and gently stir to distribute; do not let the salt dissolve.

8. Once the ice cream reaches 25°F (-5°C) or colder, pour in the dark chocolate in the last few seconds of churning to create freckles.

9. Transfer the ice cream mixture to the chilled loaf pan. Press a piece of wax paper directly on top of the ice cream and freeze for at least 4 hours before serving.

CHAPTER 11

cheese
& y

Whether we know it or not, we all have implicit biases when it comes to food. I first realized some of my own at a young age, hearing about my mom's favorite ice cream flavor: cheese. Not mascarpone or cream-cheese ice cream, but bright-orange cheddar cheese ice cream. Although it was a standard in my mom's home country, I thought it to be an odd, grimace-inducing flavor. Until my mom posed a question—"But you like cheesecake, don't you?" It opened my eyes to a world of possibilities with other cheeses and dairy products, like the fact that the same ricotta

dairy
yogurt

that stuffs lasagna fills a sweet cannoli. Or that the same thick, cheese-like yogurt used as a savory dip can be flipped into sweet breakfast with fruit. Burrata on a salad is great, but have you ever had it as an ice cream flavor with a milky pistachio spread swirled through it? My favorite melty, stretchy cheese situation isn't found between two tortillas or in a folded slice of pepperoni pizza, but in a Middle Eastern dessert underneath buttery strings of pastry soaked in perfumy syrup. This chapter is an ode to all of it.

LABNEH & POMEGRANATE ROSE JAM

Makes about 1 quart (1 liter)

In the year I was in the throes of launching Wanderlust Creamery, my friends took a vacation to Greece without me. They went island hopping around the Aegean Sea and raved about Naxos, an idyllic island they claimed was their favorite of all. On Naxos they had traveled down winding roads lined with verdant valleys of endless olive groves, passing by white-washed houses to reach an ancient mountain village constructed predominantly from Venetian marble. There they rewarded themselves with freshly made yogurt—made from the milk of a ewe that was grazing just feet away—strewn with rose preserves and pomegranate seeds. I found that flavor combination far too captivating not to re-create in some way. I turned it into an ice cream flavor. But here I use labneh, the Levantine nod to Greek yogurt, which is left to drain for longer and has a thicker texture, making for an even creamier ice cream.

For the labneh base

¾ cup + 3 tablespoons (190 g) granulated sugar

5 tablespoons + 2 teaspoons (40 g) nonfat dry yogurt powder or nonfat dry milk powder

½ teaspoon (2 g) tara gum (optional; see page 24)

Scant ¾ teaspoon (3 g) lecithin (optional)

1 cup + 3½ tablespoons (300 g) whole milk

1 cup + 3 tablespoons (275 g) heavy cream

9 ounces (250 g) full-fat labneh

For the pomegranate-rose jam

½ cup (100 g) granulated sugar

¾ teaspoon (1.5 g) agar-agar

½ cup (120 g) 100% pomegranate juice

½ cup (150 g) rose jam (see Note)

NOTE: Rose jam can be purchased at many gourmet or specialty food shops, however my favorites are the thick and concentrated Greek ones found in Middle Eastern supermarkets.

1. Prepare an ice bath (see page 39).

2. **Make the labneh base:** In a small bowl, whisk together the sugar, yogurt powder, tara gum (if using), and lecithin (if using). In a tall cylindrical 1½-quart (1.5 liter) mixing vessel, blend the whole milk and heavy cream with a hand blender. Slowly add the dry ingredients while blending and blend thoroughly to dissolve all the solids.

3. Pour the mixture into a small saucepan and cook over medium-low heat, whisking constantly, until it reaches 165°F (75°C) on an instant-read thermometer.

4. Once the base reaches 165°F (75°C), immediately remove from the heat and pour it back into the tall mixing vessel. Add the labneh and blend with a hand blender for 2 minutes to fully homogenize.

5. Pour the base through a fine-mesh sieve into the prepared ice bath to cool. Once completely cool, transfer to an airtight container. Cover and refrigerate for at least 12 hours and up to 3 days.

6. **Make the pomegranate-rose jam:** In a small bowl, mix together the sugar and agar-agar.

7. In a small saucepan, heat the pomegranate juice with the sugar and agar-agar mixture over medium heat. Whisk the mixture, making sure the solids dissolve completely. Bring the mixture to a boil, allow it to boil for 30 seconds, then remove it from the heat and allow it to cool to room temperature.

8. Stir in the rose jam, and transfer mixture to an airtight container.

9. **Churn the ice cream:** When ready to begin, place a loaf pan and the jam in the freezer to chill. Quickly blend the ice cream base once more with a hand blender or whisk before pouring it into an ice cream machine. Churn the ice cream until it reaches the texture of very stiff soft-serve and the surface looks dry, about 25°F (-5°C) or colder on a thermometer gun.

10. Spread half of the ice cream mixture into the chilled loaf pan. Pour half of the jam on top. Repeat the layering process once more. Immediately place the ice cream into the freezer for 15 minutes to firm it up.

11. Using a spatula, gently fold the ice cream and jam layers to create swirls. Three or four folds should be sufficient for visible ribbons throughout the pan; any more than that will overmix the jam into the ice cream base, which may affect freezing and final texture.

12. Press a piece of wax paper directly on top of the ice cream and freeze for at least 4 hours before serving.

KNAFEH

When my in-laws visited Bethlehem and asked if I wanted souvenirs, I asked for "whatever you think is absolutely worth bringing home." Instead of some religious tchotchke, they brought home what looked from the outside like restaurant leftovers wrapped in foil. Yet inside was something definitely worthy: It was a slice of authentic Palestinian knafeh—a square of mild cheese covered with crispy string-thin strands of buttery, Mediterranean sun-scented pastry soaked in orange flower syrup and dotted with green bits of pistachio.

For the base

¼ cup + 1½ teaspoons (30 g) nonfat dry milk powder

¾ cup (150 g) granulated sugar

½ teaspoon (1 g) salt

¼ cup + 1 tablespoon (45 g) glucose powder

½ teaspoon (2 g) tara gum (optional; see page 24)

Scant ¾ teaspoon (3 g) lecithin (optional)

1¾ cups + 1 tablespoon (415 g) whole milk

1 cup + 2 teaspoons (240 g) heavy cream

4 ounces (115 g) mascarpone cheese

4 ounces (115 g) whole-milk ricotta cheese

For the ice cream

1 cup (295 g) Kadaifi Crisp (recipe follows)

¾ cup (120 g) finely chopped pistachios

1. Prepare an ice bath (see page 39).

2. **Make the base:** In a small bowl, whisk together the milk powder, sugar, salt, glucose powder, tara gum (if using), and lecithin (if using). In a tall cylindrical 1½-quart (1.5 liter) mixing vessel, blend the milk with a hand blender while slowly adding the dry ingredients. Blend thoroughly to dissolve all the solids.

3. Pour the mixture into a small saucepan and cook over medium-low heat, whisking constantly, until it reaches 165°F (75°C) on an instant-read thermometer.

4. Once the base reaches 165°F (75°C), immediately remove from the heat and pour it back into the tall mixing vessel. Add the heavy cream, mascarpone, and ricotta cheese and blend with a hand blender for 2 minutes to fully homogenize.

5. Pour the base through a fine-mesh sieve into the prepared ice bath to cool. Once completely cool, transfer to an airtight container. Cover and refrigerate for at least 12 hours and up to 2 days.

TIP: The knafeh I had was made with Nabulsi cheese, which has a very mild flavor and the texture of mozzarella. The cheese becomes elastic when heated, so it doesn't melt well into an ice cream base. I've found that a blend of mascarpone and ricotta with a generous amount of salt imitates the flavor pretty closely for ice cream.

Method continued on next page

6. **Churn the ice cream:**
   When ready to begin, place a loaf pan in the freezer to chill. Quickly blend the ice cream base once more with a hand blender or whisk before pouring into an ice cream machine. Churn until the ice cream reaches the texture of very stiff soft-serve and the surface looks dry, about 25°F (−5°C) or colder on a thermometer gun. Gradually add the cooled kadaifi and pistachios in the last few seconds of churning.

7. Transfer the ice cream to the chilled loaf pan. Press a piece of wax paper directly on top of the ice cream and freeze for at least 4 hours before serving.

KADAIFI CRISP
Makes about 2 cups (590 g)

Kadaifi are angel hair–like strands of pastry dough found in most Middle Eastern markets. If you don't have access to kadaifi, you can substitute it by taking half a 1-pound (455 g) package of phyllo dough, tightly rolled, and then thinly slicing it crosswise into noodles.

1¼ cups (250 g) granulated sugar

½ cup (120 g) water

2 tablespoons (30 g) orange flower water

8 ounces (230 g) kadaifi dough (half a 16 oz/455 g package)

8 tablespoons (115 g) unsalted butter, melted and cooled slightly

1. In a small saucepan, combine the sugar and water and bring to a boil over medium heat. Remove from the heat and add the orange flower water. Let cool to room temperature.

2. Meanwhile, preheat the oven to 350°F (180°C). Line a baking sheet with parchment paper.

3. Place the kadaifi dough in a large bowl. Working carefully with your hands, gently pull apart and separate the strands to make a fluffy mass. Gradually drizzle in the melted butter and toss to coat all the strands.

4. Carefully spread out the strands evenly on the prepared baking sheet. Bake until golden and crispy, about 1 hour.

5. While the baked kadaifi is still hot, transfer it to a large bowl and drizzle some of the cooled syrup over the strings. Using tongs, toss to evenly coat. Allow the kadaifi to completely absorb the syrup before adding more and tossing to coat once again. Repeat until all the syrup has been used. Spread the kadaifi on the baking sheet and let cool to room temperature.

TEA-RAMISU

For the base

Mascarpone Base (page 51), with changes (see step 1)

For Royal Milk Tea-Ramisu: 5 tablespoons (25 g) loose Ceylon or Assam tea leaves

For Thai Tea-Ramisu: 5 tablespoons (25 g) loose Thai tea leaves

For Matcha Tea-Ramisu: 1½ teaspoons (3 g) matcha powder

1 vanilla bean, split lengthwise

For the Royal Milk boozy tea syrup

¼ cup (60 g) aged or dark rum

1 tablespoon + 1 teaspoon (17 g) granulated sugar

¼ cup (60 g) strongly brewed Ceylon tea or Assam tea (made with at least 2 tablespoons/ 10 g loose tea leaves)

For the Thai boozy tea syrup

¼ cup (60 g) Licor 43 (see Tip) or other vanilla liqueur

1 tablespoon + 1 teaspoon (17 g) granulated sugar

¼ cup (60 g) strongly brewed Thai tea (made with at least 2 tablespoons/10 g loose tea leaves)

For the Matcha boozy tea syrup

1 tablespoon (13 g) granulated sugar

2 teaspoons (4 g) matcha powder

4 tablespoons (60 g) water

¼ cup (60 g) Licor 43 or other vanilla liqueur

For the ice cream

Sponge Cake (page 276), cut into finger-size strips, or 24 store-bought ladyfingers

Everyone loves tiramisu. There's something about the marriage of a sweet cream with bitter, boozy coffee. But coffee can get boring, in my opinion. I find that a wide variety of teas can provide an equally bitter and bold dynamic to mascarpone yet transcend with nuances that are highlighted by sweet liqueurs and spirits. What follows are my three favorite iterations of tea-ramisu ice cream: made with Royal Milk tea (a strong and malty black tea), Thai tea, and matcha. Each is completely different in flavor profile from the next. I prefer to use sponge cake instead of the traditional ladyfingers, which tend to have an overpowering citrus flavor. However, you can still use them, or a store-bought sponge cake. These ice cream recipes utilize the blank canvas of the mascarpone base.

1. **Make the base:** *For Royal Milk and Thai Tea-Ramisu*: Before making the mascarpone base, start by infusing the whole milk with tea. Place it in a saucepan and bring to a boil. Add the tea leaves, remove from the heat, and let steep for 25 minutes. Pour through a fine-mesh sieve lined with cheesecloth and transfer to the mixing vessel. *For Matcha Tea-Ramisu*: Simply add the matcha powder to the dry ingredients.

2. *For all versions*: Follow the directions for step 2 of the base recipe by blending the milk with the dry ingredients. In step 3, when heating the mixture, scrape in the vanilla seeds and add the vanilla pod. Remove the pod before blending in the heavy cream and mascarpone. Follow the rest of the recipe as directed, chilling the base for at least 12 hours and up to 3 days.

3. **Make the boozy tea syrup:** *For Royal Milk and Thai Tea-Ramisu*: In a small bowl, combine all the ingredients and whisk thoroughly to dissolve the sugar. *For Matcha Tea-Ramisu*: Using a whisk (a matcha whisk, if you have one), combine the sugar and matcha powder in a small bowl. Whisk in 2 tablespoons (30 g) of the water. Once the matcha has completely dissolved and no lumps remain, add the remaining water and the liqueur.

4. **Churn the ice cream:** When ready to begin, place a loaf pan in the freezer to chill. Quickly blend the ice cream base once more with a hand blender or whisk before pouring it into an ice cream machine. Churn the ice cream until it reaches the texture of very stiff soft-serve and the surface looks dry, about 25°F (−5°C) or colder on a thermometer gun.

5. Meanwhile, using a pastry brush, moisten the sponge cake strips or ladyfingers with the boozy tea syrup, making sure not to oversoak them or they may be difficult to handle. Set aside.

6. Spread half of the ice cream into the chilled loaf pan. Arrange a layer of soaked cake strips or ladyfingers on top of the ice cream. Using a pair of kitchen scissors, snip each cake strip or ladyfinger into small squares. Working quickly, repeat this layering process once more. Immediately place the ice cream into the freezer for 15 minutes to firm it up.

7. Using a spatula, gently fold the ice cream and cake pieces twice. Rotate the pan 180 degrees, then do two more folds. Press a piece of wax paper directly on top of the ice cream and freeze for at least 4 hours before serving.

TIP: Licor 43 is a Spanish liqueur that tastes of honeyed vanilla with a whisper of sweet orange. If you can't find it, any vanilla liqueur, such as Tuaca or vanilla schnapps, will suffice.

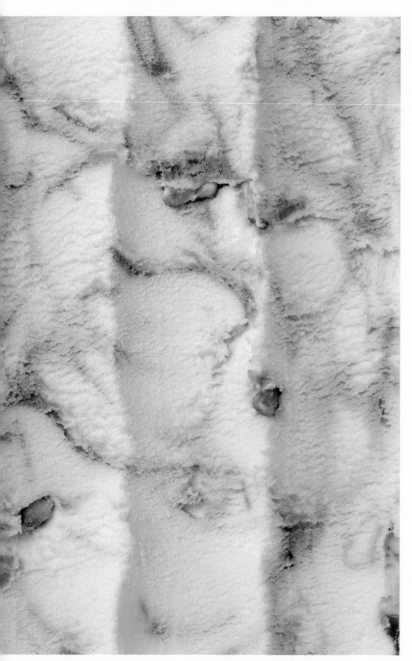

BURRATA & CREMA DI PISTACCHIO

For the base

2 ½ tablespoons (20 g) nonfat dry milk powder

⅔ cup (130 g) granulated sugar

¼ cup + 2 ½ tablespoons (60 g) glucose powder

½ teaspoon (2 g) tara gum (optional; see page 24)

Scant ¾ teaspoon (3 g) lecithin

1 ½ cups + 1 ½ tablespoons (365 g) whole milk

¾ cup + 3 tablespoons (215 g) heavy cream

8 ounces (225 g) burrata

For the ice cream

1 cup (280 g) Italian crema di pistacchio (see Tip), tempered to 90°F (25°C)

¼ cup + 2 tablespoons (50 g) pistachios, chopped

TIP: Italian crema di pistacchio (pistachio cream) is a jarred, olive-hued spread, much like Nutella but made with at least 50% pistachios, milk, sugar, and sometimes white chocolate or olive oil. You can find it online or at specialty food shops.

Fior di latte is an Italian term that translates to *flower of milk*. It generally implies that something is made with the best-quality cow's milk. Italians use this only when referring to two things: gelato and mozzarella. If you've ever tasted fior di latte ice cream in Italy, you'd understand how closely related in flavor the two are. Stateside, the only way I've found to make a fior di latte ice cream that's as immensely milky and buttery—yet with a clean finish—is to use high-quality burrata melted right into a base of the best milk and cream you can find.

1. Prepare an ice bath (see page 39).

2. **Make the base:** In a small bowl, whisk together the milk powder, sugar, glucose, tara gum (if using), and lecithin. In a tall 1½-quart (1.5 liter) mixing vessel, blend the milk with a hand blender while slowly adding the dry ingredients. Blend thoroughly to dissolve all the solids.

3. Pour the mixture into a medium saucepan and cook over medium-low heat, whisking constantly, until it reaches 165°F (75°C) on an instant-read thermometer. Meanwhile, place the heavy cream and burrata in a stand blender.

4. Once the base reaches 165°F (75°C), immediately remove from the heat and pour into the blender and blend for 2 minutes to fully homogenize.

5. Transfer the base to the prepared ice bath to cool. Once completely cool, pour through a fine-mesh sieve into an airtight container. Cover and refrigerate for at least 12 hours and up to 2 days.

6. **Churn the ice cream:** When ready to begin, place a loaf pan in the freezer to chill. Quickly blend the ice cream base once more with a hand blender or whisk before pouring it into an ice cream machine. Churn the ice cream until it reaches the texture of very stiff soft-serve and the surface looks dry, about 25°F (−5°C) or colder on a thermometer gun.

7. Meanwhile, in a medium bowl, mix the pistachio cream with the chopped pistachios.

8. Spread half of the ice cream onto the bottom of the chilled loaf pan. Spread half of the pistachio cream mixture on top. Repeat the layering process once more. Immediately place the ice cream into the freezer for 15 minutes to firm it up.

9. Using a spatula, gently fold the ice cream and pistachio layers to create swirls. Three or four folds should be sufficient for visible ribbons throughout the pan.

10. Press a piece of wax paper directly on top of the ice cream and freeze for at least 4 hours before serving.

KOLDSKÅL

In Denmark, summer is officially marked by cold bowls of sweet buttermilk soup flecked with vanilla seeds and lemon zest. Slurping what tastes like cheesecake in liquid form sounds absolutely gluttonous, but is actually quite light, not too sweet, and refreshing on a warm day. Koldskål is traditionally topped with crushed Danish kammerjunker biscuits that remind me of Nilla wafers, and is sometimes dotted with blueberries or sliced strawberries, which you can imitate with freeze-dried berries in this ice cream iteration.

For the base

2 tablespoons + ½ teaspoon (15 g) nonfat dry milk powder or nonfat dry yogurt powder

⅔ cup + ½ tablespoon (140 g) granulated sugar

½ teaspoon (2 g) tara gum (optional; see page 24)

2 tablespoons + ¾ teaspoon (20 g) glucose powder

1½ cups + 1½ tablespoons (365 g) heavy cream

3 tablespoons (60 g) sweetened condensed milk

70 grams egg yolks (from about 4 large eggs)

1¾ cups (410 g) full-fat buttermilk

Grated zest of ⅓ lemon

1 tablespoon (15 g) fresh lemon juice

For the ice cream

⅓ cup (150 g) crushed kammerjunker, Nilla wafer cookies, or shortbread cookies

¼ cup (7 g) freeze-dried whole blueberries or strawberry slices (optional)

1. Prepare an ice bath (see page 39).

2. **Make the base:** In a small bowl, whisk together the milk powder, sugar, tara gum (if using), and glucose. In a tall cylindrical 1½-quart (1.5 liter) mixing vessel, blend the heavy cream, condensed milk, and egg yolks with a hand blender. Slowly add the dry ingredients while blending and blend thoroughly to dissolve all the solids.

3. Pour the mixture into a small saucepan and cook over medium-low heat, whisking constantly, until it reaches 165°F (75°C) on an instant-read thermometer.

4. Once the base reaches 165°F (75°C), immediately remove from the heat and pour into the mixing vessel and add the buttermilk; blend with a hand blender for 2 minutes to fully homogenize.

5. Pour the base through a fine-mesh sieve into the prepared ice bath to cool. Once completely cool, stir in the lemon zest and lemon juice. Transfer to an airtight container and refrigerate for at least 12 hours and up to 3 days.

6. **Churn the ice cream:** When ready to begin, place a loaf pan and the crushed cookies in the freezer to chill. Quickly blend the ice cream base once more with a hand blender or whisk before pouring it into an ice cream machine. Churn the ice cream until it reaches the texture of very stiff soft-serve and the surface looks dry, about 25°F (−5°C) or colder on a thermometer gun. Add the cookies and freeze-dried fruit (if using) in the last few seconds of churning.

7. Transfer the ice cream to the chilled loaf pan. Press a piece of wax paper directly on top of the ice cream and freeze for at least 4 hours before serving.

CHAPTER 12

rice
cre

In 2015, when I started letting people in on my little secret—that I was starting an ice cream shop with travel-inspired flavors—my boyfriend JP's cousin Mark suggested making "Thai mango-sticky rice ice cream." I thought, *Well, how do I do that?* Here lies the classic ice cream conundrum—how to make a specific flavor while respecting the balance of ice cream. Whole rice grains, even when cooked, freeze into hard bits. Dairy masks the subtle flavor of rice . . . so does coconut. Too much pureed rice renders the recipe too high in solids and unscoopable. It took about four weeks of daily recipe

ams

revisions and tweaks to get the perfect balance of a scratch-made sticky rice milk and coconut, so one didn't overpower the other, with a soft and scoopable end result. A few years later, I reiterated the recipe using heavy cream in place of coconut cream, and to my surprise, it still tasted like rice, but in a different way—like sweet rice cake or horchata sans cinnamon. I quickly realized how versatile the mother recipe was . . . it spawned so many ice creams inspired by rice desserts.

STICKY RICE & MANGO

This is the flavor that put us on the map. There were at least thirty different recipe versions, until I landed on a dense and smooth ice cream that tastes equally of all the hallmark elements: sweet rice, slightly salty coconut cream, and very ripe Southeast Asian mango. Everyone who tries this ice cream is amused by how it tastes exactly like the famous Thai dessert. Because this recipe is made primarily with the ingredients that are in the namesake dessert, it's also unintentionally vegan. Many people are surprised to find out that there's no dairy in this ice cream. Its thick and creamy texture is achieved with the "sticky rice milk" and added fat from coconut oil.

For the base

Sticky Rice Milk (page 53)

½ cup + 1 tablespoon (114 g) granulated sugar

1 cup + 2 tablespoons (160 g) glucose powder

1 teaspoon (3 g) Nondairy Stabilizer (optional; page 33)

2 cups + 2½ tablespoons (381 g) coconut cream (see Tip)

½ teaspoon (1 g) tapioca flour

3 tablespoons (45 g) water

2 tablespoons + 1 teaspoon (30 g) virgin coconut oil

For the ice cream

Mango Jam (recipe follows)

1. Prepare an ice bath (see page 39).

2. **Make the base:** Pour the sticky rice milk into a tall mixing vessel. In a small bowl, whisk together the sugar, glucose, and stabilizer (if using).

3. In a small saucepan, cook the coconut cream over medium-low heat, whisking occasionally until it reaches 115°F (45°C). Add the dry ingredients and blend with a hand blender until completely dissolved.

4. Continue cooking, whisking constantly, until the mixture reaches 165°F (75°C) on an instant-read thermometer. Meanwhile, in a small bowl, whisk together the tapioca flour and water to make a slurry.

5. When the mixture reaches 165°F (75°C), whisk in the tapioca slurry. Bring the mixture to a boil and cook, stirring, until thickened, about 1 minute. Immediately remove the base from the heat and pour it into the tall mixing vessel containing the rice milk. Add the coconut oil and blend with a hand blender for 2 minutes to fully homogenize the base.

6. Pour the base through a fine-mesh sieve into the prepared ice bath to cool. Once completely cool, pour into an airtight container. Cover and refrigerate for at least 12 hours and up to 3 days.

TIP: Be snobby about your coconut cream; not all of them are made equal. Because this is a Thai flavor, I use only the Thai brands Mae Ploy, Aroy-D, and Savoy. Stay away from coconut products with UHT (ultra-high temperature) on the label, as they have a slight oxidized flavor that doesn't work well in this specific recipe. And be sure to use full-fat coconut cream—not coconut milk.

Method continued on next page

7. **Churn the ice cream:** When ready to begin, place a loaf pan and the mango jam in the freezer to chill. Quickly blend the ice cream base once more with a hand blender or whisk before pouring it into an ice cream machine. Churn the ice cream until it reaches the texture of very stiff soft-serve and the surface looks dry, about 25°F (-5°C) or colder on a thermometer gun.

8. Spread half of the ice cream into the frozen loaf pan. Pour half of the mango jam on top of the ice cream. Repeat the layering process once more. Immediately place the ice cream into the freezer for 15 minutes to firm it up.

9. Using a small spatula, gently fold the ice cream and mango jam layers to create swirls. Three to four folds should be sufficient for visible ribbons throughout the pan; any more than that will mix the mango jam into the ice cream base, which may affect freezing and texture.

10. Press a piece of wax paper onto the top of the ice cream and freeze for at least 3 hours before serving.

MANGO JAM
Makes 1 cup (265 g)

½ pound (225 g) very ripe Ataulfo mangoes (see Tip), peeled and diced (1 to 2 mangoes)

¼ cup (50 g) granulated sugar

In a stand blender, process the mangoes with the sugar until completely smooth. Place the puree in an airtight container and refrigerate for up to 3 days.

TIPS:

Mango sticky rice is typically made with Alphonso mangoes, which are hard to find outside of Asia. Stateside, Ataulfo mangoes (sometimes labeled "champagne mango" or "honey mango") are similar tasting and used in this recipe. You can also use any other Southeast Asian mango like Kesar or Keitt.

Always choose the smaller, yellow, oblong mangoes and not the larger and rounder red kind from South America. The former should never be substituted with the latter.

Make sure the mangoes you use are very ripe, to the point where they are just beginning to wrinkle and have bright orange skin and the soft feel of a peach when gently squeezed. You can speed up ripening by placing the mangoes in a closed paper bag together with a ripe banana or apple and leaving it at room temperature for a few days. Never refrigerate your mangoes before they are ripe, as this will irreversibly stop the ripening process.

If yellow mangoes are not in season, you can substitute the mango jam with 1 cup (250 g) canned kesar mango puree (found at most Indian and South Asian grocers) mixed with 3 tablespoons corn syrup.

BIKO

In the early days of Wanderlust Creamery, before we could afford any machinery or equipment beyond what we inherited from the Cold Stone Creamery that inhabited the space before us, we made our sticky rice ice cream base just two gallons at a time. That's because we only had one stockpot and one induction burner. Steven, RJ, or Fernando (the kitchen team at the time) were often tasked with standing over the pot and continuously whisking, painstakingly waiting for the temperature of the mix to hit 185°F (85°C)—the hydration point of our stabilizer at the time. As you can imagine, a shift in that corner of the kitchen was a lesson in patience. I'm not sure which of the guys it was who got impatient and decided to multitask with another chore during sticky rice duty, but one day a batch went unstirred for a while and the bottom of the pot burned. With every penny critical in that first year of business, the thought of throwing it out pained us. I frantically stirred, hoping that maybe the burnt part would be diluted, but instead, every turn of the whisk only colored the batch a darker shade of tan. Taking it off the burner, though, it smelled familiar: like biko—a Filipino rice cake baked with brown sugar and coconut cream until caramelized. Feeling hopeful, I returned the pot to the heat to be "burned" more. An hour later, this batch that started out as sticky rice and mango base ended up being an outrageously popular biko ice cream instead.

For the base

Sticky Rice Milk (page 53)

1 teaspoon (3 g) Nondairy Stabilizer (page 33)

1¼ cups (180 g) glucose powder

¾ cup (150 g) granulated sugar

1¾ cups (385 g) coconut cream (see Note on page 29)

½ cup + 1½ tablespoons (140 ml) water

1 by 4-inch (2.5 by 10 cm) strip of banana leaf, for steeping (optional)

Heaping ¼ teaspoon (1 g) tapioca flour

3 tablespoons (45 g) water

2 tablespoons + 1 teaspoon (30 g) virgin coconut oil

For the ice cream

Latik (page 237)

1. Prepare an ice bath (see page 39).

2. **Make the base:** Pour the sticky rice milk into a tall cylindrical 1½-quart (1.5 liter) mixing vessel. In a small bowl, whisk together the stabilizer and glucose. Add the mixture to the sticky rice milk and blend thoroughly with a hand blender. Set aside.

3. Make a caramel: In a medium saucepan, melt the granulated sugar over medium-high heat. Do not stir; pick up the pot and swirl it around occasionally as it melts. Continue heating until the sugar caramelizes, 8 to 10 minutes. Once the sugar approaches 365°F (185°C) on an instant-read thermometer, keep a very close eye on it. As soon as the temperature hits 375°F (190°C), turn off the heat and add the coconut cream; the mixture will violently bubble up and create a lot of steam. Return to medium-high heat, whisking to dissolve the caramel completely. Bring the mixture to a boil, and let it boil for 2 minutes.

4. After 2 minutes of boiling, add in the ½ cup + 1½ tablespoons (140 ml) of water, along with the sticky rice milk and the banana leaf (if using).

5. Continue cooking over medium-high heat, whisking frequently. Meanwhile, in a small bowl, whisk together the tapioca flour and 3 tablespoons (45 g) of water to make a slurry.

6. Whisk in the tapioca slurry and bring the mixture to a boil for 2 minutes. Remove the mixture from the heat (remove the banana leaf if using) and pour it back into the tall mixing vessel along with the coconut oil; blend with a hand blender for 2 minutes to fully homogenize.

7. Once completely cool, transfer the ice cream base into an airtight container. Cover and refrigerate for at least 12 hours and up to 3 days.

8. **Churn the ice cream:** When ready to begin, place a loaf pan in the freezer to chill. Quickly blend the ice cream base once more with a hand blender or whisk before pouring it into an ice cream machine. Churn the ice cream until it reaches the texture of very stiff soft-serve and the surface looks dry, about 25°F (−10°C) or colder on a thermometer gun. Sprinkle in the crispy latik in the last few seconds of churning.

9. Spread the ice cream mixture into the chilled loaf pan. Press a piece of wax paper onto the top of the ice cream and freeze for at least 3 hours before serving.

STRAWBERRY DAIFUKU

Makes 1 quart (1 liter)

Daifuku is a type of wagashi, or Japanese confectionery, made of a sweet filling (think red bean paste, crème caramel, or Japanese plum) encased in a thin skin of chewy mochi. Perhaps the most famous is a modern one, invented in the 1980s: ichigo daifuku, aka strawberry daifuku. A whole juicy strawberry hides in sweetened red bean paste, enveloped in a chewy, bouncy rice confection. Similarly, this ice cream recipe tucks strawberry jellies in swirls of smooth red bean paste and sweet rice ice cream. Note: Anko koshian can be found in any Japanese supermarket.

For the base

1 recipe Rice Cream Base with Dairy (page 52; follow the recipe through Step 7)

For the ice cream

⅓ cup Strawberry Jellies (page 281)

½ cup Mochi Pieces (page 286)

½ cup anko koshian (smooth sweet red bean paste)

1. Once the rice cream base is completely chilled, place a loaf pan, the strawberry jellies, and mochi pieces in the freezer to chill. Process the ice cream base in an ice cream machine according to the manufacturer's instructions.

2. Churn the ice cream until it reaches the texture of very stiff soft-serve and the surface begins to look dry (about 25°F/-5°C with a thermometer gun).

3. Spread half of the ice cream mixture into the chilled loaf pan. Spread half of the anko on top, then sprinkle with half of the strawberry jellies and mochi pieces. Repeat the layering process once more. Immediately place the ice cream into the freezer for 15 minutes to allow it to firm up.

4. Using a spatula, gently fold the ice cream and anko layers to create swirls. Three or four folds should be sufficient for visible ribbons throughout the pan. Press a piece of wax paper directly on top of the ice cream and freeze for at least 4 hours before serving.

VARIATIONS:

Coffee Daifuku:
Add 1 teaspoon of instant coffee or espresso to the red bean paste and omit the strawberry jellies.

Purin Daifuku:
Fold mochi ice cream with ice cream made from the Pasteis de Nata ice cream base (page 58).

Yomogi Daifuku:
Add 25 to 30 g of Japanese mugwort powder to the base and coat the mochi with kinako powder.

RISALAMANDE

Makes about 1 quart (1 liter)

My friend Sabina is a Danish expat living in Los Angeles. Among the many things she misses from home, the biggest thing is Christmastime in Denmark. In comparison to the archetypal snowy Scandinavian Christmas, December in Los Angeles can feel a little flat, especially when it's a sunny 65°F (20°C) outside. Every year, four Sundays before Christmas, we get together for an evening of hygge over holiday food and drinks while making advent wreaths, a Danish tradition of adorning a wreath to hold four candles—one candle to be lit each Sunday leading up to December 25, to count down the weeks to Christmas. After the wreaths are made, to kick off holiday season gluttony, we eat multiple servings of risalamande, a cold creamy rice pudding dotted with vanilla bean and almonds and topped with hot, saucy cherries. This is the ice cream version—cold "Rice Cream" with hot cherries à la mode. As in the Danish risalamande tradition, a whole almond is hidden somewhere in the entire batch of ice cream. Whoever finds it in their sundae gets a prize or gift.

For the rice pudding base

Rice Cream Base with Dairy (page 52), with changes (see step 1 below)

1 vanilla bean, split lengthwise, or ½ teaspoon (2 g) vanilla extract

For the ice cream

1 whole almond

⅓ cup (35 g) slivered almonds, lightly toasted

2 cups (640 g) Amarena or Luxardo cherries, or preserved sour cherries in their syrup

TIP: If preferred, puree the saucy cherries and swirl it throughout the ice cream instead.

1. **Make the base:** Make the rice cream base as directed, but when you heat the mixture in step 4, scrape in the vanilla seeds and add the pod. Remove the vanilla pod before blending in step 6. If using vanilla extract, add it to the base after cooling in the ice bath.

2. **Churn the ice cream:** When ready to begin, place a loaf pan and both the whole and slivered almonds in the freezer to chill. Quickly blend the ice cream base once more with a hand blender or whisk before pouring it into an ice cream machine. Churn the ice cream until it reaches the texture of very stiff soft-serve and the surface looks dry, about 25°F (–5°C) or colder on a thermometer gun. Add the whole almond and slivered almonds in the final few seconds of churning.

3. Transfer the ice cream to the chilled loaf pan and press a piece of wax paper directly on top of the ice cream. Freeze for at least 4 hours before serving.

4. To serve, warm the cherries in their syrup and top each scoop of ice cream with 3 cherries and a drizzling of warm cherry syrup on top.

INJEOLMI

Injeolmi is a type of tteok, or Korean rice cake, that's generously dusted with toasted soybean powder (which in Japanese is called kinako). I've represented this idea many times with a "rice cream" that has the soybean powder mixed directly into the base for a nutty, almost peanut butter-like, sweet rice ice cream.

Rice Cream Base with Dairy (page 52)

¼ cup + 2 tablespoons (45 g) kinako (roasted soybean powder)

½ cup (125 g) Mochi Pieces (page 286), cornstarch omitted

1. Make the rice cream base, adding the 20 g kinako powder along with the dry ingredients in step 3.

2. Place the mochi pieces in a large bowl and sprinkle the 3 tablespoons kinako powder on top. Gently toss the mochi in the bowl until each square is completely covered in kinako powder. Transfer the coated mochi back into an airtight container and keep frozen until ready to use.

3. **Churn the ice cream:** When ready to begin, place a loaf pan in the freezer to chill. Quickly blend the ice cream base once more with a hand blender or whisk before pouring it into an ice cream machine. Churn the ice cream until it reaches the texture of very stiff soft-serve and the surface looks dry, about 25°F (–5°C) or colder on a thermometer gun. Add the mochi pieces in the last few seconds of churning.

4. Transfer the ice cream to the chilled loaf pan and press a piece of wax paper directly on top of the ice cream. Freeze for at least 4 hours before serving.

CHAPTER 13

flov

For centuries, flowers have been the chosen flavor of desserts. In 1682, the first-ever written recipe for ice cream was titled "Snow of Orange Flowers," and was scented with blossoms of the orange tree. In the Middle East, floral flavors are as standard as vanilla, which is incidentally also from a flower. Flowers also add another dimension of taste experience through their aroma, transporting the eater to a far-off secret garden in some corner of the world. But the taste of blossoms often sparks reactions from opposite ends of the spectrum. I've overheard our Violet Marshmallow ice cream compared to "Victoria's Secret lotion." Yet whenever we take it off the menu, customers write long emails pleading for us to bring it back.

I find that ice cream is the perfect medium for floral flavors. The cream-

vers

iness and richness in an ice cream cut the intensity of a floral essence and seem to soften the astringency into lighter notes of sweetness: Rose evokes berries and lychee; elderflower gives citrus vibes; orange blossoms emit hints of sunny coconut, while violet's musk is diluted to an airy cloud of cotton candy.

But when making floral ice creams, there is a fine line to tread between "subtly fragrant" and "soapy." My tip for floral recipes: Use a light hand when dosing ice cream bases with essences and extracts, then taste thoughtfully, staying mindful that the flavor will be dulled slightly once churned and frozen. (Read more in chapter 1 about how air or "overrun" and temperature affect taste.) When you taste, ask yourself, *Is the floralness detectable yet subtle enough for me not to be tired of it halfway through a pint?* Consider a *yes* the goal.

BLUEBERRY ELDERFLOWER

Makes about 1 quart (1 liter)

On a trip to Sweden I fell in love with all details quintessentially Scandinavian: cardamom (kardemumma) in everything baked, salted black licorice (not a fan personally, although I found the country's obsession with it intriguing), and locally foraged fruit and flowers like lingonberries, bright orange cloudberries, and my favorite, elderflower everything. These dainty white flowers grow on elderberry bushes, which produce berries that remind me of blueberries but with a floral undertone of acacia. The elderflowers are sweet and honey-scented, and are used to infuse teas, cordials, and liqueurs that end up tasting like lychee but with a pronounced lemon note. I imagined a bursting blueberry-elderflower jam smeared through mascarpone ice cream brightened with lemon.

For the base

Mascarpone Base (page 51)

Finely grated zest of ½ lemon

For the blueberry elderflower jam

¼ cup + 1½ tablespoons (70 g) granulated sugar

8 ounces (225 g) blueberries, fresh or frozen (see Tips)

5 tablespoons (90 g) corn syrup

¼ teaspoon agar-agar powder

1 ounce (30 g) freeze-dried blueberries (optional; see Tips)

¼ cup + 3½ tablespoons (115 g) elderflower syrup or cordial (see Tips)

½ teaspoon (3 g) fresh lemon juice (see Tips)

TIPS:

Fresh blueberries don't matter here, as they will be cooked down anyway to evaporate as much water as possible to reduce any iciness.

If you like a lot of fruit pieces in your ice cream, I highly recommend using freeze-dried blueberries (regularly stocked at Trader Joe's) as their complete lack of water will give you an un-icy bite of blueberry, and they'll help to further dehydrate your jam, making it more concentrated and bursting with flavor.

You can find several kinds of elderflower cordial at most liquor stores, and any of them will do. I do find, however, that elderflower syrups pack a more flavorful punch than cordials. The ones by Monin, or even IKEA, are easily accessible.

The lemon juice is key in the jam, as it truly highlights the citrusy notes in the elderflower. It's important to use freshly squeezed lemon juice in the jam as the oil from the rind will make all the difference.

1. **Make the base:** Make the mascarpone base recipe as directed, adding the lemon zest when you blend in the mascarpone. Chill as directed.

2. **Make the blueberry elderflower jam:** In a medium saucepan, combine the sugar, blueberries, and corn syrup and bring to a boil over high heat. Reduce the heat to a simmer and continue to cook, stirring occasionally, until most of the berries have deflated and the syrup has thickened, about 10 minutes. Remove from the heat.

3. If you will be adding freeze-dried blueberries at the end, you can skip the following: Using a slotted spoon, transfer one-third of the berries to a small bowl.

4. Add the agar-agar powder to the saucepan and use an immersion blender to puree the berries and juices with the agar-agar. (Alternatively, carefully transfer the hot mixture to a stand blender and puree it until smooth, then return the puree to the saucepan.)

5. Add the elderflower cordial and return to medium heat. Bring the mixture to a boil for 10 seconds. Remove from the heat and add the reserved whole berries and or the freeze-dried blueberries.

6. Let the jam cool to room temperature, then add the lemon juice. Transfer to an airtight container and refrigerate until ready to use, up to 3 days. If you used the freeze-dried fruit, refrigerate the jam for at least 6 hours to allow the fruit to soak up some syrup.

7. **Churn the ice cream:** When ready to begin, place a loaf pan and the blueberry jam in the freezer to chill. Quickly blend the ice cream base once more with a hand blender or whisk before pouring it into an ice cream machine. Churn the ice cream until it reaches the texture of very stiff soft-serve and the surface looks dry, about 25°F (–5°C) or colder on a thermometer gun.

8. Spread half of the ice cream mixture into the chilled loaf pan. Pour half of the blueberry jam on top. Repeat the layering process once more. Immediately place the ice cream into the freezer for 15 minutes to firm it up.

9. Using a spatula, gently fold the ice cream and jam layers to create swirls. Three or four folds should be sufficient for visible ribbons throughout the pan; any more than that will overmix the jam into the ice cream base, which may affect freezing and final texture.

10. Press a piece of wax paper directly on top of the ice cream and freeze for at least 4 hours before serving.

SAKURA CRUNCH

Makes about 1 quart (1 liter)

In Japan, you'll know spring has officially arrived when patisseries, wagashi shops, and cafes start advertising sakura-flavored items and sakura matcha lattes. At the same time, the country's trees explode in soft pink blooms within a two-week span. Sakura, also known widely as cherry blossom, refers to the flowers of ornamental (non-fruit-bearing) cherry trees, an emblem of Japan. Sakura's flavor (which comes from the leaves of the tree) is floral and sweet, with a hint of light spice, almost reminiscent of cinnamon. And while the flavor of cherry blossom tastes nothing like cherries, the leaves contain coumarin (a compound found in cherry pits), which lends a familiar yet ever-so-subtle note that's evocative of bitter almond or *noyaux*. My sister once sent me a touristy photo from Tokyo, of her Japanese Kit Kat haul on a picnic blanket beneath a blooming sakura tree. It sparked inspiration for this ice cream of crunchy strawberry and matcha Kit Kat pieces nestled in a softly sakura-flavored cream. It's a tourist's *hanami* (flower viewing) in a scoop. At Wanderlust Creamery, we make this flavor every spring, and it's so popular that we keep it on the menu until summer starts.

For the base

¾ teaspoon (2 g) sakura leaf powder (see Notes)

⅔ cup + ½ tablespoon (140 g) granulated sugar

⅓ cup + 1 teaspoon (50 g) glucose powder

2 tablespoons + 2 ½ teaspoons (20 g) nonfat dry milk powder

½ teaspoon (2 g) tara gum

1¾ cups + 1 ½ tablespoons (450 g) whole milk

3½ tablespoons (70 g) sweetened condensed milk

70 grams egg yolks (from about 4 large eggs)

1½ cups + 2 tablespoons (375 g) heavy cream

2 drops natural red food coloring (optional)

For the ice cream

10 Kit Kat bars, 5 each of strawberry and matcha, finely chopped (see Notes)

NOTES:

Sakura leaf powder can be found online and is preferred for a cleaner flavor. However, salt-pickled sakura leaves are more widely available at Japanese supermarkets. If that's all you can find, use 4 whole (7 g) salt-pickled sakura leaves. Before using, soak them in a bath of warm water for 30 minutes to remove the brine. Rinse once more under cool water, then pat dry with a paper towel. Place in a stand blender, add the milk, and puree until smooth. Blend the milk as usual when directed.

Matcha and strawberry Kit Kats can also be found in Asian supermarkets as well as online. If necessary, you can substitute for them by dipping a package of strawberry wafer cookies in Matcha Chocolate Freckle (page 279), and freezing them before chopping.

1. Prepare an ice bath (see page 39).

2. **Make the base:** In a tall cylindrical 1½-quart (1.5 liter) mixing vessel, whisk together the sakura leaf powder, sugar, glucose, milk powder, and tara gum. Add the whole milk, condensed milk, and egg yolks and blend with a hand blender to dissolve.

3. Pour the mixture into a medium saucepan and cook over medium-low heat, whisking constantly, until it reaches 165°F (75°C) on an instant-read thermometer.

4. Once the base reaches 165°F (75°C), immediately remove it from the heat and pour it back into the tall mixing vessel. Add the heavy cream and food coloring (if using), then blend with a hand blender for 2 minutes to fully homogenize.

5. Pour the base through a fine-mesh sieve into the prepared ice bath to cool. Once completely cool, transfer into an airtight container and refrigerate for at least 12 hours and up to 3 days.

6. **Churn the ice cream:** When ready to begin, place a loaf pan and the chopped Kit Kats in the freezer to chill. Quickly blend the ice cream base once more with a hand blender or whisk before pouring into an ice cream machine. Churn the ice cream until it reaches the texture of very stiff soft-serve and the surface looks dry, about 25°F (–5°C) or colder on a thermometer gun. Add the chopped Kit Kats in the last few seconds of churning.

7. Transfer the ice cream to the chilled loaf pan. Press a piece of wax paper directly on top of the ice cream and freeze for at least 4 hours before serving.

VIOLETTE MARSHMALLOW

Makes about 1 quart (1 liter)

2 ½ tablespoons (20 g) nonfat dry milk powder

¼ cup + ⅛ teaspoon (120 g) granulated sugar

½ teaspoon (2 g) tara gum (optional; see page 24)

¼ cup + 1 tablespoon (45 g) glucose powder

1¾ cups + 1 tablespoon (415 g) whole milk

3½ tablespoons + 1 teaspoon (75 g) sweetened condensed milk

70 grams egg yolks (from about 4 large eggs)

1½ cups + 1½ tablespoons (365 g) heavy cream

½ teaspoon natural purple food coloring

½ teaspoon (2 g) marshmallow flavor extract

¼ teaspoon (1 g) violet flavor extract, plus more to taste

TIP: Violet, like any floral flavor, is very polarizing. Start with the amount stated in the recipe, then add more to your liking. However, don't forget that the final flavor will be slightly muted once frozen.

In the south of France, glaciers, or ice cream makers, enchanted me with their rare flavors of flowers. Their glass cases featured pastel-colored creams like rainbows of gemstones in a jeweler's display. The names read Coquelicot (red poppy flower), Jasmin, Mimosa (tiny yellow pom-poms of blossoms)—each one delicately perfumed with just enough floralness to make me chase the flavor with another spoonful. My favorite was a lightly purple-hued ice cream that tasted of violets. The flavor of violet actually tastes as floral and powdery as an old lady's perfume, but it's light. There's an airy sweetness about it—almost like cotton candy, or marshmallow. In this recipe, which served as a longstanding signature flavor at Wanderlust Creamery, I intensify the ethereal sweet back note of violet with marshmallow flavoring.

1. Prepare an ice bath (see page 39).

2. In a small bowl, whisk together the milk powder, sugar, tara gum (if using), and glucose. In a tall cylindrical 1½-quart (1.5 liter) mixing vessel, blend the milk, condensed milk, and egg yolks together with a hand blender. Slowly add the dry ingredients while blending and blend thoroughly to dissolve all the solids.

3. Pour the mixture into a medium saucepan and cook over medium-low heat, whisking constantly, until it reaches 165°F (75°C) on an instant-read thermometer. Place the heavy cream and food coloring (if using) into the tall mixing vessel.

4. Once the base reaches 165°F (75°C), immediately remove from the heat and pour into the tall mixing vessel; blend with a hand blender for 2 minutes to fully homogenize.

5. Transfer the base to the prepared ice bath to cool. Once completely cool, stir in the extracts and adjust to taste. Pour through a fine-mesh sieve into an airtight container. Cover and refrigerate for at least 12 hours and up to 3 days.

6. **Churn the ice cream:** When ready to begin, place a loaf pan in the freezer to chill. Quickly blend the ice cream base once more with a hand blender or whisk before pouring it into an ice cream machine. Churn the ice cream until it reaches the texture of very stiff soft-serve and the surface looks dry, about 25°F (−5°C) or colder on a thermometer gun.

7. Transfer the ice cream to the chilled loaf pan. Press a piece of wax paper onto the top of the ice cream pan and freeze for a minimum of 4 hours before serving.

ROSE & BERRY STRACCIATELLA

Makes about 1 quart (1 liter)

Balanced Base (page 49), with changes (see step 2 below)

1 teaspoon (5 g) granulated sugar

1 tablespoon (15 g) rose water, plus more to taste

Berry Stracciatella (recipe follows), tempered to 80°F (25°C)

NOTE: You can use any type or combination of freeze-dried berry powders, but I find that rose is best complemented by raspberry. I recommend using a powder with a minimum of 50% raspberries. You can also make your own powder by pulverizing whole freeze-dried berries into a powder in a spice grinder.

Of all the stores we've opened, the most memorable opening was Pasadena. Leading up to opening day, we were apprehensive. Within a stone's throw of our location were at least five different ice cream shops—some seemingly more popular than us, and others considered Pasadena institutions. Luckily, our space in Pasadena is tiny—two hundred square feet inside a shared food hall in a historic Art Deco building. We were hoping for just a small slice of the entire neighborhood of ice cream goers. Instead, on opening day, our line spanned three city blocks, eventually wrapping around to a back alley. It was too long for me to walk to the end of it myself, so I didn't quite believe others' estimation of it . . . until someone climbed to the rooftop of a building across the street and sent me an aerial view of the line. It was so outrageous that the fire marshal and police arrived for crowd control. So grateful and humbled, I decided to make a flavor as an ode and thank you to Pasadena. A rose-flavored ice cream for "The City of Roses," speckled with berry-tinged white chocolate freckles throughout.

1. Prepare an ice bath (see page 39).

2. Make the balanced base recipe as directed, increasing the amount of sugar by 1 teaspoon (5 g) and adding the rose water after the base has cooled in the ice bath.

3. **Churn the ice cream:** When ready to begin, place a loaf pan in the freezer to chill. Quickly blend the ice cream base once more with a hand blender or whisk before pouring it into an ice cream machine. Churn until the ice cream reaches the texture of very stiff soft-serve and the surface looks dry, about 25°F (-5°C) or colder on a thermometer gun.

4. Meanwhile, make sure the stracciatella is cooled to 80°F (25°C).

5. Pour in all the liquid chocolate quickly in the last few seconds of churning to make freckles.

6. Transfer the ice cream to the chilled loaf pan. Press a piece of wax paper directly on top of the ice cream and freeze for at least 4 hours before serving.

BERRY STRACCIATELLA

Makes ¾ cup (245 g)

3 tablespoons (42 g) refined coconut oil

6 ounces (170 g) white or ruby chocolate, chopped

7 tablespoons (35 g) freeze-dried berry powder (see Note)

1. In a glass bowl, microwave the coconut oil until it registers at least 130°F (55°C) on an instant-read thermometer.

2. Add the chocolate and use a whisk or silicone spatula to stir the mixture until all the chocolate has melted.

3. Transfer the mixture to a container that can be poured from, such as a glass measuring cup. Cool the chocolate to a tepid temperature at which it is still liquid and pourable, about 80°F (25°C), then whisk in the berry powder. If using at a later time, transfer and store the chocolate in an airtight container instead. Remelt the chocolate in a double boiler, or in a microwave, heating in 30-second increments and stirring after each. Cool the chocolate again to 80°F (25°C) just before ice cream assembly.

ORANGE FLOWER
BAKLAVA

Makes about 1 quart (1 liter)

I was never a baklava fan until I tasted it in Egypt, where it was made exclusively with bright green pistachios and buttery pastry flakes in tandem with a beachy scent of orange flower water. I later learned that this was characteristic of North African–style baklava, which forgoes spiced honey and walnuts or almonds that other regions use. My preference would later be confirmed by my Paris-born Algerian best friend, when his mother would occasionally ship her homesick son a tin of her home-baked goods—an assortment of neroli-fragrant pastries, baklava included.

For the base

¼ cup +1½ teaspoons (55 g) granulated sugar

2 tablespoons + 2½ teaspoons (25 g) glucose powder

2 tablespoons + 2½ teaspoons (20 g) nonfat dry milk powder

½ teaspoon (2 g) tara gum (optional; see page 24)

1½ cups + 3½ tablespoons (420 g) whole milk

3½ tablespoons + 1 teaspoon (75 g) sweetened condensed milk

3 tablespoons + 1 teaspoon (70 g) honey

70 grams egg yolks (from about 4 large eggs)

1¾ cups (400 g) heavy cream

1 tablespoon (15 g) orange flower water, plus more to taste

For the ice cream

10 ounces (300 g) pistachio baklava (3 or 4 squares), crumbled

1. Prepare an ice bath (see page 39).

2. **Make the base:** In a small bowl, whisk together the sugar, glucose, milk powder, and tara gum (if using). In a tall cylindrical 1½-quart (1.5 liter) mixing vessel, blend the whole milk, condensed milk, honey, and egg yolks with a hand blender. Slowly add the dry ingredients while blending and blend thoroughly to dissolve all the solids.

3. Pour the mixture into a small saucepan and cook over medium-low heat, whisking constantly, until it reaches 165°F (75°C) on an instant-read thermometer.

4. Once the base reaches 165°F (75°C), immediately remove it from the heat and pour it back into the tall mixing vessel. Pour in the heavy cream and blend with a hand blender for 2 minutes to fully homogenize.

5. Pour the base through a fine-mesh sieve into the prepared ice bath to cool. Once completely cool, stir in the orange flower water and adjust the taste with more if desired. Transfer the ice cream base into an airtight container. Cover and refrigerate for at least 12 hours and up to 3 days.

6. **Churn the ice cream:** When ready to begin, place a loaf pan and the crumbled baklava in the freezer to chill. Quickly blend the ice cream base once more with a hand blender or whisk before pouring it into an ice cream machine.

Churn the ice cream until it reaches the texture of very stiff soft-serve and the surface looks dry, about 25°F (–5°C) or colder on a thermometer gun. Add the baklava in the last few seconds of churning.

7. Transfer the ice cream to the chilled loaf pan. Press a piece of wax paper directly on top of the ice cream and freeze for at least 4 hours before serving.

CHAPTER 14

plants, & bot

This chapter is all about green-ery, which has inspired me to embark on some very flavorful experimentations.

Ice cream infused with coconut-like fig leaf pairs exquisitely with the warm notes of honey and floral green pistachios. Basil, on the other hand, is brightened beautifully with lime and the sweetness of juicy berries. After making numerous batches, I highly rec-ommend crowning a scoop of Earl Grey

herbs
nicals

ice cream with a few scrapes of zesty, floral, lemon verbena granita, drizzled with grassy olive oil. The refreshment of a coconut lime sherbet is amplified by makrut lime leaf and a few snips from a Vietnamese herb garden.

Plants and herbs offer a vibrant "top note" quality that complements the richness of ice cream. When incorporated into fruit ice creams, fresh herbs elevate the vibrancy of the flavors, providing a delightful balance.

BASIL LIME WITH STRAWBERRY

Makes about 1 quart (1 liter)

For the basil lime puree

1¾ ounces (50 g) fresh basil leaves (about 60 large leaves)

Grated zest of 1 lime

⅓ cup + 1 tablespoon (95 g) fresh lime juice

¼ cup + 2½ tablespoons (80 g) granulated sugar

For the base

2 tablespoons + 2½ teaspoons (20 g) nonfat dry milk powder

¼ cup + 2½ tablespoons (80 g) granulated sugar

½ teaspoon (2 g) tara gum (optional; see page 24)

Scant ¾ teaspoon (3 g) lecithin (optional)

1¼ cups (315 g) whole milk

3 tablespoons (60 g) sweetened condensed milk

1½ cups + 2 teaspoons (355 g) heavy cream

For the ice cream

Strawberry Jellies (page 281)

NOTE: The ice cream base may separate while aging overnight, which is normal because of the lime juice and dairy. Blending the base just before churning will re-emulsify everything.

A refreshing and surprisingly delightful ice cream of verdant lime and green basil dotted with juicy bites of strawberry jelly throughout. It's perfect for a sunny summer afternoon by the pool.

1. Prepare an ice bath (see page 39).

2. **Make the basil lime puree:** In a stand blender, process the basil, lime zest, lime juice, and sugar until the basil is roughly pureed. Leave the puree in the blender but set it aside.

3. **Make the base:** In a small bowl, whisk together the milk powder, sugar, tara gum (if using), and lecithin (if using). In a tall cylindrical 1½-quart (1.5 liter) mixing vessel, blend the whole milk and condensed milk with a hand blender. While blending, add the dry ingredients and blend again to dissolve all the solids.

4. Pour the mixture into a medium saucepan and cook over medium-low heat, whisking constantly, until it reaches 165°F (75°C) on an instant-read thermometer.

5. Once the base reaches 165°F (75°C), immediately remove it from the heat and pour it back into the tall mixing vessel. Add the heavy cream and blend with a hand blender for 2 minutes to fully homogenize.

6. Pour the base through a fine-mesh sieve into the prepared ice bath to cool. Once completely cool, transfer the base to the stand blender with the basil puree. Process until completely smooth.

7. Transfer the base to an airtight container and refrigerate for at least 12 hours and up to 1 day.

8. **Churn the ice cream:** When ready to begin, place a loaf pan and the strawberry jellies in the freezer to chill. Quickly blend the ice cream base once more with a hand blender or whisk before pouring it into an ice cream machine. Churn the ice cream until it reaches the texture of very stiff soft-serve and the surface looks dry, about 25°F (−5°C) or colder on a thermometer gun.

9. Spread half of the ice cream into the bottom of the chilled loaf pan. Sprinkle half of the strawberry jellies on top. Repeat the layering process once more. Immediately place the ice cream into the freezer for 15 minutes to firm it up.

10. Using a spatula, gently fold the ice cream to distribute the strawberry jellies throughout the pan. Three or four folds should be sufficient.

11. Press a piece of wax paper directly on top of the ice cream and freeze for at least 4 hours before serving.

NOPAL SORBET

Makes about 1 quart (1 liter)

The end of summer's scorching weather always has me craving Mexican-style ice cream—specifically the kind you'd find from street vendors, called nieve de garrafa. "Nieve" means "snow," and garrafa refers to the container in which the ice cream is made: Vendors hand-churn water-based concoctions of local fruit and plants—think Key lime, nance (Mexican creamy yellow cherries), prickly pear—in metal buckets submerged in ice and salt. It's lighter than traditional ice cream, with a coarse consistency due to the hand-churning. My favorite and the most interesting nieve de garrafa I ever had was one made of paddle cactus, lime, and salt. It inspired a sorbet of the same ingredients, but with cooling aloe vera pulp. So what does cactus ice cream taste like? Verdant. With notes of green grapes balanced with the salinity of salt and tartness of lime. The aloe vera honey provides an essential complementary fruit flavor to the cactus and contains some stabilizers that enhance the texture of the sorbet. Be sure to use young paddle cactus (narrower in shape and not as thick) for a more subdued vegetal flavor. A quick brine in salt removes some of the slimy texture that might inhibit freezing.

5 ounces (150 g) nopal paddles (3 to 4 small), cleaned of spines and cut into strips

2 tablespoons + ¼ teaspoon (7 g) kosher salt, or more to taste

¼ cup (65 g) fresh lime juice, plus more to taste

¼ cup + 3 tablespoons (105 g) Korean aloe vera honey tea (see Note)

2½ cups (600 g) water

¾ cup (150 g) granulated sugar, plus more to taste

¾ cup + 2 tablespoons (125 g) glucose powder

1 teaspoon (3 g) Sorbet Stabilizer (optional; page 33)

Citric acid

1. Place the nopal strips in a bowl and liberally cover with 2 tablespoons (8 g) of the kosher salt, coating the nopales thoroughly. Set a timer for 10 minutes and let it sit. After 10 minutes, rinse the nopales under cool running water to wash away all salt.

2. In a blender, combine the nopales, lime juice, aloe vera honey, and remaining ¼ teaspoon salt and puree until completely smooth. Transfer the puree into another container and set aside.

3. In the same blender, combine half of the water, the sugar, glucose, and stabilizer (if using) and blend on high until all the solids have completely dispersed.

4. Pour the mixture along with the remaining water into a small saucepan and cook over medium-high heat, whisking occasionally, until the temperature reaches 122°F (50°C) on an instant-read thermometer.

VARIATION: To achieve the authentic texture of Mexican nieve de garrafa, skip the ice cream machine. After step 7, place the sorbet base in a prechilled metal mixing bowl and place in the freezer. Whisk the sorbet base every 30 minutes, returning the bowl to the freezer after every whisking. Repeat the whisking and freezing process until you have a scoopable texture and no liquid remains. Transfer the mixture to the chilled loaf pan and press a piece of wax paper onto the top of the sorbet and place back into the freezer until ready to serve.

NOTE: You can find Korean aloe vera honey (a thick green syrup in glass jars) at any Asian market. Alternatively, you can use bottled aloe vera drink (called bebida de savila at Latino food markets) in place of water and omit the aloe vera honey altogether. If doing so, make sure to use "original" flavor, not the other flavored varieties.

5. Remove the base from the heat and pour it through a fine-mesh sieve into the prepared ice bath to cool. Once the mixture has completely cooled, whisk in the nopal puree.

6. Using a refractometer (see page 37), measure the Brix of the base, verifying it is within the target range of 25 to 32 Brix. At this point, you can adjust the flavor of the base with citric acid and more sugar or salt, adding just ½ teaspoon at a time and rechecking the Brix after each addition.

7. Transfer the base to an airtight container and refrigerate for at least 12 hours and up to 2 days.

8. **Churn the sorbet:** When ready to begin, place a loaf pan in the freezer to chill. Quickly blend the base once more with a hand blender or whisk before pouring it into an ice cream machine. Churn the sorbet until it reaches the texture of a stiff slushie, about 30°F (−1°C) or colder on a thermometer gun.

9. Transfer the sorbet into the chilled loaf pan. Press a piece of wax paper directly on top of the sorbet and freeze for at least 4 hours before serving.

COCONUT LIME & VIETNAMESE HERBS

Makes about 1 quart (1 liter)

2 large makrut lime leaves

1 small sprig each of Vietnamese balm, spearmint or peppermint, and Thai basil

Grated zest of 1 lime

½ cup + 2 teaspoons (130 g) fresh lime juice

1¼ cups (250 g) granulated sugar, plus more to taste

¼ cup + 1½ teaspoons (40 g) glucose powder

1 teaspoon (3 g) Sorbet Stabilizer (optional; page 33)

2 tablespoons + 1 teaspoon (20 g) inulin (optional)

1¼ cups (300 g) water

1¾ cups (400 g) coconut cream

Citric acid

This creamy sorbet of lime and coconut cream is infused with refreshing and brightly aromatic Vietnamese herbs. Makrut lime leaf is not originally a Vietnamese herb (it's more widely known in Thai and Indonesian cooking), but it is occasionally used in Vietnamese cuisine to flavor soups, curries, and stir-fries. It has a distinctive crisp, green aroma and flavor that is citrusy and slightly floral, and is often used in combination with other Vietnamese herbs to create flavor complexity. In this recipe, it mingles with sweet anise-like húng quế (Thai basil), cooling rau thơm (fresh mint), and lemony kinh giới (Vietnamese balm).

1. In a stand blender, process the lime leaves, herbs, lime zest, and lime juice into a completely smooth puree. Transfer the puree to another container and set aside.

2. Rinse the blender, then combine the sugar, glucose, stabilizer (if using), inulin (if using), water, and coconut cream and blend on high until all the solids have completely dispersed.

3. Pour into a large saucepan and heat over medium-high heat, whisking occasionally, until the temperature reaches 122°F (50°C) on an instant-read thermometer.

4. Remove from the heat and strain the liquid through a fine-mesh sieve into the prepared ice bath to cool. Once the mixture has completely cooled, whisk in the herb-lime puree.

5. Using a refractometer (see page 37), measure the Brix of the base, verifying it is within the target range of 25 to 32 Brix. At this point, you can adjust the sweetness or tartness of the base with citric acid or more sugar, adding just ¼ teaspoon at a time and rechecking the Brix after each addition.

6. Transfer the base to an airtight container and refrigerate for at least 12 hours and up to 2 days.

7. **Churn the sorbet:** Once the base is completely chilled, place a loaf pan in the freezer to chill. Quickly blend or whisk the sorbet base thoroughly, before pouring it into an ice cream machine. Churn the sorbet until it reaches the texture of a stiff slushie, about 30°F (−1°C) or colder on a thermometer gun.

8. Spread the sorbet into the chilled loaf pan. Press a piece of wax paper directly on top of the ice cream and freeze for at least 4 hours before serving.

FIG LEAF & PISTACHIO

Makes about 1 quart (1 liter)

A few years before opening Wanderlust Creamery, I traveled to Dubrovnik, Croatia, a sun-filled, limestone medieval town on the Adriatic Sea. It's a walled city that seems to keep out any unpleasant hints of the modern world, including cars. If you've ever watched the show *Game of Thrones*, the set of King's Landing is this charming place. Just like in the show, the city is a labyrinth of narrow stone alleyways and zigzags of never-ending stairways, each turn rewarding you with something unexpected: a stunning view of terra-cotta roof-tops staggering into the ocean, a charming gelateria serving four kinds of hazelnut ice cream (the nuts prepared at varying roasting levels), a cliff where a random tattered king-sized bed was left by locals for sunbathing as the waves crash below. There were spontaneous charms everywhere. And the food was no less enthralling. A bite that stands out was one of local sheep's cheese, baked in a purse of fig leaves and covered with honey and pistachios. I managed to create an ice cream that transported me back to that Mediterranean maze.

For the fig leaf honey

4½ tablespoons (95 g) honey

30 grams (4 to 6 medium) fig leaves, finely chopped or chiffonade-cut (see Tip)

For the base

¼ cup + 1 teaspoon (30 g) nonfat dry milk powder

2 tablespoons (25 g) granulated sugar

¼ cup + 1 tablespoon (45 g) glucose powder

½ teaspoon (2 g) tara gum (optional; see page 24)

1¾ cups (425 g) whole milk

70 grams egg yolks (from about 4 large eggs)

¾ cup + 2 tablespoons (200 g) heavy cream

6 tablespoons (95 g) pure pistachio paste

For the ice cream

⅔ cup (65 g) chopped pistachios

TIP: Fig leaves have a distinctive coconut-y, grassy but sweet flavor. The older and bigger the leaves, the grassier they are, so try to pluck the younger, small to medium leaves off a fig tree.

1. **Make the fig leaf honey:** In a medium saucepan, heat the honey over medium-high heat until it starts to bubble. Add the chopped fig leaves and stir to coat. Continue heating just until they begin to shrivel around the edges, 2 to 3 minutes. Remove from the heat and allow the mixture to steep for 5 minutes. Strain the honey through a fine-mesh sieve into a tall cylindrical 1½-quart (1.5 liter) mixing vessel. Reserve the leaves and set them aside.

2. Prepare an ice bath (see page 39).

3. **Make the base:** In a small bowl, whisk together the milk powder, sugar, glucose, and tara gum (if using). Add the milk and egg yolks to the honey and blend with a hand blender. Slowly add the dry ingredients while blending and blend thoroughly to dissolve all the solids.

4. Pour the mixture into a small saucepan and cook over medium-low heat, whisking constantly, until it reaches 165°F (75°C) on an instant-read thermometer.

5. Once the base reaches 165°F (75°C), immediately remove it from the heat and pour it back into the tall mixing vessel. Add the heavy cream and pistachio paste and blend with a hand blender for 2 minutes to fully homogenize.

6. Transfer the base along with the reserved fig leaves to the prepared ice bath to cool. Once completely cool, transfer the base to an airtight container and refrigerate for at least 12 hours and up to 3 days.

7. **Churn the ice cream:** When ready to begin, place a loaf pan and the chopped pistachios in the freezer to chill. Quickly blend the ice cream base once more with a hand blender or whisk before pouring it through a fine-mesh sieve into an ice cream machine. Churn the ice cream until it reaches the texture of very stiff soft-serve and the surface looks dry, about 25°F (-5°C) or colder on a thermometer gun. Add the pistachios in the last few seconds of churning.

8. Transfer the ice cream mixture to the chilled loaf pan. Press a piece of wax paper directly on top of the ice cream and freeze for at least 4 hours before serving.

CALABRIAN SUNDAES

Makes about 6 servings

For the ice cream
Balanced Base (page 49),
with changes (see step 1)

6 tablespoons (30 g) loose
Earl Grey tea leaves

For the lemon verbena granita
½ cup + 3 tablespoons (160 g)
water

¾ cup + 1 tablespoon (160 g)
granulated sugar

2¾ cups + 2 tablespoons (680 g)
fresh lemon juice

3½ packed cups (95 g) fresh
lemon verbena leaves

For the sundaes
6 tablespoons bergamot olive oil

Flaky sea salt, for sprinkling

6 sprigs fresh lemon verbena
(optional), for garnish

This is one of many souvenir-inspired recipes you'll find throughout this book. The souvenir: a bottle of golden-green oil that smells like luxury Italian perfume. It was olive oil pressed with whole bergamot citrus fruits brought back from Calabria, Italy—and for a while, the most prized possession in my pantry. My favorite use for it was as a topping on vanilla or plain chocolate ice cream. Then when I started making ice cream at home, it was my go-to accompaniment to Earl Grey ice cream (also made with bergamot). But if you add a shaving of zesty granules of lemon granita scented with bright and perfumy lemon verbena, something magical happens. This sundae is a symphony of similar flavors (verdant, citrusy, floral, sunny) juxtaposed with contrasting textures—smooth and creamy ice cream with flaky grains of crunchy ice, all culminating in ultimate refreshment.

1. **Make the base:** Make the balanced base as directed through blending in the heavy cream (step 4). Omit the straining when adding to the ice bath (step 5) and instead stir in the Earl Grey tea leaves before cooling and refrigerating to chill.

2. **Churn the ice cream:** When ready to begin, place a loaf pan in the freezer to chill. Quickly blend the ice cream base once more with a hand blender or whisk before pouring it through a fine-mesh sieve into an ice cream machine. Churn the ice cream until it reaches the texture of very stiff soft-serve and the surface looks dry, about 25°F (-5°C) or colder on a thermometer gun.

3. **Meanwhile, make the lemon verbena granita:** Place a loaf pan in the freezer to chill.

4. In a small saucepan, bring the water to a boil over high heat. Remove from the heat and stir in the sugar to dissolve. Set the syrup aside to cool completely.

5. In a stand blender, blend the lemon juice with the lemon verbena until the leaves are finely pureed. Pour the mixture through a fine-mesh sieve into the saucepan of cooled syrup and stir to combine thoroughly.

6. Pour the mixture into the chilled loaf pan and return it to the freezer to freeze for 1 hour.

7. Using a fork, scrape the surface of the frozen liquid into small granules of ice. Return the pan to the freezer and repeat this process every 45 minutes or so for a total of 4 hours. The final product should be completely frozen, but flaky or granulated, like finely crushed ice.

8. **Make the sundaes:** Place a scoop of Earl Grey ice cream onto a plate and top it with a large mound of lemon verbena granita. Drizzle some bergamot olive oil on top and finish with a sprinkle of flaky sea salt. If desired, garnish with a sprig of lemon verbena.

CHAPTER 15

boo

In my former life, I tended bar. What was meant to be a brief stint to hold me over financially through college ended up being a decade of valuable experience. Working behind a cocktail bar is not much different than working on the line in a kitchen. A cocktail is essentially a liquid dish. It's a balance of flavors and aromas, visual and edible art. Behind a bar, there's prep—mise en place is essential—and the barback is the kitchen porter. There's juggling multiple orders at a time, making each one exactly to the chef's (lead mixologist's) exact specifications, while a printer spits a trail of order tickets spanning the length of a human body. The bar can be just as unglamorous as the kitchen—coming home late with wet socks, fingers bar-rotted, physically drained, and never having a schedule that will allow you a normal social life. Like a chef, a mixologist needs a trained palate to know how to

balance sweetness with acidity or bitterness, the nuances and notes in every different brand of spirit and liqueur, and how one will affect another. Just as the question of whether a cut of meat should be braised or seared, should a drink be shaken or stirred? Like any cook worth her salt should know how to perfectly execute a standard mother sauce before iterating a new version of it, a good mixologist will understand the history, technique, and proper ratios of any classic cocktail before using it as a template for creation. It's like making ice cream: You can add this or that, but will your additions render the formula a textural, unfreezable mess? I may not have attended culinary school like I'd always wanted to, or earned my so-called stripes in a kitchen, but the bar taught me much of what I know about exploring flavor with balance.

SICILIAN NEGRONI

Makes about 1½ quarts
(1.5 liters)

Many mixologists' take on a "Sicilian" Negroni involves blood orange because of the island's abundance of it. Yet Sicily's citrus is more than just blood oranges; the island is also one of the largest producers of bergamot—a green orange whose peel smells like cologne and gives Earl Grey tea its distinctive flavor—as well as cedro, another citrus used widely in perfumery. But when I close my eyes and think of Sicily, I not only think of hills of citrus trees, but the creamy white flowers that cover them and the intoxicating scent they emit, a scent of sun-drenched nirvana. Incidentally, there's a tincture of these citruses, their blossoms, and a handful of mysterious botanicals used in the region's baked goods that encapsulates all these things in a bottle. The tincture flavors Sicilian panettone with a distinct musky citrus-vanilla essence. It's called fior di Sicilia, which translates to "flowers of Sicily." Imagine all the redolence described above wrapped up in a Creamsicle-like ice cream steeped with gin botanicals and swirled with a blood orange/Campari sorbet with zest of bergamot. *That* is my idea of a Sicilian Negroni.

For the gin ice cream base

1 heaping tablespoon (8 g) juniper berries

½ teaspoon (1 g) coriander seeds

1¼ cups (310 g) whole milk

2 tablespoons + ¾ teaspoon (16 g) nonfat dry milk powder

½ cup + 1¼ teaspoons (105 g) granulated sugar

½ teaspoon (2 g) tara gum (optional; see page 24)

2 tablespoons + 2½ teaspoons (55 g) sweetened condensed milk

51 grams egg yolks (from about 3 large eggs)

1 cup + 2 tablespoons (260 g) heavy cream

1 teaspoon gin (see Notes)

¼ teaspoon fior di Sicilia extract (see Notes)

¾ teaspoon orange flower water

For the blood orange/Campari sorbet base

½ cup + 1 tablespoon (115 g) granulated sugar, plus more as needed

½ teaspoon (1.5 g) Sorbet Stabilizer (page 33)

3 tablespoons (45 g) water

2⅓ cups (557 g) blood orange juice

1 tablespoon + 2 teaspoons (25 g) fresh lemon juice

1 drop bergamot essential oil

2½ teaspoons (12 g) Campari

2½ teaspoons (12 g) sweet vermouth

Citric acid

NOTES:

Fior di Sicilia and orange flowers have such a delicate, nuanced flavor that can be easily masked by certain gins. For this recipe, try to find a classic London dry or Plymouth gin. Fior di Sicilia can be found online or in specialty food shops.

The usual Brix range for sorbet (25 to 32) will not work for this recipe due to the alcohol from Campari and sweet vermouth, which depresses the freezing point a few degrees. Instead, aim for 19 to 24 Brix.

1. **Make the gin ice cream base:** Pulse the juniper berries and coriander in a spice grinder until coarsely ground.

2. In a small saucepan, scald the milk. Stir in the ground juniper/coriander mixture and remove from the heat. Allow the mixture to steep and cool. Pour the mixture through a fine-mesh sieve into a tall cylindrical 1½-quart (1.5 liter) mixing vessel.

3. Prepare an ice bath (see page 39).

4. In a small bowl, whisk together the milk powder, sugar, and tara gum (if using). Add the condensed milk and egg yolks to the milk in the mixing vessel and blend with a hand blender. Slowly add the dry ingredients while blending and blend thoroughly to dissolve all the solids.

5. Pour the mixture into a small saucepan and cook over medium-low heat, whisking constantly, until it reaches 165°F (75°C) on an instant-read thermometer.

6. Once the base reaches 165°F (75°C), immediately remove it from the heat and pour it back into the tall mixing vessel. Add the heavy cream and blend with a hand blender for 2 minutes to fully homogenize.

7. Pour the base through a fine-mesh sieve into the prepared ice bath to cool. Once completely cool, stir in the gin, fior di Sicilia, and orange flower water. Transfer the mixture to an airtight container and refrigerate for at least 12 hours and up to 3 days.

8. **Make the blood orange/ Campari sorbet base:** In a small bowl, mix together the sugar and sorbet stabilizer. In a tall cylindrical 1½-quart (1.5-liter) mixing vessel, blend the water with a hand blender while gradually adding the dry ingredients.

9. Pour the mixture into a small saucepan and heat over medium heat until it registers 120°F (50°C) on an instant-read thermometer. Remove from the heat and pour it back into the tall mixing vessel. Set aside to cool.

10. Once the mixture has completely cooled, add the blood orange juice, lemon juice, bergamot oil, Campari, and sweet vermouth. Blend with a hand blender.

11. Using a refractometer (see page 37), measure the Brix of the base, verifying it is between 19 and 24 Brix. At this point, you can adjust the sweetness or tartness of the base with citric acid or more sugar, adding ½ teaspoon at a time and rechecking the Brix after each addition.

12. Transfer the base to an airtight container and refrigerate for at least 12 hours and up to 2 days.

13. **Churn the ice cream/sorbet:** When ready to begin, place a loaf pan in the freezer to chill.

14. Quickly blend the ice cream base once more with a hand blender, then pour it into an ice cream machine. Churn until the ice cream reaches the texture of very stiff soft-serve and the surface looks dry, about 25°F (−5°C) or colder on a thermometer gun.

15. Spread the ice cream mixture into the chilled loaf pan and place it in the freezer.

16. Scrape the ice cream machine clean (no need to wash it) and process the blood orange/Campari sorbet until it reaches the texture of a stiff slushie, about 30°F (−1°C) or colder on a thermometer gun.

17. Spread the sorbet into the chilled loaf pan on top of the layer of gin ice cream. Using a spatula, gently fold the ice cream layers to create visible swirls. Press a piece of wax paper directly on top of the ice cream and freeze for at least 4 hours before serving.

NESSELRODE BULA

I not only find ice cream inspiration from far-off places, I also find it wanderlusting for a different time period. Reading about history's ice cream greats, I came across a brand that was apparently very popular right here in Southern California. From the 1940s to the 1970s, Wil Wright's was a chain of charming old-school ice cream parlors decked out in its trademark pink and red stripes, with full service. Customers sat down at marble bistro tables or along the candy jar–lined bar, where a waiter would take their orders and serve up super-high-butterfat scoops (rumored to be over 20%!) in stemmed coupes, like delicate cocktails. The whipped cream was hand-whipped, the Creamsicle shakes made from freshly squeezed oranges, and the rum raisin ice cream was boozy enough to make a child tipsy. Celebrities like Clark Gable, Marlon Brando, and Marilyn Monroe would sneak into the Westwood and Sherman Oaks locations late at night for a scoop or quart to take home. There was even one just a few blocks from where our Tarzana location now stands. Among many favorites, such as Peppermint Stick and Chocolate Burnt Almond, Wil Wright's famed flavor was Nesselrode Bula. It was a boozy concoction of rum, brandy, and chestnut custard ice cream packed with liquor-soaked fruit and nuts. Inspired, I made a version of it—with roasted hazelnut paste in place of chestnut puree. It was divine. Holiday decadence in a scoop.

For the boozy fruit and raisins

½ cup (75 g) diced assorted glacé fruit (apricot, peaches, cherries, etc.)

Heaping ½ cup (90 g) raisins

1 vanilla bean, split lengthwise, or ½ teaspoon (2 g) vanilla extract

3 tablespoons rum

3 tablespoons brandy

For the base

1 cup + 2 ½ tablespoons (270 g) heavy cream

2 tablespoons + ½ teaspoon (15 g) nonfat dry milk powder

½ cup + 1 ¼ teaspoons (105 g) granulated sugar

½ teaspoon (2 g) tara gum (optional; see page 24)

1 ⅓ cups (325 g) whole milk

3 tablespoons (60 g) sweetened condensed milk

119 grams egg yolks (from about 7 large eggs)

3 tablespoons + 2 teaspoons (60 g) pure hazelnut paste or pure chestnut paste

For the ice cream

⅓ cup (35 to 45 g) hazelnuts, pecans, or walnuts, toasted

NOTE: Because of its alcohol content, this ice cream should be ready to scoop at 0°F—straight out of the freezer after 4 to 6 hours of hardening.

VARIATION: For Tropical Nesselrode Bula, substitute dried coconut, papaya, jackfruit, pineapple, and diced Philippine dried mango for the dried glacé fruit. Substitute soft-dried bananas (aka "natural dried bananas" at Trader Joe's) for the raisins. Omit the brandy and double the rum. Instead of the hazelnut paste, use roasted purple sweet potato or unsweetened ube paste. For the nuts added during churning, use toasted pili nuts or chopped Brazil nuts.

1. **Prepare the boozy fruit and raisins:** Do this the day before you make the ice cream. Place the dried glacé fruit in a small and narrow jar. Place the raisins in another. If using a vanilla bean, scrape the seeds into the jar with the raisins and add the pod. In a small saucepan, warm the rum and brandy to a simmer, then remove from the heat. Measure 2 tablespoons (30 ml) of the hot alcohol into the jar with the dried fruit; pour the remainder into the jar with the raisins and vanilla pod. Cover each jar and let the infusions sit at room temperature for a minimum of 24 hours and up to 2 days.

2. Prepare an ice bath (see page 39).

3. **Make the base:** Remove the vanilla pod (if it was used) from the raisin infusion and reserve for another use. In a stand blender, combine the raisins and their soaking liquid, vanilla extract (if using), and heavy cream and blend until completely smooth. Set aside.

4. In a small bowl, whisk together the milk powder, sugar, and tara gum (if using). In a tall cylindrical 1½-quart (1.5 liter) mixing vessel, blend the whole milk, condensed milk, and egg yolks with a hand blender. Add the dry ingredients and blend again thoroughly to dissolve all the solids.

5. Pour the mixture into a small saucepan and cook over medium-low heat, whisking constantly, until it reaches 165°F (75°C) on an instant-read thermometer.

6. Once the base reaches 165°F (75°C), immediately remove from the heat and pour it back into the tall mixing vessel. Add the raisin/cream puree and hazelnut paste. Blend the mixture with a hand blender for 2 minutes to fully homogenize it.

7. Pour the base through a fine-mesh sieve into the prepared ice bath to cool. Once completely cool, transfer the ice cream base to an airtight container. Refrigerate for at least 12 hours and up to 3 days.

8. **Churn the ice cream:** When ready to begin, place a loaf pan and the dried fruits and nuts in the freezer to chill. Quickly blend the ice cream base once more with a hand blender or whisk before pouring it into an ice cream machine. Churn the ice cream until it reaches the texture of very stiff soft-serve and the surface looks dry, about 25°F (−5°C) or colder on a thermometer gun. Add the dried fruits and nuts in the last few seconds of churning.

9. Transfer the ice cream mixture to the chilled loaf pan. Press a piece of wax paper directly on top of the ice cream and freeze for at least 4 to 6 hours before serving.

OATMEAL & SCOTCH HONEY CARAMEL

Makes about 1 quart (1 liter)

Can you wanderlust for a place that doesn't actually exist? I do. On two separate occasions, the fictional geographical regions in the HBO series *Game of Thrones* inspired a "Game of Cones" seasonal menu at Wanderlust Creamery. Out of a fortress called The Wall, I imagined a black icy sorbet of dark chocolate and bitter Russian imperial stout, dubbed "Dragon Glace" (*glace*, French for *ice cream* and pronounced "dragon glass," like the magical weapon in the show). The fertile flora of the Reach inspired a lemon verbena ice cream with candied roses and violets, while "A Flavor of Ice and Fire"—a spicy chile/*dragon* fruit sorbet— was envisioned from Essos. The flavor of this ice cream, a hearty oatmeal ice cream with peaty Scotch whiskey–spiked honey caramel, was born out of imagination for the Stark family hearth at Winterfell.

For the oatmeal
¾ cup + 1½ tablespoons (205 g) whole milk

3½ tablespoons (25 g) rolled oats

1 cinnamon stick

For the base
2 tablespoons + ½ teaspoon (15 g) nonfat dry milk powder

½ cup + 1 tablespoon (115 g) granulated sugar

2 tablespoons + ¾ teaspoon (20 g) glucose powder

¾ cup + 1½ tablespoons (205 g) whole milk

3½ tablespoons (70 g) sweetened condensed milk

70 grams egg yolks (from about 4 large eggs)

1⅓ cups (300 g) heavy cream

For the Islay Scotch honey caramel
¾ cup (150 g) granulated sugar

⅔ cup (225 g) honey

3½ tablespoons (50 g) unsalted butter

¼ cup + 3 tablespoons (100 g) heavy cream

2 tablespoons (30 g) Islay Scotch whisky

¾ teaspoon (1.5 g) salt

1. **Make the oatmeal:** In a small saucepan, bring the milk to a boil. Stir in the oats and cinnamon stick and cook over medium heat, stirring occasionally, until the oats are tender and most of the liquid has absorbed, 5 to 6 minutes. Remove from the heat and cool to warm temperature.

2. Once the oatmeal has cooled a bit, remove the cinnamon stick and set it aside. Process the oatmeal in a stand blender until completely smooth. Pour the puree back into the saucepan and set aside.

3. Prepare an ice bath (see page 39).

4. **Make the base:** In a small bowl, whisk together the milk powder, sugar, and glucose. In a tall cylindrical 1½-quart (1.5 liter) mixing vessel, blend the whole milk, condensed milk, and egg yolks. Slowly add the dry ingredients while blending and blend thoroughly to dissolve all the solids.

5. Pour the mixture into the saucepan containing the oatmeal puree and cook over medium-low heat, whisking constantly, until it reaches 165°F (75°C) on an instant-read thermometer.

6. Once the base reaches 165°F (75°C), immediately remove it from the heat and pour it back into the tall mixing vessel. Add the heavy cream and blend with a hand blender for 2 minutes to fully homogenize.

7. Pour the base through a fine-mesh sieve into the prepared ice bath to cool. Once completely cool, transfer the ice cream base along with the reserved cinnamon stick to an airtight container. Cover and refrigerate for at least 12 hours and up to 3 days.

8. **Make the Islay Scotch honey caramel:** In a medium stockpot, melt the sugar over medium-high heat. Do not stir; pick up the pot and swirl it around occasionally as it melts. Continue heating until the sugar caramelizes, 15 to 20 minutes.

9. Once the sugar approaches 365°F (185°C) on an instant-read thermometer, keep a *very* close eye on it. As soon as the temperature hits 375°F (190°C), remove from the heat and add the honey and butter, stirring to combine. Pour in the heavy cream; the mixture will violently bubble up and create a lot of steam. Return the mixture to medium heat and whisk to dissolve the caramel. Bring the caramel to a boil for 2 minutes. Remove from the heat and stir in the whisky and salt. Allow the caramel to cool completely before pouring it into an airtight container. Keep refrigerated until use, up to 3 days.

10. **Churn the ice cream:** When ready to begin, place a loaf pan in the freezer to chill. Remove the cinnamon stick, then quickly blend the ice cream base once more with a hand blender or whisk before pouring it into an ice cream machine. Churn the ice cream until it reaches the texture of very stiff soft-serve and the surface looks dry, about 25°F (−5.5°C) or colder on a thermometer gun.

11. Spread half of the ice cream into the bottom of the loaf pan. Spread half of the caramel on top of the ice cream. Repeat the layering process with the remaining ice cream and caramel. Immediately place the ice cream into the freezer for 15 minutes to firm it up.

12. Using a spatula, gently fold the ice cream and caramel layer to create swirls. Three or four folds should be sufficient for visible ribbons throughout the pan.

13. Press a piece of wax paper directly on top of the ice cream and freeze for at least 3 hours before serving.

PEARL DIVER FLOAT

One of my favorite cocktails is a new rendition of a classic tiki drink called a Pearl Diver. It's traditionally made from two types of rum, freshly squeezed citrus, "gardenia mix" (a spiced emulsion of butter and honey), and falernum (think: limey orgeat). But in this new version famously found at Latitude 29 in New Orleans, passion fruit is added to play off the funkiness found in pot-still Jamaican rum. In this recipe, the gardenia mix takes form in an ice cream of browned butter and honey, with a hint of cinnamon and allspice. The result is an indulgent frou-frou cocktail that's part dessert—the kind you're too ashamed to order in public—that you can enjoy in the privacy of your own backyard.

For the gardenia mix ice cream

Ice cream base from Brown Butter Sans Rival (page 238), with changes (see step 1 below)

¼ teaspoon ground cinnamon

¼ teaspoon ground allspice

For each Pearl Diver float

1 ½ ounces Jamaican rum

¾ ounce aged demerara rum

¾ ounce freshly squeezed orange juice

½ ounce fresh lime juice

1 ½ tablespoons passion fruit puree

1 teaspoon falernum (see Note)

Ice, for shaking

1 orchid or pineapple spear, for garnish

1. Prepare an ice bath (see page 39).

2. **Make the base:** Make the base recipe as directed, but omit the glucose and use 105 grams of honey instead of the granulated sugar (add it to the browned butter as it's cooling). Add the cinnamon and allspice to the dry ingredients. Chill the base as directed.

3. **Churn the ice cream:** When ready to begin, place a loaf pan in the freezer to chill. Quickly blend the ice cream base once more with a hand blender or whisk before pouring it into an ice cream machine. Churn the ice cream until it reaches the texture of very stiff soft-serve and the surface looks dry, about 25°F (−5.5°C) or colder on a thermometer gun.

4. Transfer the ice cream mixture to the chilled loaf pan. Press a piece of wax paper directly on top of the ice cream and freeze for at least 4 hours before serving.

5. **Make the floats:** In a cocktail shaker, combine all the liquid ingredients. Place a scoop of gardenia mix ice cream in a pearl diver glass or tiki mug. Add ice to the shaker and shake vigorously for 20 seconds. Strain the cocktail over the scoop of ice cream and top with your garnish of choice.

NOTE: Falernum is a zero- to low-alcoholic cordial made from lime, spices, and almond milk. While it's available at most liquor stores, there are tons of simple recipes online to make your own. If you do, try swapping out the almonds for macadamias to up the creaminess.

ROYAL PRUNE ARMAGNAC

Makes about 1 quart (1 liter)

For the Armagnac prunes

⅓ cup (80 g) Armagnac

3 tablespoons (10 g) loose Ceylon or Assam tea leaves

Generous ½ cup (90 g) pitted prunes

For the base

1 tablespoon + 1¼ teaspoons (10 g) nonfat dry milk powder

½ cup + 1½ tablespoons (120 g) granulated sugar

1 teaspoon (4 g) tara gum (optional; see page 24)

1 cup + 3½ tablespoons (295 g) whole milk

3½ tablespoons + ¾ teaspoon (70 g) sweetened condensed milk

135 grams egg yolks (from about 8 large eggs)

1½ cups + 1½ tablespoons (365 g) heavy cream

1 teaspoon (4 g) vanilla extract

For serving (optional)

Armagnac-soaked prunes

Whipped cream

Waffle cone chip

This ice cream is inspired by the famed Parisian glacier Berthillon, where I had my first taste of prune Armagnac ice cream. From all the possible flavor options there were to choose from—the usual in-season fruits, nuts, and nougats—I decided to choose one that seemed least likely to be enjoyed, the flavor that sounded like it was designed specifically for a ninety-year-old man: Prune Armagnac. Unexpectedly, it's a flavor of ice cream I now can't knock from the top of my list. Prunes soaked in the amber Chuck Norris of brandies churned into a custard cream elicit so many nuanced flavors, like black tea, leather, and tobacco. In my version, I add malty tea leaves to the prune maceration for a rum-raisin-meets-royal-milk-tea ice cream.

1. **Make the Armagnac prunes:** About 2 days in advance, in a glass jar, combine the Armagnac and tea leaves, cover with a lid, and infuse at room temperature for a minimum of 12 hours (and up to 2 days).

2. After infusing, pour the Armagnac through a fine-mesh sieve into another jar. Add the prunes and allow the prunes to macerate for a minimum of 12 hours and up to 2 days.

3. In a stand blender, puree the prunes and soaking liquid to your desired consistency (see Notes). Set aside.

4. Prepare an ice bath (see page 39).

5. **Make the base:** In a small bowl, whisk together the milk powder, sugar, and tara gum (if using). In a tall cylindrical 1½-quart (1.5 liter) mixing vessel, blend the whole milk, condensed milk, and egg yolks with a hand blender. Add the dry ingredients and blend again to dissolve all the solids.

6. Pour the mixture into a small saucepan and cook over medium-low heat, whisking constantly, until it reaches 165°F (75°C) on an instant-read thermometer.

7. Once the base reaches 165°F (75°C), immediately remove it from the heat and pour it back into a tall mixing vessel. Add the heavy cream and blend with a hand blender for 2 minutes to fully homogenize.

8. Pour the base through a fine-mesh sieve into the prepared ice bath to cool. Once completely cool, whisk in the prune/Armagnac puree and vanilla extract. Transfer to an airtight container and refrigerate for at least 12 hours and up to 3 days.

9. **Churn the ice cream:** When ready to begin, place a loaf pan in the freezer to chill. Quickly blend the ice cream base once more with a hand blender or whisk before pouring it into an ice cream machine. Churn the ice cream until it reaches the texture of very stiff soft-serve and the surface looks dry, about 25°F (−5°C) or colder on a thermometer gun.

10. Transfer the ice cream mixture to the chilled loaf pan. Press a piece of wax paper directly on top of the ice cream and freeze for 4 to 6 hours before serving.

NOTES:
If you prefer bigger booze-soaked bits and pieces of prune in your ice cream, make a chunkier puree. For a smoother ice cream, puree the prunes a little finer. Don't, however, puree the prunes completely smooth: Because they hold some of the alcohol, if you puree the prunes completely, they will release all the alcohol into the base, which will make the ice cream difficult to freeze.

Because of its alcohol content, this ice cream should be ready to scoop at 0°F—straight out of the freezer 4 to 6 hours after hardening.

CHAPTER 16

filip american

Ice cream making is in my blood. Shortly after I started Wanderlust Creamery, it was pointed out to me that my grandfather had worked as a flavor chemist at an iconic ice cream company since the 1930s. The ice cream plant is where he also met my grandmother. The company they worked for originally made classic American flavors, targeting members of the American Navy stationed in the Philippines. Lolo Ely (my grandfather) and the team would work on formulation for these products. But they were also quietly making batches for themselves and the factory workers from local produce like langka (jackfruit), mangga (mango), ube, corn, and, most famously, the factory's proprietary cheese—ice cream flavors that

ino
childhood

would eventually make it to market and greatly outsell their "classic" predecessors. It's a story that reminds me of ours. To be honest, making Filipino flavors was the furthest thing from my mind. Our Ube Malted Crunch (page 225) was supposed to be a temporary seasonal flavor—now it's a mainstay that outsells all other flavors by three times. But looking back, I see that by starting our brand the way we did—celebrating cultures and flavors from all parts of the world and not just ours—we've captured a much broader audience. So when we do pay tribute to our roots, we get to share Filipino flavors with so many more people who may not have tried them otherwise.

PANDAN TRES LECHES

Makes about 1 quart (1 liter)

Having made several popular variations of tres leches ice creams one year—guava, passion fruit, and "cuatro leches" (with cajeta as the fourth milk)—this was a flavor I had dreamed up but was saving in my back pocket for the perfect occasion. Nothing like it, not even an actual cake, existed. Then October (Filipino American History Month) came, presenting a perfect opportunity to tell the story of being both Filipino and American. "American" to me means being of a culture that's a culmination of not only my family's culture, but others' as well. In this case, the ice cream depicts how Latino cuisine is just as much a part of my upbringing in Los Angeles as is pandan, a quintessential Southeast Asian flavor. After making cameos in the dipping case every October, overwhelming demands from customers finally made this ice cream a staple on Wanderlust Creamery's signature menu in 2017. Understandably, when people read the word "pandan" they automatically anticipate an overwhelming pandan and/or coconut flavor. Instead, Pandan Tres Leches is all about nuance. In keeping with the true essence of tres leches cake, it's simply evaporated milk, sweet cream, and coconut cream ice cream, a ribbon of condensed milk, and soft pandan cake pieces—the only pandan part about the entire thing. Coconut cream in both the ice cream base and condensed milk swirl give just a whisper of something tropical.

For the ice cream base

2½ tablespoons (18 g) nonfat dry milk powder

½ teaspoon (2 g) tara gum (optional; see page 24)

Scant ½ teaspoon (2 g) lecithin (optional)

½ cup + 1 tablespoon (110 g) granulated sugar

¼ cup + 2 tablespoons + ½ teaspoon (55 g) glucose powder

1½ cups (390 g) evaporated milk

3½ tablespoons (70 g) sweetened condensed milk

1 cup + 2 tablespoons (200 g) coconut cream

1 cup + 3½ tablespoons (280 g) heavy cream

For the coconut condensed milk swirl

Scant ½ cup (153 g) sweetened condensed milk

4 teaspoons (15 g) coconut cream

4½ tablespoons (60 g) refined coconut oil

Pinch of salt

For the ice cream

1 cup (120 g) Pandan Sponge Cake Pieces (page 276)

TIP: In the instance you want more of a pandan punch, add a bruised pandan leaf, tied into a knot, when you heat the ice cream base on the stovetop. Set it aside during the homogenization, then return it to the base to steep when it refrigerates to chill.

1. Prepare an ice bath (see page 39).

2. **Make the base:** In a small bowl, whisk together the milk powder, tara gum (if using), lecithin (if using), sugar, and glucose. In a tall cylindrical 1½-quart (1.5 liter) mixing vessel, blend the evaporated milk, condensed milk, and coconut cream with a hand blender. Slowly add the dry ingredients while blending and blend thoroughly to dissolve all the solids.

3. Pour the mixture into a medium saucepan and cook over medium-low heat, whisking constantly, until it reaches 165°F (75°C) on an instant-read thermometer.

4. Once the base reaches 165°F (75°C), immediately remove it from the heat and pour it back into the tall mixing vessel. Add the heavy cream and blend with a hand blender for 2 minutes to fully homogenize.

5. Pour the base through a fine-mesh sieve into the prepared ice bath to cool. Once completely cool, transfer to an airtight container. Cover and refrigerate for at least 12 hours and up to 3 days.

6. **Make the coconut condensed milk swirl:** In a small saucepan, combine the condensed milk, coconut cream, coconut oil, and salt and heat over medium-low heat, whisking until combined thoroughly. Store in an airtight container, refrigerated, for up to 1 week.

7. **Churn the ice cream:** When ready to begin, place a loaf pan, the condensed milk swirl, and cake pieces in the freezer to chill. Quickly blend the ice cream base once more with a hand blender or whisk before pouring it into an ice cream machine. Churn the ice cream until it reaches the texture of very stiff soft-serve and the surface looks dry, about 25°F (-5°C) or colder on a thermometer gun. Add the pandan cake pieces in the last few seconds of churning.

8. Spread half of the ice cream mixture into the chilled loaf pan. Spread half of the condensed milk swirl on top. Repeat this layering process once more. Immediately place the ice cream into the freezer for 15 minutes to firm it up.

9. Using a spatula, gently fold the ice cream and condensed milk swirl layers to create swirls. Three or four folds should be sufficient for visible ribbons throughout the pan.

10. Press a piece of wax paper directly on top of the ice cream and freeze for at least 4 hours before serving.

UBE MALTED CRUNCH

Makes about 1 quart (1 liter)

Before ube was everywhere in the dessert world, it was a big part of my Filipino American identity. Growing up in a predominantly white suburb of Los Angeles, my mom would buy two cakes for my childhood birthday parties. She'd buy an ube cake for me and our relatives, and a generic chocolate or vanilla cake for all the kids from school. She and I both knew from experience that they'd refuse to eat the ube cake. Never mind the mild vanilla-like flavor; it looked "weird and purple" and that was enough for a kid to refuse a slice. Looking back on this, I wanted to encapsulate my experience as a Filipino American in a flavor. So, I combined a classic flavor of Americana—a malted shake—with this emblematic Filipino purple yam. Incidentally, the wheaty, cereal flavor of malt combined with ube tastes just like the ube birthday cake from my childhood. With both the malted milk and malted crunch, it's classic ube ice cream reinvented—Filipino ice cream grown up as American. Nearly eight years after making this a signature flavor at Wanderlust Creamery, it is still our bestseller by miles. To this day, the child in me is astonished to see kids of all races walk out with a purple ice cream mustache.

For the base

1 tablespoon + ½ teaspoon (8 g) nonfat dry milk powder

2 tablespoons (22 g) malted milk powder

¼ cup + 2 tablespoons (75 g) granulated sugar

2 tablespoons + ¾ teaspoon (20 g) glucose powder

¼ teaspoon salt

½ teaspoon (2 g) tara gum (optional; see page 24)

1¾ cups (430 g) whole milk

3½ tablespoons + 1 teaspoon (75 g) sweetened condensed milk

1 tablespoon + 1½ teaspoons (70 g) ube halaya (purple yam jam)

1¾ cups (405 g) heavy cream

2½ teaspoons (12 g) ube extract (see Notes)

For the ice cream

1 cup (185 g) Malted Crunch (page 272)

1. Prepare an ice bath (see page 39).

2. **Make the base:** In a small bowl, whisk together the milk powder, malted milk powder, sugar, glucose powder, salt, and tara gum (if using). In a tall cylindrical 1½-quart (1.5 liter) mixing vessel, blend the whole milk, condensed milk, and ube halaya with a hand blender. Slowly add the dry ingredients while blending and blend thoroughly to dissolve all the solids.

3. Pour the mixture into a medium saucepan and cook over medium-low heat, whisking constantly, until it reaches 165°F (75°C) on an instant-read thermometer.

4. Once the base reaches 165°F (75°C), immediately remove it from the heat and pour it back into the tall mixing vessel. Add the heavy cream and blend with a hand blender for 2 minutes to fully homogenize.

5. Pour the base through a fine-mesh sieve into the prepared ice bath to cool. Once completely cool, stir in the ube extract and transfer to an airtight container and refrigerate for at least 12 hours and up to 3 days.

6. **Churn the ice cream:** When ready to begin, place a loaf pan in the freezer to chill. Quickly blend the ice cream base once more with a hand blender or whisk before pouring it into an ice cream machine. Churn the ice cream until it reaches the texture of very stiff soft-serve and the surface looks dry, about 25°F (-5°C) or colder on a thermometer gun. Add the malted crunch in the last few seconds of churning.

7. Transfer the ice cream to the chilled loaf pan. Press a piece of wax paper directly on top of the ice cream and freeze for at least 3 hours before serving.

NOTES:

Ube is a purple root crop that is native to the Philippines but is rarely available in fresh form outside of the Philippines, so I find that ube halaya—sweetened ube puree sold in jars at most Asian supermarkets (often also labeled "purple yam jam")—is an easy fix.

The ube extract is essential to this recipe in order to get the full ube flavor. There are those who scoff at the idea of using US-available purple sweet potatoes in place of ube since they don't taste like ube, but the flavor that many people associate with ube is mostly artificial and comes from ube flavoring. Don't let anyone tell you otherwise—show me an ube dessert that actually tastes like "ube" but doesn't have ube flavoring . . . I'll wait.

For the malted crunch, you can swap it out for anything plain tasting and crunchy, like rice cereal. Malt ball centers (like Maltesers or Whoppers without the chocolate coating) also make a great substitute, but again, be sure that they're plain and uncoated, as the delicate flavor of ube is easily masked by chocolate.

TITA'S FRUIT SALAD PIES

Makes two 8-inch (20 cm) pies

For the crusts
Cookie Crust (page 288), made with crushed lengua de gato or otap cookies (see Note)

For the bases
½ recipe Mascarpone Base (page 51)

½ recipe jackfruit ice cream base from Sapin Sapin (page 235)

½ recipe mango ice cream base from Lolo's Philippine Mango (page 240)

For the pies
½ cup macapuno (coconut sport), rinsed of syrup and drained

½ cup halved maraschino cherries

½ cup Peach Jellies (page 281)

Whipped cream, for topping

2 maraschino cherries, for garnish

NOTE: Lengua de gato (langue de chat in France) are wafer-thin buttery egg white cookies. Otap is a puff pastry cookie, similar to French palmiers, but thinner and sometimes made with coconut included. Both are easily found at any Filipino or Asian supermarket. Either one makes the perfect crust for this recipe, but you can also substitute with a plain cookie such as shortbread, vanilla wafers, or graham crackers.

jackfruit ice cream

whipped cream

peach jellies

cookie crust

Philippine
mango ice cream

maraschino cherries

macapuno

World War II and its accompanying American presence in the Philippines left its mark on the country's cuisine by creating a nation-wide penchant for canned and processed foods. This can be seen at any spread in a Filipino household: macaroni salad tossed with raisins and canned pineapple chunks for Christmas, fried Spam and Vienna sausages or canned corned beef atop rice for break-fast, and technicolor salads concocted from canned fruits, Jell-O cubes, and tinned dairy products at holidays and special occasions. Probably the most famous of these all is the "fruit salad." Versions vary and every Filipino tita (auntie) claims theirs is the best, but the gist of a Filipino fruit salad is a jumble of cream cheese, condensed milk, and an entire tub of Cool Whip with canned fruit cocktail mixed in. My favorite versions always include jarred tropical fruits like macapuno (a type of coconut) or jackfruit, and fresh seasonal fruit as well. This kind of fruit salad is a sta-ple at every Filipino holiday gathering. But I always reimagined it as a holiday cream pie, dotted with colorful fruits, and contained within a buttery crust of crumbled Filipino cookies.

1. **Make the crusts:** Make the pie crusts as directed in the recipe.

2. **Make the ice cream bases:** Make the mascarpone, jackfruit, and mango bases as directed in their respective recipes and chill.

3. When ready to begin, line two metal loaf pans with wax or parchment paper (see page 45). (Alternatively, you can use a silicone loaf pan.) Place the loaf pans in the freezer to chill.

4. Quickly blend the jackfruit base once more with a hand blender or whisk before pouring it into an ice cream machine. Churn the ice cream until it reaches the texture of very stiff soft-serve and the surface looks dry, about 25°F (-5°C) or colder on a thermometer gun.

5. Spread the ice cream mixture into the chilled loaf pan. Press a piece of wax paper directly on top of the ice cream and freeze for at least 8 hours before unmolding. (Alternatively, use dry ice to quick-freeze the ice cream; see Blast Freezing, page 45.)

6. Scrape the ice cream machine clean (no need to wash it). Quickly blend the mango ice cream base once more with a hand blender or whisk, then churn the ice cream until it reaches the texture of very stiff soft-serve and the surface looks dry, about 25°F (-5°C) or colder on a thermometer gun.

7. Spread the mango ice cream into the second chilled loaf pan. Press a piece of wax paper directly on top of the ice cream and freeze for at least 8 hours before unmolding. (Alternatively, use dry ice to quick-freeze the ice cream; see Blast Freezing, page 45.)

8. When the two ice creams have completely hardened, unmold them onto a piece of parchment or wax paper. Working quickly with a wet chef's knife, slice the ice cream into slices 1 inch (2.5 cm) thick, then into 1-inch (2.5 cm) cubes. Place the cubes back into their loaf pans and cover with plastic wrap. Keep the ice cream cubes frozen until assembling the pies.

9. **Make the pies:** Place the pie crusts, macapuno, and cherries in the freezer to chill.

10. Quickly blend the mascarpone ice cream base once more with a hand blender or whisk before pouring it into an ice cream machine. Churn until the ice cream reaches the texture of very stiff soft-serve and the surface looks dry, about 25°F (-5°C) or colder on a thermometer gun. Add the macapuno and cherries in the last few seconds of churning.

11. Using half of the mascarpone ice cream, divide it between the two pie crusts. Evenly arrange cubes of jackfruit and mango ice cream on top, pressing them into the ice cream toward the bottom of the crusts. Sprinkle half of the peach jellies on top. Add the remaining ice cream from the machine into the pies and top with more jackfruit and mango ice cream cubes and peach jellies.

12. Press a piece of wax paper directly on top of the ice cream pies and freeze for at least 4 hours before serving.

13. To serve, top the pie with whipped cream and a single cherry in the middle before serving.

HALO HALO

For the canned milk base

2 tablespoons pinipig rice
(sweet young rice; see Notes)

½ cup + 1½ tablespoons (120 g)
granulated sugar

1 tablespoon + ½ teaspoon (10 g)
glucose powder

Scant ¾ teaspoon (3 g) lecithin
(optional)

1¾ cups + 2½ tablespoons
(480 g) evaporated milk

2½ tablespoons (50 g) sweetened
condensed milk

1 cup (230 g) heavy cream

⅔ cup + 2 tablespoons (140 g)
coconut cream

1 ounce (25 g) ripe jackfruit, fresh
or canned

2 to 3 caramelized plantains
(optional; see Notes)

For the ice cream

Halo halo mix-ins of choice
(see page 233)

NOTES:

Pinipig is sweet young rice, sold
in bags.

Caramelized plantains come in
jars labeled "matamis na saging"
in Filipino supermarkets, although
you can also make your own by
simmering sliced plantains in
equal parts water and brown
sugar until tender.

"Halo halo" means "mix mix," referring to a hodgepodge of different tastes and textures in the form of sweet odds and ends. It's a parfait of jarred fruits, candied palm fruit seeds, coconut gels, udon-shaped gelatinous coconut, with an avalanche of shaved ice and canned milks (evaporated and condensed). Anthony Bourdain once described it as "an icy, milky, Technicolor concoction of sundry sweets: mung beans, candied fruits, and gelatins," referring to the classic and more broadly known everything-but-the-kitchen-sink type of halo halo. But what resonated with me as a Filipino American most was his commentary upon finishing the parfait: "It's kind of like, if you let the Fruit Loops marinate in the milk for a while—that's what it tastes like." Dodging the beans and synthetic banana-flavored thingamabobs with a spoon to simply slurp the tropical-fruit-infused milk was the part I (and many other Filipinos born stateside) enjoyed about halo halo most. To mimic this moment in an ice cream, I infuse a base of canned milks with toasted rice, jackfruit, and plantains. The ice cream is then sweetened with chewy jellies, crispy bits, and thick jams.

Because halo halo itself is a frozen dessert, one would think that all the usual components can be thrown into ice cream as mix-ins, but NO! That's not the case. Certain ingredients used in halo halo—like fruit pieces, nata de coco (cubes of fermented coconut water gel), whole sweetened beans, and corn kernels—freeze into solid hard bits due to their water content. In halo halo ice cream, these elements must be represented as jellies or variegates instead. This ice cream base recipe can be made into any variation of halo halo you want, so feel free to get creative with the mix-ins (see Halo Halo Mix-Ins, opposite), but just make sure to consider the final frozen texture of anything you add.

1. **Make the base:** In a dry skillet, toast the pinipig over medium heat while stirring often with a wooden spoon, until the rice smells nutty and begins to turn golden brown, 5 to 6 minutes. Transfer the toasted pinipig to a spice grinder and grind into a fine powder.

2. Prepare an ice bath (see page 39).

3. In a small bowl, whisk together the toasted pinipig, sugar, glucose, and lecithin (if using). Add the evaporated milk and condensed milk to a tall cylindrical 1½-quart (1.5 liter) mixing vessel. Slowly add the dry ingredients while blending and blend thoroughly to dissolve all the solids.

4. Pour the mixture into a medium saucepan and cook over medium-low heat, whisking constantly, until it reaches 165°F (75°C) on an instant-read thermometer.

5. Once the base reaches 165°F (75°C), immediately remove it from the heat and pour it into a stand blender. Add the heavy cream, coconut cream, and jackfruit and blend for 2 minutes to puree the jackfruit and homogenize the base.

6. Transfer the base to the prepared ice bath to cool. Once completely cool, transfer the base to an airtight container along with the caramelized plantains (if using) and refrigerate for at least 12 hours and up to 3 days.

7. **Churn the ice cream:** When ready to begin, place a loaf pan and your chosen mix-ins in the freezer to chill. Remove the plantains (if using) from the base and quickly blend once more with a hand blender or whisk before pouring it through a fine-mesh sieve into an ice cream machine. Churn the ice cream until it reaches the texture of very stiff soft-serve and the surface looks dry, about 25°F (-5°C) or colder on a thermometer gun.

8. Spread half of the ice cream mixture into the chilled loaf pan. If there is a variegate, spread half on top. Sprinkle the solid mix-ins evenly on top. Repeat the layering process once more. (If making the Classic, place all of the red bean paste in the middle layer and all of the ube halaya on the top layer.) Immediately place the ice cream into the freezer for 15 minutes to firm it up.

9. Using a spatula, gently fold the ice cream and variegate layers to create swirls. Three or four folds should be sufficient for visible ribbons throughout the pan.

10. Press a piece of wax paper directly on top of the ice cream and freeze for at least 4 hours before serving.

HALO HALO MIX-INS

KAPAMPANGAN HALO HALO ICE CREAM

MIX-INS:
⅓ cup (90 g) macapuno (coconut sport; see Note)

⅓ cup (37 g) ¼-inch (6 mm) cubes of flan, store-bought or homemade

¼ cup toasted pinipig or rice cereal

⅓ cup pureed caramelized plantains (see Notes, page 231)

VARIEGATE:
⅔ cup (228 g) dulce de leche

CLASSIC HALO HALO ICE CREAM

MIX-INS:
⅓ cup chopped toddy palm seeds

⅓ cup (100 g) Pandan Jellies (page 281)

⅓ cup (90 g) macapuno (coconut sport; see Note)

VARIEGATES:
½ cup anko tsubuan (chunky sweetened red bean paste)

½ cup (136 g) ube halaya (purple yam jam)

TROPICAL FRUIT HALO HALO ICE CREAM

MIX-INS:
⅓ cup Guava Jellies (page 281)

⅓ cup "Dalandan" Jellies (page 280)

⅓ cup Passion Fruit Jellies (page 281)

⅓ cup (90 g) macapuno (coconut sport; see Note)

VARIEGATE:
⅔ cup Mango Jam (page 170)

NOTE: Macapuno is a mutant coconut with a jelly-like texture that's sold in jars in thick strings that look sort of like udon noodles. In addition to the name *macapuno*, jars are also labeled "coconut sport."

SAPIN SAPIN

At every Filipino gathering in my childhood memory, the dessert table would almost always include a platter of sapin sapin. It's a tri-colored jiggly cake, made from sticky rice flour. Colorful layers of purple, orange/yellow, and white would have any child expecting to taste something as exciting as Fruit Loops. Instead, it always just tasted plainly of rice and coconut. Each time I tried a slice, I anticipated a different outcome, only to be disappointed. It wasn't until my twenties, when attending my boyfriend JP's family gatherings, that sapin sapin hit differently. That's because it wasn't the usual sapin sapin bought from the take-out section of a Filipino turo-turo (cafeteria style) restaurant. It was Auntie Lita's homemade sapin sapin, prepared the traditional way with not just three different colors, but three different flavors: coconut, jackfruit, and ube. Each flavor stands on its own but complements the next—creamy and nutty coconut, funky-tropical and bubblegum-like jackfruit, then milky-earthy ube. This late discovery is the origin story of Wanderlust's Filipino Neapolitan ice cream.

½ recipe Coconut Rice Cream base (page 52)

½ recipe ice cream base from Ube Malted Crunch (page 225)

For the jackfruit base

6½ ounces (185 g) ripe jackfruit, fresh or canned

¾ cup + 3 tablespoons (215 g) heavy cream

1 tablespoon + 1 teaspoon (40 g) granulated sugar

½ teaspoon (2 g) tara gum (optional; see page 24)

Scant ½ teaspoon (2 g) lecithin (optional)

1 tablespoon + ½ teaspoon (8 g) nonfat dry milk powder

2 tablespoons + ¾ teaspoon (20 g) glucose powder

3 tablespoons (50 g) whole milk

1½ tablespoons (30 g) sweetened condensed milk

Natural yellow food coloring (optional)

For the ice cream

Latik (recipe follows) or ⅓ cup (185 g) darkly toasted coconut (see Note)

NOTE: Making this kind of latik is a long process, but here's an optional shortcut: Use the same amount of darkly toasted shredded coconut instead. Toast the coconut in a 350°F (180°C) oven until it's a shade darker than normal toasted coconut.

TIP: If you prefer a scooped ice cream instead of a sliced terrine, fold the ice cream layers at the end of assembly, just before freezing the finished pan.

1. Make the rice cream base and the malted ube ice cream base as directed in those recipes and chill.

2. Prepare an ice bath (see page 39).

3. **Make the jackfruit base:** In a stand blender, process the jackfruit and heavy cream into a completely smooth puree. Set aside.

4. In a small bowl, whisk together the sugar, tara gum (if using), lecithin (if using), milk powder, and glucose. Pour the whole milk and condensed milk into a tall cylindrical 1½-quart (1.5 liter) mixing vessel and blend with a hand blender while gradually adding the dry ingredients.

5. Pour the mixture into a small saucepan and cook over medium-low heat, whisking constantly, until it reaches 165°F (75°C) on an instant-read thermometer.

6. Once the base reaches 165°F (75°C), immediately remove it from the heat and pour it back into the tall mixing vessel. Add the jackfruit puree and yellow food coloring (if using) and blend with a hand blender for 2 minutes to fully homogenize.

7. Pour the base into the prepared ice bath to cool. Once completely cool, transfer to an airtight container and refrigerate for at least 12 hours and up to 2 days.

8. **Churn the ice cream:** Once all three of the ice cream bases are completely chilled, line a metal loaf pan with wax or parchment paper (see page 45). (Alternatively, you can use a silicone loaf pan.) Place the loaf pan in the freezer to chill. Quickly blend each ice cream base with a whisk or hand blender.

9. Churn the jackfruit ice cream until it reaches the texture of very stiff soft-serve and the surface looks dry, about 25°F (-5°C) or colder on a thermometer gun. Spread the ice cream mixture into the chilled loaf pan and place it in the freezer.

10. Scrape the ice cream machine clean (no need to wash it), then churn the rice cream base as directed above. Add the latik or toasted coconut in the last seconds of churning. Spread the coconut rice cream mixture into the chilled loaf pan on top of the layer of jackfruit ice cream and return it to the freezer.

11. Clean and dry the ice cream machine completely, then churn the malted ube ice cream base as for the other ice creams. Spread the malted ube ice cream into the chilled loaf pan on top of the layer of coconut rice ice cream.

12. Press a piece of wax paper directly on top of the ice cream and freeze for at least 8 hours before unmolding. (Alternatively, use dry ice to quick-freeze the ice cream; see Blast Freezing, page 45.)

13. When the ice cream has completely hardened, unmold the ice cream onto a piece of parchment or wax paper. Working quickly with a wet chef's knife, slice the ice cream into slices 1½ inches (4 cm) thick and serve.

LATIK
Makes ⅓ cup (185 g)

Latik is a Filipino culinary term that refers to burnt coconut. It can refer to a caramelized coconut syrup/sauce, or my favorite kind of latik—crispy fried curds of coconut milk.

1 can (19 oz/560 ml) coconut cream

1. In a medium pot, bring the coconut cream to a boil. Reduce the heat to medium and continue to simmer, occasionally scraping the coconut solids from the bottom using a wooden spoon or heatproof silicone spatula. Simmer until the liquid evaporates, about 12 minutes.

2. Adjust the heat between low and medium and continue to cook until the coconut solids begin to separate from the coconut oil, about 12 minutes.

3. Once the coconut solids begin to change color, continue to cook, stirring constantly, until the color turns a medium golden brown, about 5 minutes. Immediately remove from the heat (the solids will continue to brown from residual heat) and allow to cool to warm.

4. Drain the solids (the latik) in a sieve set over a bowl to catch the coconut oil. Reserve the oil for another use, such as Coconut Rice Cream Base (page 52).

5. Spread the latik on a plate lined with paper towels to absorb the remaining oil. Transfer to an airtight container until ready to use.

BROWN BUTTER
SANS RIVAL

Makes about 1 quart (1 liter)

For the base

5 tablespoons (70 g) unsalted butter

½ cup + 1½ teaspoons (60 g) nonfat dry milk powder

½ teaspoon (2 g) tara gum (optional; see page 24)

½ cup + 1¼ teaspoons (105 g) granulated sugar

¼ cup + 2½ tablespoons (60 g) glucose powder

1¾ cups + 2 teaspoons (425 g) warm water

3½ tablespoons (70 g) sweetened condensed milk

70 grams egg yolks (from about 4 large eggs)

¾ cup + 2 tablespoons (200 g) heavy cream

½ teaspoon (2 g) vanilla extract

For the ice cream

Crispy Nut Dacquoise (page 273), made with cashews

1 cup (105 g) chopped store-bought butter toffee cashews

My abnormal love for butter stems from the fact that growing up, my family, following the erroneous nutritional guidelines of the time, only kept margarine in the house. Any food that had actual real butter was literal gold to my taste buds. And the dish that took the cake (pun intended) in my book was sans rival. Born from a French dessert made of layers of almond meringue sandwiched between whipped egg yolks and butter, the Filipino sans rival utilizes native buttery cashews baked into crispy thin meringue layers encased in even more butter. It is one of my favorite things on earth—so much so that I once ate an entire Filipino-party-sized sans rival cake in the hospital while waiting to birth twins. Every October for Filipino American History Month at Wanderlust Creamery, we make an ice cream version of sans rival with toasted brown butter, crispy cashew dacquoise (whose butteriness is intensified with browned milk solids), and cashews candied in (you guessed it) butter.

1. **Make the base:** In a small saucepan, melt the butter over medium heat until it begins to bubble and the milk solids begin to separate from the fat, 5 to 6 minutes. Whisk in the dry milk powder and continue to cook, whisking frequently, until the milk solids just begin to turn color. Remove from the heat and allow it to cool for 5 minutes; the milk solids will continue to darken and brown. Pour the warm butter, along with every bit of browned milk solids scraped from the pot, into a tall cylindrical 1½-quart (1.5 liter) mixing vessel.

2. Prepare an ice bath (see page 39).

3. In a small bowl, whisk together the tara gum (if using), sugar, and glucose. Add the warm water, condensed milk, and egg yolks to the mixing vessel with the browned butter.

Blend with a hand blender, slowly adding the dry ingredients while blending and blend thoroughly to dissolve all the solids.

4. Pour the mixture into a small saucepan and cook over medium-low heat, whisking constantly, until it reaches 165°F (75°C) on an instant-read thermometer.

5. Once the base reaches 165°F (75°C), immediately remove it from the heat and pour it back into the tall mixing vessel. Add the heavy cream and blend with a hand blender for 2 minutes to fully homogenize.

6. Pour the base into the prepared ice bath to cool. Once completely cool, stir in the vanilla extract and transfer to an airtight container. Cover and refrigerate for at least 12 hours and up to 3 days.

7. **Churn the ice cream:** When ready to begin, place a loaf pan, the cashew dacquoise, and the butter toffee cashews in the freezer to chill. Quickly blend the ice cream base once more with a hand blender or whisk before pouring it into an ice cream machine. Churn the ice cream until it reaches the texture of very stiff soft-serve and the surface looks dry, about 25°F (-5°C) or colder on a thermometer gun. Add the cashew dacquoise and butter toffee cashews in the last few seconds of churning.

8. Transfer the ice cream to the chilled loaf pan. Press a piece of wax paper directly on top of the ice cream and freeze for at least 4 hours before serving.

LOLO'S PHILIPPINE MANGO (MANGGA)

Makes about 1 quart (1 liter)

I'll never forget my first scoop of mangga ice cream. It came in a clear plastic tub that would later become a family heirloom form of Tupperware. "Philippine mango," my mom said, "the best in the world." Barely any tartness, the flavor had an almost toffee-like aftertaste that I couldn't quite put my finger on, chasing it with every spoonful. It ruined all other mango ice creams for me. It made me a snob. Companions at ice cream dates would swoon over mango sorbet at a generic gelateria and offer me a taste of their cone, but I declined, knowing better.

After opening my own ice cream shop, I discovered that my late grandfather Lolo was among the flavor chemists who developed that mango ice cream from my childhood. The secret to this ice cream? I still don't know. But I can guess.

For starters, it's the king of mangoes—the oblong yellow Philippine mango. And the toffee-like notes? Allowing the mangoes to ripen to a point of partial dehydration. When the fruit has wrinkled, it's given up some of its moisture; the sugars condense and concentrate into a caramelized flavor. Any tartness the fruit had ripens into an ethylene—a funky tropical flavor that can only come from a Southeast Asian mango.

3 tablespoons + ¾ teaspoon (23 g) nonfat dry milk powder

½ cup (100 g) granulated sugar

½ teaspoon (2 g) tara gum (optional; see page 24)

Scant ½ teaspoon (2 g) lecithin (optional)

¾ cup + 1 tablespoon (200 g) whole milk

1¾ cups + 1 tablespoon (415 g) heavy cream

3½ tablespoons + 1 teaspoon (75 g) sweetened condensed milk

10 slices (70 g) dried Philippine mangoes

1 cup (230 g) kesar mango pulp (see Tip)

TIP: Kesar mango is a South Asian tropical mango from India that comes readily pureed and canned, available year-round at any South Asian or Middle Eastern grocery. I find its flavor very close to that of a Philippine mango, which isn't available year-round, making the kesar an easier alternative. Moreover, the flash-heating process involved in making the kesar pulp shelf stable condenses and concentrates the mango flavor, which seems to echo the taste that was unique to Lolo's mangga ice cream. To further accentuate this, Philippine-style dried mangoes pureed right into the base imitate the sweet, musky intensity of a wrinkly ripened mango.

1. Prepare an ice bath (see page 39).

2. In a small bowl, whisk together the milk powder, sugar, tara gum (if using), and lecithin (if using). In a tall cylindrical 1½-quart (1.5 liter) mixing vessel, blend the whole milk, heavy cream, and condensed milk with a hand blender. Slowly add the dry ingredients while blending and blend thoroughly to dissolve all the solids.

3. Pour the mixture into a small saucepan and cook over medium-low heat, whisking constantly, until it reaches 165°F (75°C) on an instant-read thermometer.

4. Once the base reaches 165°F (75°C), immediately remove it from the heat and pour it back into the tall mixing vessel; blend with a hand blender for 2 minutes to fully homogenize.

5. Transfer the base to the prepared ice bath to cool. Once completely cool, pour through a fine-mesh sieve into a stand blender. Add the dried mangoes and blend until fully pureed. Add the kesar mango pulp and blend again until completely smooth.

6. Transfer the base to an airtight container and refrigerate for at least 12 hours and up to 2 days.

7. **Churn the ice cream:** When ready to begin, place a loaf pan in the freezer to chill. Quickly blend the ice cream base once more with a hand blender or whisk before pouring it into an ice cream machine. Churn the ice cream until it reaches the texture of very stiff soft-serve and the surface looks dry, about 25°F (–5°C) or colder on a thermometer gun.

8. Transfer the ice cream mixture to the chilled loaf pan. Press a piece of wax paper directly on top of the ice cream and freeze for at least 4 hours before serving.

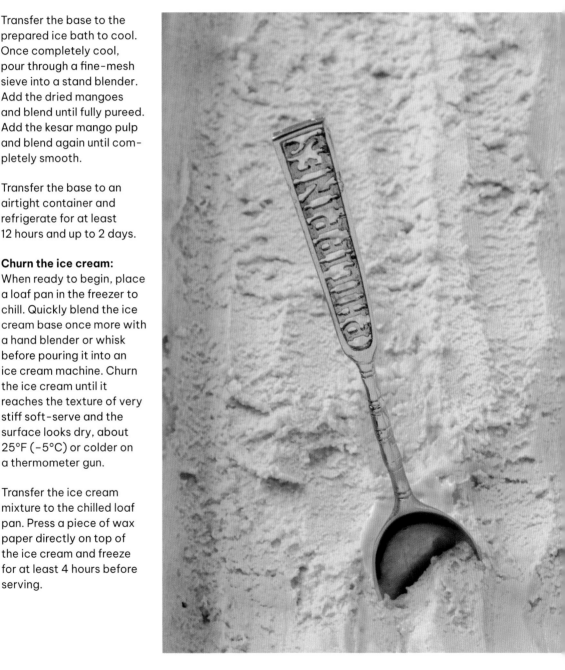

CHAPTER 17

reinve
cla

Despite the name "Wanderlust Creamery," we still get customers confused about the concept of foreign ice cream flavors. "Where's the cookies 'n' cream? Butter pecan?" Luckily for us, ice cream is ice cream. It's a medium no one can refuse. We use it to trick people into exploring new flavors. Oftentimes, reinventing classics is the only way you'll get someone to try

nted
ssics

something new. This chapter is all about taking classic American ice cream formats like rocky road, Neapolitan, and mint chip, and making them with new flavors to ignite unadventurous ice cream eaters with curiosity of what else is possible when you roam outside the norm.

PALO SANTO MINT CHIP

Makes about 1 quart (1 liter)

While vacationing in Asia in 2014, I was sharing accommodations with my boyfriend, JP, and his sister. Being the hippie that she is, she often burned sage and incense in our shared space, or a stick of wood that smelled like a Catholic church, mint, and sweet marshmallow—all at the same time. "It's Peruvian holy wood," she said. In Ecuador and Peru, sticks of palo santo from a sacred tree found in the Amazon and Yucatán are believed to have purifying powers when burned. Coincidentally I had an uncle who was living in Peru at the time, so I asked him to bring me some palo santo on his next visit home. What arrived in my souvenir bag from Peru were not sticks, but wood shavings in tea bags. "You wanted palo santo, right? In Peru, it's tea," my uncle shrugged. I made myself a cup, and all I could taste past an initial mild oak flavor were pastel-colored, pillow-shaped butter mints.

This discovery would later inspire a palo santo version of mint chip ice cream on Wanderlust Creamery's opening menu a year later. Back then, people scoffed at the menu description. "Wood ice cream? Pass." "Palo what?!" Then there were others who would complain that there was an "off-flavor" to our mint chip. We got tired of explaining, so it disappeared from the menu. But just a year later, palo santo had become a staple in every hipster household. And a year after that, every wide-brimmed-hat-wearing girl on LA's Westside had a stick of palo santo in a bowl on her coffee table. That's when palo santo mint chip started making cameos in our dipping case again, and we haven't had to explain a thing since.

For the palo santo milk

1¾ cups (425 g) whole milk

¼ cup (10 g) palo santo tea (aka loose shavings; see Note)

For the base

2 tablespoons + 2½ teaspoons (20 g) nonfat dry milk powder

½ cup + 2 tablespoons (125 g) granulated sugar

⅓ cup + 1 teaspoon (50 g) glucose powder

½ teaspoon (2 g) tara gum (optional; see page 24)

Scant ¾ teaspoon (3 g) lecithin (optional)

3½ tablespoons + 1 teaspoon (75 g) sweetened condensed milk

1¾ cups (400 g) heavy cream

⅛ teaspoon peppermint extract

For the crème de menthe freckle

1½ tablespoons refined coconut oil

4 ounces (113 g) white chocolate, chopped

¼ teaspoon peppermint extract or 2 drops peppermint essential oil

A few drops natural green food coloring

For the ice cream

½ recipe Chocolate Freckles (page 279), made with dark chocolate

NOTE: This recipe combines traditional peppermint and palo santo for a serene mint flavor. When shopping for palo santo tea, also called "loose shavings," "shredded," or "incense dust," look for a coarsely shredded product that looks like thick sawdust and not actual powder or wood chips. Use the freshest palo santo you can find, which you can decipher by how strongly fragrant it is through its packaging. If palo santo loose tea is not readily available, you can use palo santo essential oil instead: Place one drop of the oil onto a spoon, and shake off as much oil as you can. Use that spoon to stir the base after cooling, scenting the entire mixture with the residual oil left behind on the spoon.

1. **Make the palo santo milk:** In a small saucepan, scald the whole milk over medium-low heat. Remove from the heat and stir in the palo santo shavings. Pour the mixture along with the palo santo shavings into a tall cylindrical 1½-quart (1.5 liter) mixing vessel.

2. Prepare an ice bath (see page 39).

3. **Make the base:** In a small bowl, whisk together the milk powder, sugar, glucose, tara gum (if using), and lecithin (if using). Add the condensed milk to the palo santo milk and blend with a hand blender to combine. Add the dry ingredients and blend again to fully incorporate.

4. Pour the mixture into a medium saucepan and cook over medium-low heat, whisking constantly, until it reaches 165°F (75°C) on an instant-read thermometer.

5. Once the base reaches 165°F (75°C), immediately remove it from the heat and pour it back into the tall mixing vessel. Add the heavy cream and blend with a hand blender for 2 minutes to fully homogenize.

6. Pour the base through a fine-mesh sieve into the prepared ice bath to cool. Once completely cool, add the peppermint extract. Transfer the base to an airtight container and refrigerate for at least 12 hours and up to 3 days.

7. **Make the crème de menthe freckles:** In a microwave-safe bowl, microwave the coconut oil until it registers at least 130°F (55°C) on an instant-read thermometer.

8. Add the white chocolate and food coloring and let sit for 30 seconds. Using a whisk or flexible spatula, stir the mixture until all the chocolate has melted.

9. Transfer the mixture to a container that can be poured from, such as a liquid measuring cup. Cool the white chocolate to a tepid temperature in which it is still liquid and pourable, about 80°F (25°C). (If made ahead, microwave in 30-second increments, stirring after each, to remelt. Cool it again to 80°F/25°C just before ice cream assembly.)

10. **Churn the ice cream:** When ready to begin, place a loaf pan in the freezer to chill. Quickly blend the ice cream base once more with a hand blender or whisk before pouring it into an ice cream machine. Churn until the ice cream reaches the texture of very stiff soft-serve and the surface looks dry, about 25°F (−5°C) or colder on a thermometer gun. Pour in the dark chocolate, then follow with the crème de menthe chocolate in the last few seconds of churning. Stop the machine as soon as you see "freckles."

11. Transfer the ice cream to the chilled loaf pan. Press a piece of wax paper on top of the ice cream and freeze for at least 4 hours before serving.

VIETNAMESE ROCKY ROAD

This ice cream is literally inspired by an actual Vietnamese road. Although not quite rocky, it is very windy. My twin sister traveled this road on the back of a stranger's motorcycle, from Hội An to Huế. It's called the Hải Vân Pass, which translates to "Sea Cloud" Pass. Sea mist rises into the green mountaintops through which the road winds and bends, so "passing through sea clouds" sounds like an accurate description of the journey. Every sharp turn and steep ascent yields a different breathtaking scene—turquoise sea, lone beaches, rice paddies, vast emerald-hued jungle, punctuated with roadside coffee stops along the way. Dark, earthy Vietnamese coffee ice cream, wound through with "clouds" of condensed milk marshmallow, studded with rocky chocolate is not only my reinvention of rocky road ice cream, but a page out of my sister's travel diary written along the Hải Vân Pass.

For the base

2 tablespoons (15 g) nonfat dry milk powder

⅔ cup + 1 tablespoon (145 g) granulated sugar

½ (1 g) teaspoon cocoa powder

½ teaspoon (2 g) tara gum (optional; see page 24)

3 tablespoons + 1 teaspoon (30 g) glucose powder

1¾ cups (425 g) whole milk

70 grams egg yolks (from about 4 large eggs)

3 tablespoons + 1 teaspoon (65 g) sweetened condensed milk

1⅔ cups (380 g) heavy cream

⅓ cup (30 g) ground Vietnamese coffee

For the Vietnamese "rocky" chocolate

3 tablespoons + 2½ teaspoons (50 g) refined coconut oil

8 ounces (225 g) white chocolate, chopped

4 teaspoons (20 g) unsalted butter

Generous ¼ cup (25 g) ground Vietnamese coffee

Pinch of salt

3½ ounces (100 g) cacao nibs (about ¾ cup)

½ cup (10 g) crispy rice cereal or feuilletine (optional)

For the ice cream

1 cup (300 g) Marshmallow Crème (page 292)

1. Prepare an ice bath (see page 39).

2. **Make the base:** In a small bowl, whisk together the milk powder, sugar, cocoa powder, tara gum (if using), and glucose powder. In a tall cylindrical 1½-quart (1.5 liter) mixing vessel, blend the whole milk, egg yolks, and condensed milk with a hand blender. Slowly add the dry ingredients while blending and blend thoroughly to dissolve all the solids.

3. Pour the mixture into a small saucepan and cook over medium-low heat, whisking constantly, until it reaches 165°F (75°C) on an instant-read thermometer.

4. Once the base reaches 165°F (75°C), immediately remove it from the heat and pour it back into the tall mixing vessel. Add the heavy cream and coffee grounds and blend with a hand blender for 2 minutes to fully homogenize.

5. Transfer the base to the prepared ice bath to cool. Once completely cool, pour through a fine-mesh sieve into an airtight container. Cover and refrigerate for at least 12 hours and up to 3 days.

6. **Make the Vietnamese "rocky" chocolate:** In a microwave-safe bowl, microwave the coconut oil until it registers at least 130°F (55°C) on an instant-read thermometer.

7. Add the white chocolate, butter, and ground coffee and let sit for 30 seconds. Using a whisk or rubber spatula, stir the mixture until all the chocolate has melted. Let the mixture steep for 10 minutes before straining through a fine-mesh sieve into a container that can be poured from, such as a liquid glass measuring cup. Cool the chocolate to a tepid temperature in which it is still liquid and pourable, about 78°F (25°C), then stir in the cacao nibs and rice cereal. (If made ahead, microwave in 30-second increments, stirring after each, to remelt. Cool it again to 78°F/25°C just before ice cream assembly.)

8. **Churn the ice cream:** When ready to begin, place a loaf pan and the marshmallow crème in the freezer to chill. Quickly blend the ice cream base once more with a hand blender or whisk before pouring it through a fine-mesh sieve into an ice cream machine. Churn the ice cream until it reaches the texture of very stiff soft-serve and the surface looks dry, about 25°F (−5°C) or colder on a thermometer gun. Pour in the "rocky" chocolate in the final seconds of churning. Stop the machine just before the chocolate begins to break into fine pieces; you should aim for small chunks rather than fine freckles.

9. Spread half of the ice cream mixture into the chilled loaf pan. Spread half of the marshmallow crème on top. Repeat the layering process once more. Immediately place the ice cream into the freezer for 15 minutes to firm it up.

10. Using a spatula, gently fold the ice cream and marshmallow layers to create swirls. Three or four folds should be sufficient for visible ribbons throughout the pan.

11. Press a piece of wax paper directly on top of the ice cream and freeze for at least 4 hours before serving.

ALMOND COOKIES & LYCHEE CREAM

Makes about 1 quart (1 liter)

For the base

1½ cups (230 g) drained canned lychees

¾ cup (240 g) lychee syrup

2½ tablespoons (18 g) nonfat dry milk powder

½ teaspoon (2 g) tara gum (optional; see page 24)

Scant ½ teaspoon (2 g) lecithin (optional)

¾ cup + 2½ tablespoons (220 g) whole milk

2¾ teaspoons (20 g) sweetened condensed milk

1¾ cups + 3 tablespoons (445 g) heavy cream

2 teaspoons (10 g) lychee flavor extract (optional; see Note)

For the ice cream

⅓ cup (150 g) crushed Chinese almond cookies

NOTE: Lychee flavor extract (Butterfly brand is my favorite) can be found in many Asian groceries or online.

Lychee and almond are a common flavor pairing in Asian desserts, perhaps due to their complementary flavors and aromas. Some of the aromatic compounds of almond include phenethyl alcohol, which gives it a warm rose aroma similar to notes found in lychee. At Wanderlust Creamery, we'd often iterate this as lychee sorbet swirled with almond milk sherbet. Then one day, our friend Jasmine challenged us: "Can you make a lychee flavor, but as ice cream?" Lychee in sorbet form is very commonly found, but rarely do you see it translated into creamy ice cream, because of its high water content. In this recipe, some of the water in milk is displaced by pureed lychees, and sugar comes in the form of lychee-perfumed syrup. The result is an unexpected juicy lychee flavor presented in a creamy texture, contrasted by hits of marzipan in crunchy Chinese almond cookies—my kind of "cookies 'n' cream."

1. **Make the base:** In a stand blender, process the lychees and lychee syrup into a completely smooth puree. Set aside.

2. Prepare an ice bath (see page 39).

3. In a small bowl, whisk together the milk powder, tara gum (if using), and lecithin (if using). In a tall cylindrical 1½-quart (1.5 liter) mixing vessel, blend the whole milk and condensed milk together with a hand blender while slowly adding the dry ingredients. Blend thoroughly to dissolve all the solids.

4. Pour the mixture into a medium saucepan and cook over medium-low heat, whisking constantly, until it reaches 165°F (75°C) on an instant-read thermometer.

5. Once the base reaches 165°F (75°C), immediately remove it from the heat and pour it back into the tall mixing vessel. Add the heavy cream and blend with a hand blender for 2 minutes to fully homogenize.

6. Pour the base through a fine-mesh sieve into the prepared ice bath to cool. Once completely cool, whisk in the lychee puree and lychee extract (if using), then transfer to an airtight container and refrigerate for at least 12 hours and up to 2 days.

7. **Churn the ice cream:** When ready to begin, place a loaf pan and the crushed almond cookies in the freezer to chill. Quickly blend the ice cream base once more with a hand blender or whisk before pouring it through a fine-mesh sieve into an ice cream machine. Churn until the ice cream reaches the texture of very stiff soft-serve and the surface looks dry, about 25°F (-5°C) or colder on a thermometer gun. Add the crushed almond cookies in the last few seconds of churning.

8. Transfer the ice cream to the chilled loaf pan. Press a piece of wax paper directly on top of the ice cream and freeze for at least 4 hours before serving.

JAPANESE NEAPOLITAN

Makes about 1½ quarts
(1½ liters)

At the beginning of our ice cream journey, we kept getting the same type of customer—the kind who would peruse our select offerings and ask, "Where are the classic flavors?" Instead of conforming to their demands, I thought of a Neapolitan to showcase what's "classic" in other parts of the world. This recipe incorporates matcha, black sesame, and hojicha—three popular and "classic" ice cream flavors in Japan. It's bittersweet matcha ice cream contrasted with swirls of nutty black sesame and caramel-like hojicha. To this day, our Japanese Neapolitan is one of our most renowned flavors. Sometimes, if it's scooped just right, it looks like a globe on a cone—a reminder that ice cream belongs to the whole world.

TIP: After making this flavor for eight years, I've learned that people have a varying love and tolerance for the bitterness of matcha. Some like it weak, and others like it strikingly strong. For this recipe, start with the amount stated, then add to your liking. There is less black sesame ice cream than there is matcha and hojicha, because the nuttiness of the black sesame can overpower the nuances of the other flavors. If you have a large-capacity ice cream machine (bigger than 1.6 quarts), I would suggest doubling the recipes to meet the volume requirements for proper churning.

MATCHA ICE CREAM BASE

Makes about ⅔ quart (600 ml)

3 tablespoons (20 g) matcha powder

¼ cup + 3 tablespoons (85 g) granulated sugar

2 tablespoons + 1 teaspoon (10 g) nonfat dry milk powder

¼ teaspoon (1 g) tara gum (optional; see page 24)

1¼ cups + 1 tablespoon (210 g) whole milk

2 tablespoons (40 g) sweetened condensed milk

2 egg yolks (35 g total)

1¼ cups + 1 tablespoon (200 g) heavy cream

1. Prepare an ice bath (see page 39).

2. In a small bowl, whisk together the dry ingredients thoroughly (make sure that the matcha has completely blended into the sugar and milk powder). In a stainless-steel bain-marie pot, blend the whole milk, condensed milk, and egg yolks with a hand blender. Slowly add the dry ingredients while blending; blend thoroughly to dissolve all the solids.

3. Pour the mixture into a medium saucepan and cook over medium-low heat, whisking constantly until it reaches 165°F (75°C). Place the heavy cream in the bain marie pot.

4. Once the base reaches 165°F (75°C), immediately remove from the heat and pour into the bain-marie pot containing the heavy cream. Blend with a hand blender for 2 minutes to fully homogenize.

5. Pour the base through a fine-mesh strainer into the prepared ice bath to cool. Once completely cool, transfer to an airtight container. Cover and refrigerate for at least 12 hours and up to 3 days.

BLACK SESAME ICE CREAM BASE

Makes about ⅓ quart (300 ml)

3½ tablespoons (45 g) granulated sugar

1½ tablespoons (6 g) nonfat dry milk powder

⅛ teaspoon tara gum (optional)

½ cup + 1 tablespoon (140 g) whole milk

7 tablespoons (100 g) heavy cream

1 generous tablespoon (60 g) sweetened condensed milk

1 egg yolk (15 g total)

1 tablespoon (15 g) black sesame paste

1. Prepare an ice bath (see page 39).

2. In a small bowl, whisk together the dry ingredients thoroughly. In a stainless-steel bain-marie pot, blend the whole milk, heavy cream, condensed milk, and egg yolk with a hand blender. Slowly add the dry ingredients while blending; blend thoroughly to dissolve all the solids.

3. Pour the mixture into a medium saucepan and cook over medium-low heat, whisking constantly until it reaches 165°F (75°C) on an instant-read thermometer. Place the black sesame paste into the bain-marie pot.

4. Once the base reaches 165°F (75°C), immediately remove from the heat and pour into the bain-marie pot containing the black sesame paste. Blend with a hand blender for 2 minutes to fully homogenize.

5. Pour the base through a fine-mesh strainer into the prepared ice bath to cool. Once completely cool, transfer to an airtight container. Cover and refrigerate for at least 12 hours and up to 3 days.

HOJICHA
ICE CREAM BASE

Makes about ⅔ quart (600 ml)

2 tablespoons (25 g) granulated sugar

¼ cup + 1 teaspoon (18 g) nonfat dry milk powder

¼ teaspoon (1 g) tara gum (optional; see page 24)

1 cup + 1½ tablespoons (265 g) whole milk

⅞ cup (210 g) heavy cream

3 tablespoons (65 g) honey

3 egg yolks (50 g total)

6½ tablespoons (20 g) hojicha leaves

1. Prepare an ice bath (see page 39).

2. In a small bowl, whisk together the dry ingredients thoroughly. In a stainless-steel bain-marie pot, blend the whole milk, heavy cream, condensed milk, and egg yolks with a hand blender. Slowly add the dry ingredients while blending; blend thoroughly to dissolve all the solids.

3. Pour the mixture into a medium saucepan and cook over medium-low heat, whisking constantly until it reaches 165°F (75°C) on an instant thermometer. Place the hojicha leaves into the bain-marie pot.

4. Once the base reaches 165°F (75°C), immediately remove from the heat and pour into the bain-marie pot containing the hojicha leaves; blend with a hand blender for two minutes to fully homogenize.

5. Pour the base into the prepared ice bath to cool. Once completely cool, transfer to an airtight container. Cover and refrigerate for at least 12 hours and up to 3 days.

6. **To Assemble:** Once the ice cream bases are completely chilled, place a loaf pan in the freezer to chill. Quickly blend each ice cream base once more with a hand blender or whisk. Strain the hojicha ice cream base through a fine-mesh strainer into the ice cream machine, and process it according to the manufacturer's directions.

7. When the temperature of the surface of the ice cream registers 5°F (-15°C) or colder with a thermometer gun (or reaches the texture of very stiff soft-serve ice cream), the ice cream is finished churning.

8. Spread the ice cream mixture into the chilled loaf pan, and place in the freezer.

9. Wash and dry the ice cream machine canister, then process the black sesame ice cream base until the temperature of the surface of the ice cream registers 25°F (-5°C) or colder with a thermometer gun (or reaches the texture of very stiff soft-serve ice cream).

10. Spread the black sesame ice cream mixture into the chilled loaf pan, on top of the layer of hojicha ice cream, and place back into the freezer.

11. Wash and dry the ice-cream-machine canister, then process the matcha ice cream base until the temperature of the surface of the ice cream registers 25°F (-5°C) or colder with a thermometer gun (or reaches the texture of very stiff soft-serve ice cream).

12. Spread the matcha ice cream mixture into the chilled loaf pan, on top of the layer of black sesame ice cream.

13. Using a spatula, gently fold the ice cream layers to create visible swirls. Three or four folds should be sufficient.

14. Press a piece of wax paper directly on top of the ice cream and freeze for at least 3 hours before serving.

PINK NEAPOLITAN

Makes about 1½ quarts
(1.5 liters)

Every February, I reimagine a classic Neapolitan where fruity and bright pink ruby chocolate (see page 78) replaces the usual chocolate for a scoop that's visually reminiscent of Valentine's Day with hues of red, pink, and white.

½ recipe **Mascarpone Base**
(page 51), with changes
(see step 1 below)

½ vanilla bean, split lengthwise, or
1 teaspoon (4 g) vanilla extract

½ recipe **Strawberriest base**
(page 98)

½ recipe **Ruby Chocolate base**
(page 78)

TIP: If you have a large-capacity ice cream machine (bigger than 1.6 quarts), I would suggest doubling the recipes to meet the volume requirements for proper churning.

1. Follow the recipe for the Mascarpone Base, scraping the vanilla seeds and adding the vanilla pod to the mixture in the saucepan in step 3. Remove the vanilla pod just after the ice cream base reaches temperature and you pour it back into the mixing vessel. If using vanilla extract, add it to the base after cooling in the ice bath. Refrigerate the vanilla mascarpone base as directed.

2. Make the strawberry and ruby chocolate ice cream bases, following their respective recipes.

3. **Churn the ice creams:** Once all three bases are completely chilled, place a loaf pan in the freezer to chill.

4. Quickly blend the strawberry base once more with a hand blender or whisk before pouring it into an ice cream machine. Churn the ice cream until it reaches the texture of very stiff soft-serve and the surface looks dry, about 25°F (-5°C) or colder on a thermometer gun.

5. Transfer the ice cream to the chilled loaf pan, pushing all of it to one end of the pan. Place the ice cream pan back into the freezer.

6. Scrape the ice cream machine clean (no need to wash it), then quickly blend the chocolate ice cream base once more and churn until it reaches the texture of very stiff soft-serve and the surface looks dry, about 25°F (-5°C) or colder on a thermometer gun.

7. Transfer the ice cream to the chilled loaf pan, pushing all of it to the other side of the pan, opposite the strawberry ice cream, leaving a gap in the middle of the pan between the two ice creams. Place the ice cream pan back into the freezer.

8. Clean and dry the ice cream machine completely, then quickly blend the vanilla mascarpone ice cream base once more and churn until it reaches the texture of very stiff soft-serve and the surface looks dry, about 25°F (-5°C) or colder on a thermometer gun.

9. Transfer the ice cream into the chilled loaf pan, between the strawberry and chocolate ice creams.

10. Press a piece of wax paper directly on top of the ice cream and freeze for at least 4 hours before serving.

CHAPTER 18

asian

After eight years of making different ice cream flavors, I still don't have a pulse on which ones will be a hit. Oftentimes, I'll predict the batch size of a seasonal flavor needed to last the month, and be completely off. Flavors that I had no idea would be so popular end up flying out the door at unbelievable speed, faster than we can replenish. One thing I notice about these surprisingly popular flavors: It's always the ones modeled after a food that sparks emotion. Namely, it's the ones that are replicated after something iconic, or emblematic. I'm not talking about flavors like Cherry Coke,

icons

or Fruity Pebbles. It's the foods that are iconic to a subculture; the ones that are rarely ever translated outside of that subculture. In this chapter we explore all the crazy viral flavors whose popularity took us by surprise at Wanderlust Creamery—they're mainly Asian icons.

These ice creams are ones that people beg us to keep on the menu as staples. But because we're always innovating and keeping room on the menu for something new, here are the recipes so that you can make them whenever you can't find them in our case.

RAMUNE SHERBET

Makes about 1 quart (1 liter)

Ramune, a type of Japanese soda, is an emblem of summertime in Japan. It's also a drink that reminds me of my childhood, going to an Asian grocery and being marketed to by colorful variations of ramune in flavors like melon or strawberry, with Sanrio-like characters adorning the bottles. But I always preferred the simplicity of the "original" ramune flavor, in its iconic blue bottle. Its name comes from the Japanese transliteration of "lemonade," but it tastes almost like a lemon-lime soda kissed with bubblegum. It's a fan-favorite seasonal sherbet flavor at Wanderlust Creamery, but this version is so much more fun because it's actually carbonated like the drink. Carbonated ice cream? Yes! It's done with a technique using a stand mixer and dry ice in place of an ice cream machine. As the dry ice changes from a solid to gas, it leaves carbon dioxide bubbles in the ice cream as well as some carbonic acid (don't worry, it's safe!), leaving a "fizzy" taste and sensation in the mouth during the sherbet's meltdown.

For the base

6½ tablespoons (80 g) granulated sugar, plus more to taste

1 cup + 3 tablespoons (170 g) glucose powder

¾ teaspoon (3 g) Sorbet Stabilizer (optional; page 33)

2½ teaspoons (20 g) inulin (optional)

3⅓ cups (800 ml) lemon-lime soda (such as Sprite or 7 Up)

¼ cup (60 g) heavy cream

1¼ teaspoons (6 g) bubble gum extract

Natural blue food coloring (optional)

For the sherbet

2 pounds (900 g) dry ice, in a plastic bag

1. Prepare an ice bath (see page 39).

2. **Make the base:** In a small bowl, whisk together the sugar, glucose, stabilizer (if using), and inulin (if using). In a tall cylindrical 1½-quart (1.5 liter) mixing vessel, blend together the lemon-lime soda and dry ingredients until dissolved.

3. Pour the mixture into a small saucepan and cook over medium-high heat, whisking occasionally, until the temperature reaches 122°F (50°C) on an instant-read thermometer.

4. Remove from the heat, then strain the liquid through a fine-mesh sieve back into the tall mixing vessel. Add the heavy cream and blend for 2 minutes to homogenize.

5. Pour the base into the prepared ice bath to cool. Once completely cooled, stir in the bubblegum extract and blue food coloring (if using). Transfer the base to an airtight container and refrigerate for at least 12 hours and up to 2 days.

Method continued on next page

6. **Make the sherbet:** When ready to begin, quickly blend the base once more with a hand blender or whisk. If you're not planning on serving the sherbet immediately, place a loaf pan in the freezer to chill.

7. Place the sherbet base in a stand mixer fitted with the paddle.

8. Using insulated hands (cloth oven mitts work well), place the bag of dry ice between two layers of kitchen towels. Using a rolling pin or mallet, crush the dry ice into small pieces.

9. Turn the stand mixer on low speed and add the dry ice to the mixer just a spoonful at a time. Make sure all the CO_2 vapor has evaporated from the dry ice after each addition.

10. When the sherbet starts to look stiff and frozen, stop adding dry ice. Continue to mix the sherbet with the mixer (or manually with a spatula, if the sherbet has hardened too much) until all of the dry ice has completely sublimated. Inspect the sherbet for any remaining dry-ice particles by manually stirring it one last time. You'll know when all the dry ice is gone when the sherbet stops "smoking" or vaporizing.

11. Wait 3 to 5 minutes after all the vapor is gone, then serve the sherbet. The carbonation will gradually fizzle as it's stored, so it's best to eat it freshly churned. Alternatively, spread the sherbet into the chilled loaf pan and place it in the freezer. Press a piece of wax paper directly on top of the sherbet.

NOTES:
You might be wondering why this is called Ramune Sherbet but doesn't call for actual ramune. The soft drink itself is so mildly flavored that when it's frozen it doesn't taste as strong as the actual drink. Instead, we use lemon-lime soda for the lemon-lime flavor and pair it with bubblegum extract. Do not substitute ramune for the lemon-lime soda, as the end result will be too heavy on the bubblegum flavor.

Dry ice is available in 5- to 10-pound blocks at many chain grocery stores.

VARIATION: Make this with root beer or cola instead of ramune and substitute vanilla extract for the bubblegum extract for a carbonated "ice cream float" sherbet.

Working with Dry Ice

- Never touch dry ice with your bare hands.
- Always use temperature-insulating gloves (cloth oven mitts work well) to handle dry ice.
- Dry ice often comes in a bag. Handle it by lifting it by the bag only.
- Never consume dry ice.
- Always use dry ice in a well-ventilated area.
- Do not attempt to store dry ice in a freezer or refrigerator—it might damage the compressor of your unit.
- To make dry ice last longer, store it in a small insulated container such as a cooler or Styrofoam box. The less open space there is around a block of dry ice, the longer it will last. If your insulated cooler is large relative to the size of your dry ice, tuck some newspaper into the empty spaces of the cooler, around it.

OOLONG PINEAPPLE CAKE

Makes about 1 quart (1 liter)

Souvenirs from Taiwan (China) inspired this ice cream. My stepdad was given a short list of must-haves to bring home. Among them, Taiwanese pineapple cakes and unique teas. Unboxing each pineapple cake from its ornate container, you get an immediate whiff of butter. Each block or pineapple-shaped shortbread cookie encased a center of golden jammy pineapple paste that tasted like a field of the most fragrant ripe pineapples condensed into a single square inch. Every bite was washed down with a sip of Jin Xuan tea—a rare Taiwanese oolong with vegetal-floral notes, but with an unexpected buttery and milky aftertaste and aroma.

For the base

1 tablespoon + 2 teaspoons (12 g) "Toasted" Milk Powder (page 289; see Notes)

½ cup + 2½ teaspoons (110 g) granulated sugar

½ teaspoon (2 g) tara gum (optional; see page 24)

¼ cup + 1½ teaspoons (40 g) glucose powder

1½ cups (370 g) whole milk

3½ tablespoons (70 g) sweetened condensed milk

70 grams egg yolks (from about 4 large eggs)

1¼ cups + 3 tablespoons (330 g) heavy cream

7 tablespoons (35 g) Jin Xuan oolong tea leaves (see Notes)

For the ice cream

⅔ cup (280 g) Pineapple Jam (recipe follows)

¾ cup (340 g) coarsely crumbled or chopped all-butter shortbread cookies, such as Walker's Shortbread

1. Prepare an ice bath (see page 39).

2. **Make the base:** In a small bowl, whisk together the milk powder, sugar, tara gum (if using), and glucose. In a tall cylindrical 1½-quart (1.5 liter) mixing vessel, blend the whole milk, condensed milk, and egg yolks with a hand blender. Slowly add the dry ingredients while blending and blend thoroughly to dissolve all the solids.

3. Pour the mixture into a small saucepan and cook over medium-low heat, whisking constantly, until it reaches 165°F (75°C) on an instant-read thermometer.

4. Once the base reaches 165°F (75°C), immediately remove it from the heat and pour it back into the tall mixing vessel. Add the heavy cream and blend with a hand blender for 2 minutes to fully homogenize.

5. Pour the base through a fine-mesh sieve into the prepared ice bath and stir in the oolong tea leaves. Once completely cool, transfer the base to an airtight container. Cover and refrigerate for at least 12 hours and up to 3 days.

NOTES:
This recipe uses toasted dry milk powder to bring out the "baked pastry" aspect of a pineapple cake, but you can always use regular dry milk powder as well.

Jin Xuan oolong can be found online or at specialty tea stores. The rolled leaf variety will be of better quality than loose leaf varieties, releasing more flavor into your base during the long steep.

Method continued on next page

6. **Churn the ice cream:**
   When ready to begin, place a loaf pan, the pineapple jam, and cookie crumbles in the freezer to chill. Quickly blend the ice cream base (with the tea leaves in it) once more with a hand blender or whisk before pouring it through a fine-mesh sieve into an ice cream machine. Churn until the ice cream reaches the texture of very stiff soft-serve and the surface looks dry, about 25°F (–5°C) or colder on a thermometer gun. Add the cookie crumble in the last few seconds of churning.

7. Spread half of the ice cream mixture into the chilled loaf pan. Spread half of the pineapple jam on top. Repeat this layering process once more. Immediately place the ice cream into the freezer for 15 minutes to firm it up.

8. Using a spatula, gently fold the ice cream and pineapple layers to create swirls. Three or four folds should be sufficient for visible ribbons throughout the pan; any more than that will overmix the jam into the ice cream base, which may affect freezing and final texture.

9. Press a piece of wax paper directly on top of the ice cream and freeze for at least 4 hours before serving.

PINEAPPLE JAM
Makes about 1⅓ cups (560 g)

3 cups (18 ounces/510 g) diced extra-ripe pineapple

1 cup (200 g) granulated sugar

⅓ cup + 1 teaspoon (50 g) glucose syrup or corn syrup

3 tablespoons (60 g) unsalted butter

1¾ ounces (50 g) freeze-dried pineapple, crumbled into coarse crumbs (optional)

1. In a stand blender, puree the diced pineapple and sugar into a smooth puree.

2. Transfer the puree to a medium saucepan along with the glucose or corn syrup, bring the mixture to a boil over high heat, and boil for 10 minutes.

3. Reduce the heat to medium and continue cooking, stirring occasionally and scraping the sides of the pot with a heatproof spatula, until most of the moisture has evaporated and the mixture has reduced by half, 30 to 40 minutes. The final mixture will be thick, a shade darker, and somewhat translucent.

4. Remove from the heat and stir in the butter. Allow the mixture to cool completely, then stir in the freeze-dried pineapple, if using. Transfer the jam to an airtight container and store refrigerated for up to 1 week.

JASMINE MILK TEA WITH BOBA

Makes about 1 quart (1 liter)

For the base

1 tablespoon + 2 teaspoons (12 g) nonfat dry milk powder

½ cup + 1½ tablespoons (120 g) granulated sugar

¼ cup + 1½ teaspoons (40 g) glucose powder

½ teaspoon (2 g) tara gum (optional; see page 24)

1½ cups (370 g) whole milk

3½ tablespoons (70 g) sweetened condensed milk

70 grams egg yolks (from about 4 large eggs)

1¼ cups + 3 tablespoons (330 g) heavy cream

7 tablespoons (35 g) jasmine tea leaves

¼ teaspoon (1 g) pure jasmine extract (optional), plus more to taste (see Note)

For the ice cream

Ice Cream "Boba" (page 284), with changes (see step 6, opposite)

NOTE: For a stronger jasmine flavor without having to use more tannic tea, use pure jasmine extract, available online. Steer clear of bottled jasmine flavoring sold in Asian supermarkets, which have a chemical-like flavor.

Boba ice cream became all the rage during the pandemic. It's also what saved us from financial ruin in 2020. Stuck at home with nothing to do but watch viral videos and eat, every foodie seemed obsessed with these imported boba ice cream bars. Being in the ice cream biz myself, naturally I bought some to see what the hype was about. What I had anticipated would blow me away instead fell flat. It was simply a low-quality, flavorless milk ice pop with brown sugar–flavored mochi. At home, motivated by disappointment and inspired by my go-to boba order, I made a jasmine milk tea ice cream with chewy pearls of dark mochi and topped it with sea-salted whipped cream. By the following week, we were packing pints of it by the hundreds and selling out online in less than ten minutes. Maybe the pandemic was making people stir-crazy in their homes, but customers commented that snagging a pint online before it sold out was like buying Taylor Swift concert tickets. In April 2020, our empty stores became packed fulfillment centers, with boxes of pints and dry ice piled to the ceiling. Soon, we rehired anyone who was down to work, shipping ice cream all over the country, delivering an edible travel experience to people quarantined in their homes.

1. Prepare an ice bath (see page 39).

2. **Make the base:** In a small bowl, whisk together the milk powder, sugar, glucose, and tara gum (if using). In a tall cylindrical 1½-quart (1.5 liter) mixing vessel, blend the whole milk, condensed milk, and egg yolks with a hand blender. Slowly add the dry ingredients while blending and blend thoroughly to dissolve all the solids.

3. Pour the mixture into a small saucepan and cook over medium-low heat, whisking constantly, until it reaches 165°F (75°C) on an instant-read thermometer.

4. Once the base reaches 165°F (75°C), immediately remove it from the heat and pour it back into the tall mixing vessel. Add the heavy cream and blend with a hand blender for 2 minutes to fully homogenize. Stir in the jasmine tea leaves.

5. Pour the base into the prepared ice bath to cool. Once completely cool, transfer the base to an airtight container. Cover and refrigerate for at least 12 hours and up to 3 days.

6. **For the ice cream:** Make the boba as directed in the recipe, using strongly brewed osmanthus tea in place of water and honey in place of molasses. Transfer to the freezer to freeze solid before adding to the ice cream.

7. **Churn the ice cream:** When ready to begin, place a loaf pan in the freezer to chill. The boba should be completely frozen as well. Quickly blend the ice cream base once more with a hand blender or whisk before pouring it through a fine-mesh sieve into an ice cream machine. Churn the ice cream until it reaches the texture of very stiff soft-serve and the surface looks dry, about 25°F (-5°C) or colder on a thermometer gun. Add the frozen boba pieces in the last few seconds of churning.

8. Transfer the ice cream mixture to the chilled loaf pan. Press a piece of wax paper directly on top of the ice cream and freeze for at least 4 hours before serving.

9. To serve, the ice cream must be tempered fully for the boba to be soft and chewy.

WHITE RABBIT

Makes about 1 quart (1 liter)

White Rabbit, for those of you unfamiliar, is a Chinese candy not unlike a plain, white, milk-flavored Tootsie Roll. They come wrapped twice: once in a thin edible rice paper and again in a wax wrapper printed with blue and red rabbits—an emblem to many of Asian childhood.

Although Chinese in origin, many Asians around the world grow up eating this candy. Upon inspection of the ingredients, White Rabbit is mostly milk and sugar, so I figured a White Rabbit ice cream would taste like . . . nothing. A few days later, while planning the seasonal menu for the upcoming Lunar New Year, I revisited the idea of a White Rabbit ice cream. Unwrapping one, I was determined to taste what made it distinctly "White Rabbit." Eyes closed, I tasted condensed milk . . . and butter, but like, the funkiness butter picks up when clarified . . . ghee!

When we introduced it in our lineup, there was an unexpected social media frenzy, and it seemed like everyone was posting about it. Customers were driving in from all over, sometimes as far as eight hours away, just to try the ice cream. Someone even messaged us to say they'd flown in from Hong Kong (China) just to see what it tasted like.

Naturally, we decided to keep the flavor on the menu a little longer, but we could barely keep it in stock—a testament to the power of nostalgia, unlocked by such simple flavors.

For the White Rabbit syrup
1½ cups + 1½ tablespoons (380 g) water

6 ounces (175 g) unwrapped White Rabbit candies, but keep the inner rice paper on

For the base
2½ tablespoons (20 g) nonfat dry milk powder

4½ teaspoons (20 g) granulated sugar

Scant ½ teaspoon (2 g) lecithin (optional)

3½ tablespoons (70 g) sweetened condensed milk

1½ cups (350 g) heavy cream

1 tablespoon + 1 teaspoon (20 g) ghee

1. **Make the White Rabbit syrup:** In a small saucepan, bring the water to a boil. Reduce the heat to medium-low and add the White Rabbit candies. Continue cooking, stirring occasionally, until all the candy has melted into a thin syrup, about 30 minutes.

2. Once the candy has completely dissolved, remove it from the heat and pour the mixture into a tall mixing vessel. Allow the mixture to cool to at least 120°F (50°C).

3. Prepare an ice bath (see page 39).

4. **Make the base:** In a small bowl, whisk together the milk powder, sugar, and lecithin (if using). Add the condensed milk to the White Rabbit syrup and blend while gradually adding the dry ingredients; blend until all the solids have dissolved.

5. Pour the mixture back into the saucepan and cook over medium-low heat, whisking constantly, until it reaches 165°F (75°C) on an instant-read thermometer.

6. Once the base reaches 165°F (75°C), immediately remove it from the heat and pour it back into the tall mixing vessel. Add the heavy cream and ghee and blend with a hand blender for 2 minutes to fully homogenize.

7. Pour the ice cream base through a fine-mesh sieve into the prepared ice bath to cool. Once completely cooled, transfer to an airtight container. Refrigerate for at least 12 hours and up to 2 days.

8. **Churn the ice cream:** When ready to begin, place a loaf pan in the freezer to chill. Quickly blend the ice cream base once more with a hand blender or whisk before pouring it through a fine-mesh sieve into an ice cream machine. Churn the ice cream until it reaches the texture of very stiff soft-serve and the surface looks dry, about 25°F (−5°C) or colder on a thermometer gun.

9. Transfer the ice cream mixture to the chilled loaf pan. Press a piece of wax paper directly on top of the ice cream and freeze for at least 4 hours before serving.

CHAPTER 19

toppings, special in

In cooking, balancing a dish isn't just about taste; it's also about how the textural and visual elements either complement or contrast one another. Ice cream isn't much different. Great ice cream isn't about only the ice cream itself, but the thoughtfulness that goes into the mix-ins, swirls, and ripples that punctuate its flavor.

Just as with ice cream bases, there's a science to accompanying additions. A cookie piece may be soft at room temperature, but what happens when you freeze it? If something is crunchy on top of the ice cream, will it be so if we buried it inside? We know that to keep things from completely freezing, we need the anti-freezing

sauces & ingredients

power of sugar, but how do we make it not too sweet?

Open any ice cream cookbook and you'll probably find tons of recipes for seasonal fruit ripples, fudge, butterscotch, brownies, cookies, cakes, and pralined nuts. They usually cover the bases of saucy, fudgy, chunky, and crunchy. In this chapter, you'll find some of that, in addition to a lot of what's in between and largely neglected: mix-ins that are airy and cloud-like, or bouncy-chewy (referred to in Asian culture as QQ) . . . swirls that have the rich, gooey, and unctuous texture without all the sweetness . . . inclusions that serve dual purposes—initially crunchy, but eventually liquefied into pools of sauces within the ice cream.

MALTED CRUNCH

Makes about 1 cup (300 g)

The namesake feature in our Ube Malted Crunch (page 225) and Abuelita Malted Crunch (page 72), this recipe can be used as either a mix-in or a topping for any ice cream. It's essentially the same as the inside of chocolate-coated malt balls (aka Whoppers or Maltesers), but because it has no chocolate, it is so much more versatile, especially for ice creams where chocolate may not belong. This mix-in stays crunchy in ice cream for a day or two, but after that, the malted crunch pieces melt into little pools of liquid malty-caramel within the ice cream. If you want to keep them crispy, just give them a quick toss in melted refined coconut oil or any of the freckling chocolate recipes in this chapter.

1½ cups + 2 tablespoons (300 g) malted milk powder (see Note)

1. Adjust two oven racks to the very bottom and middle positions. Fill a baking pan with 1 inch (2.5 cm) of hot water and place it on the bottom rack. Preheat the oven to 350°F (180°C). If your oven has convection, turn off the fan (to prevent blowing away any malted milk powder).

2. Line a quarter sheet pan (13 by 9 inches/33 by 23 cm) with wax paper. Pour out the malted milk powder onto the pan as evenly as possible. Place another sheet of wax paper onto the malted milk powder, followed by another quarter-sheet pan. Press down and wiggle the top pan to form the malted milk powder into a layer evenly ¼ inch (6 mm) thick. Once you've formed an even layer, press down firmly on the top pan once more to compress the powder.

3. Place the whole thing—malted milk powder sandwiched between the two pans—into the oven, then immediately reduce the oven temperature to 300°F (150°C). Bake until the malted milk powder has formed into a solid block but not browned at all, 7 to 9 minutes.

4. Allow the malted crunch to cool before peeling off the wax paper and breaking it into ¼-inch (6 mm) pieces with your hands. Store the malted crunch pieces in an airtight container, in a cool and dry place until ready to use, for up to 2 weeks.

NOTE: Not all malted milk powders are the same. Some contain sugar, while others do not. For this recipe, it's essential that you use the kind with sugar, so that the powder will melt together into one piece. If the malted milk powder you have doesn't have sugar listed as an ingredient, use 1⅓ cups (280 g) of it mixed with 2 tablespoons (20 g) of sugar.

VARIATIONS: For varying flavors of malted crunch, sift the malted milk powder with 1 tablespoon (8 g) of cocoa powder, matcha, or freeze-dried fruit powder before baking.

CRISPY NUT DACQUOISE

Makes about 2 cups (385 g)

This crispy mix-in is made with cashews for Brown Butter Sans Rival (page 238), but it can be made into any kind of nut or seed dacquoise.

Butter and flour for the pan

½ cup (60 g) chopped nuts

¾ cup + 1 tablespoon (165 g) granulated sugar

1 tablespoon (5 g) "Toasted" Milk Powder (page 289)

2 tablespoons (15 g) all-purpose flour

Pinch of salt

110 grams egg whites (from 3 to 4 large eggs)

¼ cup (30 g) whole or halved nuts, for sprinkling

1. Preheat the oven to 300°F (150°C). Line a sheet pan with parchment paper. Butter and flour the parchment as well as the sides of the pan.

2. Grind the chopped nuts in a food processor until they're finely ground. Add 1 tablespoon (15 g) of the sugar, the toasted milk powder, 2 tablespoons (15 g) flour, and a pinch of salt to the food processor and pulse to combine into the texture of a fine nut flour. Transfer to a large bowl.

3. In a stand mixer fitted with the whisk, beat the egg whites at medium speed until they become a very fine foam. Increase the mixer speed to medium-high and very

gradually add the remaining ¾ cup (150 g) granulated sugar. Increase the speed to high and continue beating until stiff peaks form, about 5 minutes. The egg whites should hold sharp peaks when the whisk is lifted from bowl.

4. Using a rubber spatula, gradually fold the nut flour into the beaten egg whites. Fold in big motions, being careful not to deflate the meringue. Continue folding until completely combined.

5. Pour the mixture onto the prepared pan and spread it out evenly using an offset spatula.

6. Transfer the pan to the oven and reduce the

temperature to 250°F (120°C). Bake for 1 hour.

7. Reduce the oven temperature to 225°F (110°C) and bake until firm but just barely toasted, 30 to 40 minutes.

8. Turn off the oven and allow the dacquoise to cool inside the oven with the door slightly ajar.

9. Once the dacquoise has completely cooled, it should be dry and crispy. Break it into ¼- to ½-inch (6 mm to 1.5 cm) pieces using a knife or your hands. Store in an airtight container in a cool, dry place until needed, for up to 1 week.

BROWN BUTTER NUT CAKE

Makes one 13 by 9-inch (33 by 23 cm) sheet cake

A delicious cake on its own, this turns any plain ice cream into delicious renditions of patisserie masterpieces. Make it with almonds and crumble into a custard ice cream swirled with spiced plum jam, or make a pistachio version churned into noyaux ice cream with raspberry jam. Made with hazelnuts, it's a must-have mix-in for chocolate ice cream or Amalfi Pear Torte (page 143).

2 sticks (8 oz/225 g) unsalted butter

1 teaspoon nonfat dry milk powder, processed in a spice grinder to a very fine powder

1 teaspoon (4 g) vanilla extract

1 heaping cup (140 g) nuts (see Note)

1⅓ cups (165 g) powdered sugar

½ teaspoon (1 g) salt

⅓ cup (45 g) all-purpose flour

½ teaspoon baking powder

6 large egg whites (180 g total)

3 tablespoons (45 g) granulated sugar

NOTE: This recipe can be made with any nut. For almonds, pistachios, or cashews, use unroasted nuts; if using hazelnuts or peanuts, use unsalted roasted ones.

1. Preheat the oven to 350°F (180°C). Line the bottom of a quarter-sheet pan (13 by 9 inches/33 by 23 cm) with parchment paper.

2. In a medium saucepan, melt the butter over medium heat and cook until the milk solids separate from the butterfat (you'll see a white substance sink to the bottom of the pot), about 5 minutes. Add the dry milk powder and continue to cook, whisking continuously and scraping up all the solids on the bottom of the pan, until the solids are light brown, about 5 more minutes. Remove from the heat and let cool to room temperature—the color will continue to deepen as it cools. Once cool, stir in the vanilla and set aside.

3. In a food processor, combine the nuts, powdered sugar, and salt and process until finely ground. Add the flour and baking powder and pulse to combine.

4. In a stand mixer fitted with the whisk, beat the egg whites at medium speed until they become a very fine foam. Increase the mixer speed to medium-high and very gradually add the granulated sugar. Increase the speed to high and continue beating until stiff peaks form, about 5 minutes. The peaks should hold when the whisk is lifted from the bowl.

5. Using a rubber spatula, fold one-third of the nut mixture into the beaten egg whites. Next, fold in one-third of the cooled brown butter. Repeat twice, until the nut mixture and browned butter are fully incorporated. Make sure to add all the browned milk solids from the butter—that's where all the flavor is! Pour the batter into the prepared pan.

6. Transfer to the oven and bake until a toothpick inserted in the center of the cake comes out clean, 20 to 25 minutes.

7. Let cool on a wire rack for 30 minutes. Run a table knife around the inside edge of the pan and invert the cake onto a cutting board. Cut into small pieces, then crumble into large crumbs. Store in an airtight container until ready to use.

ALMOND SHORTBREAD

Makes 2 cups (450 g) crumble (or enough dough for 12 cookies)

This buttery shortbread can be used to make cookies for ice cream sandwiches (see Alfajores, page 92) or crumbled into a delicious mix-in for ice cream. The cornstarch and almond meal in the recipe make it even more tender than traditional shortbread, which makes it perfect for frozen temperatures.

2 sticks (8 ounces/225 g) unsalted butter

1 tablespoon granulated sugar

1¼ cups (160 g) all-purpose flour

1 tablespoon + 2 teaspoons (15 g) cornstarch

½ teaspoon (1 g) salt

⅓ cup + 1½ tablespoons (55 g) powdered sugar

2 tablespoons (15 g) almond flour

1 teaspoon (4 g) vanilla extract

1. Line a sheet pan with parchment paper.

2. In a stand mixer fitted with the paddle, cream the butter and granulated sugar on medium-high speed until light and fluffy.

3. In a large bowl, sift together the flour, cornstarch, salt, powdered sugar, and almond flour.

4. Turn the mixer to the lowest speed and beat the vanilla into the creamed butter. Gradually add the dry ingredients and mix until just combined.

5. Press the dough down onto the pan in a layer that's ¼ inch (6 mm) thick. Refrigerate the dough for 30 minutes to firm up.

6. Meanwhile, preheat the oven to 350°F (180°C).

7. Bake until lightly golden, 10 to 12 minutes.

8. Cool the shortbread completely. Once completely cooled, chop or crumble the shortbread into small pieces. Store the shortbread crumble in an airtight container at room temperature for up to 1 week.

SPONGE CAKE PIECES

Makes about one half sheet pan

Despite the name, this isn't technically a sponge cake recipe; it's a chiffon cake recipe. While sponge cake is soft at
room temperature, I find that it tends to freeze a little harder
than ideal for ice cream. Chiffon cake, however, which is
even more airy than sponge cake, freezes into a light sponge
texture. This recipe can be interpreted into so many different
flavors for your creative needs.

½ cup (65 g) cake flour
(see Notes)

½ teaspoon baking powder

Pinch of salt

2 large eggs, separated

Generous 1 tablespoon (15 g) +
¼ cup (50 g) granulated sugar

2 tablespoons vegetable, corn, or
avocado oil

¼ cup (60 g) whole milk

1 teaspoon (4 g) vanilla extract

VARIATIONS:

Chocolate Sponge Cake:
Sift 2¼ tablespoons (15 g) cocoa
powder with the flour mixture.

Matcha Sponge Cake:
Sift 2½ tablespoons (15 g) matcha
powder with the flour mixture.

Strawberry Sponge Cake:
Sift 3 tablespoons (15 g) freeze-
dried strawberry powder with
the flour mixture.

Ube Sponge Cake:
Substitute 2 teaspoons ube
extract for the vanilla.

Pandan Sponge Cake:
Substitute 1 teaspoon pandan
extract for the vanilla; substitute
coconut milk for the dairy milk.

NOTES:

If you don't have cake flour, sift
together 4 teaspoons (10 g)
cornstarch with 7 tablespoons
(55 g) all-purpose flour.

I like to use a standard half-sheet
pan to bake the cake because
it makes for faster baking and I
find the thickness is easier for
making the cake into little cubes
or crumbs. If you wish to use a
cake pan, the baking time may be
longer (the thicker the cake, the
longer the baking time). Also be
aware that any nonstick coating
on a cake pan may affect the
cake's ability to properly rise.

Don't worry if the cake comes
out seemingly dry: It will absorb
moisture in the ice cream and
become soft once mixed in and
frozen.

1. Adjust an oven rack to the middle position and preheat the oven to 375°F (190°C). Line a half-sheet pan (18 by 13 inches/46 by 23 cm) with parchment paper.

2. In a small bowl, sift together the cake flour, baking powder, and salt. Set the flour mixture aside.

3. In a large metal bowl, hand-whisk the egg yolks and 1 generous tablespoon (15 g) of the sugar until light and pale in color. Whisk in the oil, milk, and vanilla until incorporated. Whisk in the flour mixture until combined.

4. In a stand mixer fitted with a whisk, beat the egg whites at low speed until it becomes a very fine foam. Increase mixer speed to medium and very gradually add the remaining 1/4 cup (50 g) sugar. Increase the speed to high and beat until the meringue is glossy with firm peaks. The peaks should hold but fall back slightly onto itself when the whisk is lifted from the bowl and pointed upward.

5. Add one-third of the cake batter to the meringue and whisk lightly until just combined. Add the remaining batter to the meringue in two more additions, gently folding with a spatula, trying not to deflate the meringue.

6. Pour the batter into the prepared sheet pan, filling it no more than three-quarters of the way up.

7. Transfer the pan to the oven and reduce the oven temperature to 350°F (180°C). Bake until the top of the cake is lightly browned and springs back to the touch, 15 to 20 minutes.

8. Turn off the oven and let the cake cool inside the oven with the door ajar for 10 minutes, then remove the cake from the oven and let it cool in the pan on a cooling rack until completely cool.

9. Once completely cooled, run a knife along the edges of the cake to loosen it from the pan and invert it onto a cutting board. Using a serrated bread knife, cut the cake into 1/4-inch (6 mm) pieces. Transfer the cake pieces to an airtight container and keep refrigerated for up to 1 week or frozen for up to 2 months.

NAMELAKA CUBES

Makes about 2 cups (430 g)

Namelaka is a Japanese word that translates to *ultracreamy*. In the pastry world, it refers to a looser, less sweet ganache. If you're like me and shy away from fudgy-chunky-over-the-top chocolate desserts, but you still want an unctuous textured chocolate mix-in without all the sweetness, namelaka is for you.

3¼ ounces (90 g) dark chocolate (70% cacao or greater), 4½ ounces (125 g) white chocolate, or 4¼ ounces (120 g) milk chocolate

2 tablespoons (40 g) corn syrup

½ teaspoon (1 g) agar-agar powder

⅓ cup + 1 tablespoon (90 g) whole milk

¾ cup + ½ tablespoon (180 g) heavy cream

1. Line a small sheet pan with wax or parchment paper so that it comes up the walls of the pan with some overhang (for pulling out the chocolate later).

2. Place the chocolate in a heatproof bowl.

3. In a small saucepan, combine the corn syrup, agar-agar, milk, and cream and warm over medium heat. Continue cooking, whisking frequently, until it comes to a boil. Allow it to boil for 10 seconds, then remove from the heat and pour over the chopped chocolate. Whisk the mixture until all the chocolate has melted.

4. Pour the chocolate into the prepared pan. Refrigerate until set and it has the texture of a very firm flan, about 2 hours. Once set, place the pan in the freezer and freeze until hard, about 2 more hours.

5. Once hardened, unmold the chocolate from the pan by lifting the wax paper and cut into ¼-inch (5 mm) cubes. Store the namelaka cubes in an airtight container in the freezer until ready to use for up to 1 month.

VARIATIONS: Use ruby chocolate, freeze-dried fruit powder, tea powders, infused heavy cream, or essential oils to make a variety of namelaka flavors!

CHOCOLATE FRECKLES/ STRACCIATELLA

Makes about ⅔ cup (175 g)

Coconut oil is hard at cool temperatures but liquefies at 75°F (25°F). When mixed into chocolate, it makes the following phenomenon possible: chocolate that is liquid at room temperature, but hard when it touches ice cream, then instantaneously liquid again when it hits your mouth. I use this to make tiny "freckles" in the ice cream (aka stracciatella in the gelato world) or to coat ice cream novelties for a crunchy chocolate cover. This is also the same concept used for Magic Shell, the chocolate sauce drizzled over scoops of ice cream to make a crispy shell on top. This recipe can be transformed into any flavor by using any chocolate (white, ruby, dark, milk), or by adding any powdered dry ingredients (freeze-dried fruit powder, powdered tea or coffee) or oil-based flavor extracts.

2 tablespoons + 1½ teaspoons refined coconut oil (see Note)

5 ounces (150 g) chocolate (dark, ruby, milk, or white), chopped

NOTES:
Be sure to use refined coconut oil to avoid any unwanted coconut flavor.

Any water or moisture will break the emulsion of the chocolate, so make sure all the equipment and utensils you use are completely clean and dry.

The reason I use a microwave to melt the chocolate is that the steam from a double boiler can inadvertently add water to the mixture.

Most important, if using flavor extracts, they must be labeled "oil soluble" (no alcohol or water listed as ingredients). In this case, I find that essential oils work best for flavoring the liquid chocolate, such as peppermint, yuzu, lavender, etc.

VARIATIONS:
Strawberry/ Raspberry Stracciatella: Use white chocolate; completely dissolve 5 tablespoons plus 2 teaspoons (35 g) freeze-dried berry powder (strawberry or raspberry) in 1 tablespoon of the warmed refined coconut oil before adding the remaining ingredients.

Matcha Stracciatella: Use white chocolate; completely dissolve (10 g) matcha powder in 1 tablespoon of the warmed refined coconut oil before adding the remaining ingredients.

1. In a microwave-safe bowl, microwave the coconut oil until it registers at least 130°F (55°C) on an instant-read thermometer.

2. Add the chocolate and let sit for 30 seconds. Using a whisk or flexible spatula, stir the mixture until all the chocolate has melted. If the chocolate does not completely melt, microwave the mixture in 20-second increments, stirring after each.

3. Transfer the mixture to a container that can be poured from, such as a liquid measuring cup. Let the chocolate cool to a tepid temperature in which it is still liquid and pourable, about 80°F (25°C). If using at a later time, transfer and store the chocolate in an airtight container at room temperature. Gently remelt the chocolate in a double boiler or in a microwave. If using a microwave, heat in 30-second increments, stirring after each. Cool the chocolate again to 80°F (25°C) just before ice cream assembly.

JELLIES

I never put fresh fruit pieces in ice cream. Why? Because fruit is mostly water. Freeze it in ice cream, and instead of a refreshing bite of fruit one might expect, you'll get a hard, icy, and flavorless (because it's mostly water!) bite in your mouth. For this reason, I opt for dehydrated fruits or jellies. Gelatin-based jellies don't freeze well, but I've found agar-agar jellies survive a little longer in an ice cream. These work great as a mix-in or topping, serving as a vessel for not just flavor but also a textural contrast against smooth and creamy ice cream.

TIP: Agar-agar forms a very tight hydrocolloid matrix, resulting in a harder, almost brittle jelly. To counter this, the jelly must be softened with sugar. I've found that a sugar concentration of 40% (40 Brix) is just right for a soft jelly that isn't too sticky to handle for mixing into ice cream. Beware that certain fresh fruits, such as kiwi, papaya, and pineapple, cannot be made into jellies because they contain certain enzymes that inhibit the gelling of agar-agar. Their enzymes may be deactivated through heating. But before you dive into that, be prepared for trial and error.

ALMOND JELLIES

1 cup (240 g) unsweetened almond milk

⅓ cup + 1 tablespoon (80 g) granulated sugar

¼ teaspoon pure almond extract

2½ teaspoons (5 g) agar-agar powder

CITRUS JELLIES

1 cup (240 g) yuzu, lemon, or lime juice

¾ cup plus 2½ teaspoons (80 g) granulated sugar

1 tablespoon (6 g) agar-agar powder

COCONUT JELLIES

1 cup (240 g) coconut milk

¾ cup plus 2½ teaspoons (80 g) granulated sugar

2½ teaspoons (5 g) agar-agar powder

COFFEE OR TEA JELLIES

Coffee jellies suspended in sweet cream or milk tea ice cream are a dream come true.

1 cup (240 g) brewed espresso, coffee, or tea

¾ cup plus 2½ teaspoons (80 g) granulated sugar

2½ teaspoons (5 g) agar-agar powder

DALANDAN JELLIES

Dalandan oranges are a hyrbrid of mandarin and pomelo, so I combine manda-rin and pomelo juices for a dalandan-flavored jelly.

½ cup + 2 teaspoons (130 g) freshly squeezed mandarin juice

½ cup + 2 teaspoons (130 g) freshly squeezed pomelo juice

⅔ cup (130 g) granulated sugar

1 tablespoon (6 g) agar-agar powder

GUAVA JELLIES

1¼ cups (240 g) unsweetened guava pulp

¾ cup plus 2½ teaspoons (80 g) granulated sugar

1 tablespoon (6 g) agar-agar powder

JACKFRUIT JELLIES

1½ cups (300 g) unsweetened jackfruit puree

⅓ cup (45 g) glucose powder

1 teaspoon (5 g) water

2½ teaspoons (5 g) agar-agar powder

LYCHEE OR RAMBUTAN JELLIES

A delicious addition to noyaux or bitter almond ice cream.

1½ cups (300 g) unsweetened lychee or rambutan puree

½ cup (100 g) granulated sugar

2½ teaspoons (5 g) agar-agar powder

MANGO JELLIES

1¼ cups (300 g) canned kesar mango pulp

⅓ cup + 1 teaspoon (50 g) glucose powder

2½ teaspoons (5 g) agar-agar powder

PANDAN JELLIES

Cut this jelly into thin strips or "noodles" instead of cubes for Chè Thái (page 102), or ice cream inspired by Cendol (Southeast Asian shaved ice)!

1 cup (240 g) canned pandan water

¾ cup plus 2½ teaspoons (80 g) granulated sugar

2½ teaspoons (5 g) agar-agar powder

PASSION FRUIT JELLIES

1 cup + 2 tablespoons (215 g) unsweetened passion fruit pulp

¾ cup plus 2½ teaspoons (80 g) granulated sugar

2½ teaspoons (5 g) agar-agar powder

PEACH JELLIES

1½ cups (280 g) unsweetened peach puree

¼ cup +2 teaspoons (60 g) granulated sugar

2½ teaspoons (5 g) agar-agar powder

"RED RUBIES"

½ cup + 2½ teaspoons (100 g) coconut cream

7 tablespoons (100 g) unsweetened green apple puree

¼ cup + 3 tablespoons (90 g) granulated sugar

¼ teaspoon red food coloring

2½ teaspoons (5 g) agar-agar powder

STRAWBERRY OR RASPBERRY JELLIES

The raspberry version makes a striking flavor and color contrast in pistachio ice cream.

1 cup + 2 tablespoons (260 g) unsweetened strawberry or raspberry puree

⅔ cup + ½ tablespoon (140 g) granulated sugar

2½ teaspoons (5 g) agar-agar powder

1. Have a shallow 6 by 9-inch (15 by 23 cm) baking dish at the ready. (The jelly will need to come up to a depth of ⅜ inch/1 cm.)

2. In a small saucepan, whisk together all the ingredients. Whisking constantly, bring the mixture to a boil over medium heat. Allow the mixture to boil for 20 seconds.

3. Remove the mixture from the heat and pour into the baking dish. Refrigerate the jelly until it is set and is firm, about 3 hours.

4. Once set, use a paring knife to cut the jelly into ⅜-inch (1 cm) cubes. Cover the dish with plastic wrap and refrigerate until ready to use for up to 1 week.

**Mochi dusted
in kinako**

**Brown Butter
Hazelnut Cake**

Malted Crunch

Matcha Namelaka

**Dark Chocolate
Freckles**

Berry Jellies

Honeycomb Candy

Peach Jellies

Pandan Sponge Cake

Pandan Jelly "Noodles"

**Milk Chocolate
Namelaka**

**Malted Crunch with
freeze-dried coffee**

**Ruby Chocolate
Freckles**

Mochi flavored with ube

Almond Jellies

Ice Cream "Boba"

Almond Shortbread

Malted Crunch with Ube

Crispy Cashew Dacquoise

Jasmine Tea Jellies

Vanilla Bean Sponge Cake

White Chocolate Freckles

Malted Crunch with freeze-dried banana

Ube Sponge Cake

Chocolate Sponge Cake

Passion Fruit Jellies

Mochi

Mochi dusted in matcha

ICE CREAM "BOBA"

Makes ¾ cup (185 g) "boba"

In Taiwanese culinary speak, the term *QQ* is used to describe a distinctive texture found in select foods, namely boba. It denotes an alluring chewiness or resilient springiness of a perfectly cooked tapioca pearl. A ways past al dente, yet not quite, QQ is a highly coveted attribute. It's the measure by which one judges how well executed a boba drink is. QQ is also delicate and fleeting. Outside of a warm or lukewarm environment, tapioca pearls eventually firm up in a cold tea, stiffen in iced drinks, and absolutely harden into seemingly impenetrable bites in a frozen dessert. This is due to the physical properties of tapioca—which forms a hard hydrocolloid when frozen. Mochi, on the other hand, which is made with a high proportion of sugars, initially freezes hard but tempers into QQ perfection within ice cream, reminiscent of perfectly cooked tapioca pearls. Brown sugar and molasses serve dual purposes in this recipe: They have high freezing depression powers that keep the mochi soft, while also providing the distinctive boba flavor.

⅓ cup (75 g) water

Scant ¼ cup (50 g) light brown sugar

1 teaspoon (10 g) molasses

2 teaspoons (10 g) trehalose (see Note)

¼ cup (40 g) sweet rice flour

Cornstarch, for dusting

NOTES:
Trehalose (sometimes called "treha") is a naturally occurring sugar made up of two glucose molecules and is known for its unique properties, such as its ability to retain moisture, contributing to that QQ attribute we're striving for. It's used widely in Japanese confectionery and can be found at some Japanese supermarkets or online. I do not recommend using a substitute.

IMPORTANT: Due to the sugars used, the dough of this recipe is very sticky and soft at room temperature; it must be frozen thoroughly to be handled mess-free.

Make sure to let any ice cream containing this mix-in soften a bit before eating for an optimal QQ texture.

1. In a small saucepan, bring the water to just under a simmer over medium heat.

2. Remove the saucepan from the heat and stir in the brown sugar, molasses, and trehalose until dissolved.

3. Place the sweet rice flour in a small bowl. Gradually pour in the syrup, whisking after each addition until the mixture is completely smooth and lump-free. Pour the mixture into a shallow 6 by 9-inch (15 by 23 cm) microwave-safe baking dish.

4. Cover the dish tightly with plastic wrap and micro-wave until the mixture is cooked, about 1½ minutes. It should be semitranslu-cent and have the texture of a fully "set" flan or jello. Let the dough cool completely, covered.

5. Once cool, place the bak-ing dish in the freezer and allow the mochi to harden but not completely freeze, about 2 hours.

6. Remove the mochi from the freezer. You should be able to lift it from the corner of the baking dish and peel away the entire layer in one piece. (If not, it needs to be returned to the freezer to harden more.)

7. Dust a cutting board with some cornstarch. Place the mochi on the cutting board and use a knife dusted in cornstarch to cut it into ⅜-inch (1 cm) cubes.

8. At this point, you can wait for the mochi to soften a bit before rolling them into balls and lightly tossing them in more cornstarch to lightly coat. If the shape doesn't matter to you, skip this step and toss the cubes in some cornstarch to lightly coat them.

9. Place the boba pieces in a sieve and lightly shake off any excess cornstarch. Place the boba pieces in an airtight container and freeze until ready to use as a mix-in, for up to 3 months.

MOCHI PIECES

Makes ¾ cup (185 g)

Similar to boba, mochi also loses its chewy and bouncy texture when frozen. But formulating the dough with high anti-freezing sugars yields soft pillows of rice cakes in ice cream.

⅓ cup (75 g) water

¼ cup (50 g) granulated sugar

1½ teaspoons (10 g) corn syrup

2 teaspoons (10 g) trehalose

¼ cup plus ¼ teaspoon (40 g) sweet rice flour

Cornstarch, for dusting

1. In a small saucepan, bring the water to just under a simmer over medium heat.

2. Remove the saucepan from the heat and stir in the sugar, corn syrup, and trehalose until dissolved.

3. Place the sweet rice flour in a small bowl. Gradually pour in the syrup, whisking after each addition until the mixture is completely smooth and lump-free. Pour the mixture into a shallow 6 by 9-inch (15 by 23 cm) microwave-safe baking dish.

4. Cover the dish tightly with plastic wrap and micro-wave until the mixture is cooked, about 1½ minutes. It should be semitranslu-cent and have the texture of a fully "set" flan or jello. Let the dough cool com-pletely, covered.

5. Once cool, place the bak-ing dish in the freezer and allow the mochi to harden but not completely freeze, about 2 hours.

6. Remove the mochi from the freezer. You should be able to lift it from the corner of the baking dish and peel away the entire layer in one piece. (If not, it needs to be returned to the freezer to harden some more.)

7. Dust a cutting board with some cornstarch. Place the mochi on the cutting board and use a knife dusted in cornstarch to cut it into ⅜-inch (1 cm) cubes.

8. At this point, you can wait for the mochi to soften a bit before rolling them into balls and lightly tossing them in more cornstarch to lightly coat. If the shape doesn't matter to you, skip this step and toss the cubes in some cornstarch to lightly coat them.

9. Place the mochi in a sieve and lightly shake off any excess cornstarch. Place the mochi pieces in an air-tight container and freeze until ready to use as a mix-in, for up to 3 months.

HONEYCOMB CANDY

Makes about 3 cups (340 g)

This candy is a foamed toffee (thanks to a chemical reaction by way of baking soda) that's the main star in New Zealand's most famous ice cream, of vanilla and honeycomb candy, dubbed "Hokey Pokey." It's also a Korean street snack—sold in a circular shape with various designs stamped onto the candy while warm. When broken into smaller pieces and folded into ice cream, it provides textural contrast via crunch, but after a few days frozen, it eventually melts into pools of honey caramel within the ice cream. To keep the honeycomb pieces crunchy, however, you can give them a quick light coat in refined coconut oil or freckling chocolate (page 279).

1 cup (100 g) granulated sugar
¼ cup (80 g) corn syrup
2 tablespoons (40 g) honey
½ cup (120 g) water
2 teaspoons (10 g) baking soda

1. Line a sheet pan with parchment paper. Set aside.

2. In a medium saucepan, combine the sugar, corn syrup, honey, and water and set over medium-high heat. Do not stir the mixture; instead pick up the pan by its handle occasionally and swirl the mixture. Continue heating and occasionally swirling the pan until all the sugar has melted.

3. Continue cooking until the mixture reaches 300°F (150°C), 7 to 10 minutes. Have a large whisk or long-handled heatproof spatula handy nearby.

4. Remove the pan from the heat and quickly but carefully whisk in the baking soda. WARNING: The hot mixture will quickly foam up. Continue whisking or stirring until all the baking soda has been incorporated. Immediately pour the mixture onto the prepared sheet pan.

5. Let the honeycomb candy cool until completely hardened, about 1 hour.

6. Break the candy into large pieces and place them into a zip-seal plastic bag. Using a rolling pin or mallet, gently break the candy into smaller pieces. Keep the candy stored in the bag or an airtight container free of moisture for up to 3 days at room temperature.

COOKIE CRUST

Makes two 8-inch (20 cm)
pie crusts, for 1 quart (1 liter)
of ice cream

I use this recipe for all my ice cream pies (including Tita's Fruit Salad Pies on page 228), and it works with almost any cookie you have lying around or in your pantry. I've used Biscoff cookies for ice cream banoffee pies, Chinese almond cookies with lychee ice cream (page 250), or Nilla wafers for an ice cream pie made with Koldskål ice cream (page 164).

3½ cups (350 g) fine cookie crumbs

⅓ cup (65 g) granulated sugar

8 tablespoons (4 ounces/115 g) unsalted butter, melted

1. Preheat the oven to 350°F (180°C).

2. In a large bowl, combine the cookie crumbs, sugar, and melted butter and mix well with a wooden spoon or rubber spatula until completely blended.

3. Divide the mixture evenly between two 9-inch (23 cm) pie plates.

4. Place each pie plate on a separate baking sheet and bake until very lightly browned, 7 to 8 minutes.

5. Remove the crusts from the oven and allow them to cool completely before placing in the freezer to prechill them before filling with ice cream.

NOTE: Pulse the cookies in a food processor to obtain a very fine crumb, which is necessary for the crust to bind.

"TOASTED" FLAVOR POWDER

Makes 3 cups (335 g) milk powder or 1 cup (150 g) yeast

By toasting milk powder or yeast in a pressure cooker, you can make a versatile secret ingredient that lends a freshly baked or toasted flavor to ice cream bases. It even makes a great topping simply sprinkled onto plain custard or sweet cream ice cream.

3 cups (335 g) nonfat dry milk powder or 1 cup (150 g) instant dry yeast

1. If using milk powder, divide it between two to three ½-pint (236 ml) mason jars that will fit into the basket or steamer rack of your pressure cooker. If using yeast, simply fill one ½-pint (236 ml) mason jar. Make sure that the jars are only filled three-quarters full. Lightly screw the lids on each jar so they are just fingertip tight. Make sure the glass of the jars is not touching the walls of the pressure cooker at all.

2. Cook with 1 inch (2.5 cm) of water on high pressure for 2 hours.

3. Let the pressure release and naturally dissipate and allow the jars to cool completely before handling, about 1 hour. The mixture should have caramelized into a dark golden brown color.

4. Keep the toasted powder in airtight containers (they can stay in the mason jars) in a cool, dry place for up to 3 months.

WANDERLUST WAFFLE CONES

Makes about 12 cones

1¼ teaspoons (3 g) nonfat dry milk powder

⅓ cup (75 g) unsalted butter

120 grams egg whites (from about 4 large eggs)

1 cup + scant 3 tablespoons (235 g) granulated sugar

½ teaspoon (1 g) salt

¼ cup (60 g) heavy cream

1 tablespoon + 1 teaspoon (20 g) water

1 teaspoon (4 g) vanilla extract

2 cups (250 g) all-purpose flour

At any other ice cream shop, I very rarely order my ice cream on a cone. Why? Because they all taste the same, often made from a premade "just-add-water" mix with this unmistakable taste of fake vanilla-with-a-hint-of-citrus. Even worse are the kind of cones that come out of a box that taste like cardboard. When dreaming up our menu at Wanderlust Creamery, I wanted cones that actually tasted of caramelized butter and sugar and an airy crispness that comes from real egg whites. I immediately thought of lengua de gato cookies of my childhood. Reworking a basic recipe for that, it became a mother recipe that spawned endless variations.

1. In a spice grinder, process the nonfat dry milk powder into a fine powder.

2. In a small saucepan, melt the butter over medium heat until it begins to bubble and the milk solids begin to separate from the fat, about 6 minutes. Whisk in the dry milk powder and continue to cook, whisking frequently, until the milk solids begin to turn color. Remove from heat and let it cool in the saucepan; the milk solids will continue to darken and brown. Set aside.

3. In a bowl, combine the egg whites, sugar, and salt and whisk until the sugar is completely dissolved. Whisk in the heavy cream, water, vanilla, and brown butter, making sure to include all the browned milk solids, scraped from the bottom of the saucepan.

4. Gradually add the flour and mix until a completely smooth batter is obtained.

5. Bake the cones in a waffle cone baker according to the manufacturer's instructions. Store any unused batter in the refrigerator in an airtight container for up to 1 week.

VARIATIONS:

Ube Waffle Cones:
Omit the dry milk powder and simply melt the butter instead of browning it. Replace the vanilla extract with 2 tablespoons plus 1 teaspoon (35 ml) ube extract and 2 tablespoons ube halaya (purple yam jam).

Corn Waffle Cones:
Omit the dry milk powder and simply melt the butter instead of browning it. Double the amount of water in the recipe. Replace the vanilla extract with 1 tablespoon plus 1 teaspoon "cream-style" corn. Add ½ cup + 1 tablespoon (75 g) cornmeal and ½ cup (65 g) masa harina to the flour.

Coconut Pandan Waffle Cones:
Omit the dry milk powder and simply melt the butter instead of browning it. Replace the vanilla extract with 1 tablespoon (15 ml) pandan extract. Replace the heavy cream with coconut cream.

Brown Butter Hazelnut Waffle Cones:
Double the amount of water in the recipe. Add 1⅓ cups (150 g) finely ground hazelnuts (use a spice grinder) to the flour.

Black Sesame Waffle Cones:
Omit the dry milk powder and simply melt the butter instead of browning it. Double the amount of water in the recipe. Add ⅓ cup + 2 tablespoons (150 g) finely ground black sesame seeds (use a spice grinder) to the flour.

MARSHMALLOW CRÈME

Makes a little more than 1 cup (310 g)

A versatile, airy crème that can be used as a topping or swirled as a variegate in different versions of rocky road. Compared with marshmallow fluff in a jar, this recipe is much less sweet and without any artificial flavor.

60 grams egg whites (from about 2 large eggs)

¼ cup +2 ½ teaspoons (60 g) granulated sugar

Pinch of salt

¼ cup + 2 ½ tablespoons (130 g) corn syrup

¼ cup (60 g) water

¾ teaspoon unflavored gelatin powder softened in 2 teaspoons (10 g) water (optional; see Tip)

Seeds from ½ vanilla bean or ½ teaspoon (2 g) vanilla extract

1. In a stand mixer fitted with a completely clean and dry whisk and bowl, mix the egg whites on low speed until it begins to form a fine foam.

2. In a small saucepan, combine the sugar, salt, corn syrup, and water and bring to a boil over medium heat.

3. Meanwhile, increase the mixer speed to medium to form soft peaks. While the egg whites are beating and the syrup is boiling simultaneously, begin to take note of the temperature of the syrup with a thermometer gun or candy thermometer. As soon as the syrup reaches 240°F (115°C), remove it from the heat and immediately (but carefully!) pour it in a very thin stream close to the inside wall of the mixer bowl, away from the whisk (pouring it onto the whisk will splatter hot syrup everywhere!). Just as the last tablespoon of syrup is being added, add the softened gelatin, if using.

4. Once all the syrup has been added, increase the mixer speed to high. Whip until the marshmallow has tripled in size and the mixer bowl is cool to the touch, 7 to 10 minutes. Add the vanilla seeds or extract in the last few seconds of mixing. Transfer the marshmallow crème to an airtight container and store refrigerated for up to 1 day.

TIP: If you want a stable marshmallow swirl that will hold a little longer in ice cream (more than 3 days), add ¾ teaspoon of gelatin bloomed in water just after adding all of the hot syrup to the egg whites.

VARIATIONS:

Okay, Willy Wonka, go on and reimagine this marshmallow recipe with any flavor your heart desires: Replace the water with another liquid or vanilla extract for any other alcohol or water-based extract. Just be aware that any liquid you add must be heat-stable up to 240°F (115°C)—sorry, no fruit juices allowed—and anything with fat will deflate the marshmallow.

Thai Tea Marshmallow Crème:
Replace the water with very strongly brewed unsweetened Thai tea.

Soft Nougat Crème:
Substitute honey for the corn syrup. Omit the vanilla and add ½ teaspoon (1 g) almond extract.

Yuzu Creamsicle Fluff:
Omit the vanilla. Add ¼ teaspoon citric acid and 1 tablespoon finely ground yuzu zest in the very last few seconds of mixing (be careful—overmixing in the citrus zest may deflate the marshmallow). Swirl it into bittersweet matcha ice cream!

Berry Mallow Crème:
Omit the vanilla. Sift in 2 tablespoons freeze-dried berry powder in the last few seconds of mixing.

Caramel Nougat Crème:
Caramelize the sugar to a dark amber brown, then add the salt, corn syrup, and water before proceeding with the rest of the recipe.

Violet Marshmallow Crème:
Substitute ½ teaspoon violet extract for the vanilla. Add a few drops of all-natural purple food coloring.

Condensed Milk Marshmallow Crème:
Omit the vanilla. Decrease the sugar to ¼ cup (50 g). In a spice grinder, process 2 tablespoons plus 1½ teaspoons nonfat dry milk powder into a very fine powder. Add 1 tablespoon plus 1 teaspoon powdered sugar and pulse to combine. Set this milk powder/powdered sugar mixture aside. Follow the recipe as usual, but after all the hot syrup has been added and the marshmallow has finished mixing (step 4), remove the bowl from the mixer and sift the milk powder/powdered sugar mixture over the top of the marshmallow. Return the marshmallow to the mixer and mix on medium speed for 5 seconds, until just combined. Use this in Vietnamese Rocky Road (page 247).

Yogurt Marshmallow Crème:
Omit the vanilla. Decrease the sugar to ¼ cup (50 g). Sift together 2½ tablespoons dry yogurt powder and 4 teaspoons powdered sugar. Set the yogurt powder/powdered sugar mixture aside. Follow the recipe as usual, but after all the hot syrup has been added and the marshmallow has finished mixing (step 4), remove the bowl from the mixer and add the yogurt powder/powdered sugar mixture. Return the marshmallow to the mixer and mix on medium speed for 5 seconds, until just combined.

Malted Marshmallow Crème:
After all the hot syrup has been added and the marshmallow has finished mixing (step 4), remove the bowl from the mixer and add 2½ tablespoons malted milk powder. Return the marshmallow to the mixer and mix on medium speed for 5 seconds, until just combined.

ACKNOWLEDGMENTS

To my partner in life, business, and everything, JP Lopez, who has been responsible for Wanderlust Creamery's survival through some rough seas. I'm so lucky to have found someone who has the same level of passion as I do for the side of this business I *can't* do, lol.

To Hazel and Horace Lopez, for whom none of this would even exist if it weren't for their generosity and faith in us.

To Steven, for EVERYTHING. I don't think Wanderlust would be what it is today had you not been there from day one.

To Dana, for EVERYTHING, including but not limited to all your work and input that went into producing this book. To Mom, for trusting and supporting me in choosing a different path from the one you'd hoped for. I love you always. To my grandfather Eliseo Borlongan, whom I've never met. Thank you for this inherited passion. It's been the driving force in my life, and I'm fulfilled to have found its source and origin after so long. A very special thank-you to Tito Jack Borlongan and Tita "Baby" Emelita Montana for sharing precious detailed insight into our famly's history, and always making me feel welcome to it.

To the Wanderlust Creamery Team, past and present. Your daily dedication to the business allowed me time to dive into researching, creating, and innovating ice cream throughout Wanderlust Creamery's life span. I'd specifically like to shout out (but the list is not limited to): Angelica Reyes, Charlie and Maria Madrigal, Meldon Mendez, R. J. Gaerlan, Ashley Aglanao, Emily Turano, Conrad Almazar, Mark Uy, Justin Russikoff, and our supervisors, Sandy, Bia, Jason, and Tyler, who lead the store teams. Shout out to Chad Valencia, who we were so fortunate to have gracing our kitchen for a blip in time.

To my agent, Kitty Cowles, who brought about the idea for this book: I'm grateful for your expertise, wisdom, and guidance throughout every step of this project. To Garrett Snyder, who helped me propose this book. And to Zach Brooks, who made these introductions and took a chance on Wanderlust Creamery as Smorgasburg LA's first ice cream vendor.

To Betty Hallock, who, in the midst of her busy schedule, made time to organize all my rants and ideas into coherent sentences and paragraphs, I'm grateful for your patience, brilliance, and astuteness. You've made everything a thousand times easier on my end.

To Max Milla and Judean Sakimoto! On two separate occasions, you both put a weeklong pause on your lives and came to LA to shoot and style this book, then dedicated two more last-minute sessions to it. I'm forever grateful not only for your talent and those late nights, but for your company and humor during one of the most hectic times in my professional life. Max—it's insane to think how we started working together eight years ago when Wanderlust had just started, and the upward trajectory our careers have

taken since then. It only makes sense that you'd photograph this book, and I can't imagine it any other way. Again, to Dana Borlongan and Meldon Mendez—thank you for undertaking all the details of the shoot, including being pricked by cactii in pursuit of the perfect shot.

Thank you to Shira Katz, Dario Ibarra, Christian Benjamin, and CJ—who diligently tested each recipe, scrutinized measurements, carefully taste-tested, and retested some complete failures of first drafts to ensure that every ice cream formula actually worked.

To the team at Abrams, I cannot thank you all enough. To Soyolmaa, thank you for your patience, flexibility, and grace in extending deadlines, lol. I'm also thankful for your expertise; you've been invaluable to me throughout the process of making this book. To the design team, Jenice Kim and Deb Wood, thank you for transforming my vision into reality, while reining in my wild ideas. Thank you to Lisa Silverman, and to Holly Dolce for trusting my vision for this book and giving me the encouragement to geek out as hard as I wanted.

And lastly, I want to send my deepest gratitude to every loyal customer, stan, anyone who has walked into a Wanderlust Creamy and felt excitement, nostalgia, pride, or that they're "seen" when tasting the flavors. You understand me; you *get it*. You're what makes my unconventional ideas and dreams into a viable business, and for that my family and I are forever grateful.

INDEX

A

Abuelita Malted Crunch, 72, 73, 74, 272
AFP. *See* anti-freezing power
agar-agar, 30, *31*
aging process, 41
air, 21-22
alcohol. *See* boozy flavors
Alfajores, 92, *93*
Almond Cookies & Lychee Cream, *250*, 250-51
Almond Jellies, 280, *283*
Almond Shortbread, 275, *283*
Amalfi Pear Torte, 143
ancient China, 15
anti-freezing power (AFP), 20, 21, 87
Arab expansion, 15
Argentina, 92
aromatic compounds, 115
"artisanal" ice cream, 8, 22
Asian recipes, 258-59
   Jasmine Milk Tea with Boba, *266*, 266-67
   Oolong Pineapple Cake, 263-64, *265*
   Ramune Sherbet, *260*, 261-62
   White Rabbit, 268-69
Australia, 147

B

baking, 140-41
   Amalfi Pear Torte, 143
   Australian Pavlova, *146*, 146-47
   Creole Coffee & Donuts, 144-45, *145*
   Okinawan Mont Blanc, 148, *149*
   Pa Amb Xocolata, *150*, 150-51
baking dish, small, 37, *37*
baklava
   Orange Flower Baklava, 192, *193*
Balanced Base, 49
bars
   Elote Ice Cream Bars, 136, *137*, 138-39
   Klondike Bar, 65
   Nanaimo Bars, 65-66, *67*
bartending, 8, 206
bases, 25, 46-47
   Balanced Base, 49
   Black Sesame Ice Cream Base, 254
   Blank Base, 48
   Custard Base, 50
   Hojicha Ice Cream Base, 255
   Mascarpone Base, 51, 257
   Matcha Ice Cream Base, 254
   meringue, 146-47
   Rice Cream Base, 52-53
   techniques for, *39*, 39-44, *40*, *41*, *42*, *43*, *44*
   Vegan Base, 54, *55*
basil, 194
   Basil Lime with Strawberry, *196*, 196-97
Baskin-Robbins, 19
beignets, 144
beni imo (Okinawan purple sweet potatoes), 148
benzaldehyde, 115
berries
   Basil Lime with Strawberry, *196*, 196-97
   Berry Jellies, *282*
   Berry Mallow Crème, 293
   Berry Stracciatella, 191
   Blueberry Elderflower, 183-84
   Rose & Berry Stracciatella, *190*, 190-91
   Strawberriest Ice Cream, 98-99, *99*
   Strawberry Daifuku, *174*, 175
   Strawberry or Raspberry Jellies, 281
   Strawberry/Raspberry Stracciatella, 279
   Strawberry Sponge Cake, 276
Berthillon, 219
Biko, 171-72, *173*
bitter almond. *See noyaux*
Black Sesame Ice Cream Base, 254
Black Sesame Waffle Cones, 291
Blank Base, 48
blast freezer, 18
blast freezing, 45, *46*
blender, hand (immersion), 36, *36*
blood orange
   Sicilian Negroni, *208*, 209-10
Blueberry Elderflower, 183-84
boba
   Ice Cream "Boba," *283*, 284-85
   Jasmine Milk Tea with Boba, *266*, 266-67
Bon Appétit (magazine), 7
boozy flavors, 206-7
   Nesselrode Bula, 211-12, *213*
   Oatmeal & Scotch Honey Caramel, *214*, 214-15
   Pearl Diver Float, *216*, 217
   Royal Prune Armagnac, *218*, 218-19
   Sicilian Negroni, *208*, 209-10
Borlongan, Eliseo, 13-14, *14*
botanicals. *See* plants, herbs, and botanicals
Bourdain, Anthony, 232
Brando, Marlon, 211
Breyers, 19
Brix, 25
Brix refractometer, 37, *37*
Brooks, Zach, 10
Brown Butter Halva, *124*, 124-25

Brown Butter Hazelnut Cake, *282*
Brown Butter Hazelnut Waffle Cones, 291
Brown Butter Nut Cake, 274
Brown Butter Sans Rival, *238*, 238-39, 273
Burnt Honey Hojicha, 87
butter
   Brown Butter Halva, *124*, 124-25
   Brown Butter Hazelnut Cake, *282*
   Brown Butter Hazelnut Waffle Cones, 291
   Brown Butter Nut Cake, 274
   Brown Butter Sans Rival, *238*, 238-39, 273
butterfat, 19
   for gelato, 23

C

cacao
   Passion Fruit Cacao, *100*, 101
Café Du Monde (New Orleans), 144
cakes
   Amalfi Pear Torte, 143
   Brown Butter Hazelnut Cake, *282*
   Brown Butter Nut Cake, 274
   Chocolate Sponge Cake, 276, *283*
   Matcha Sponge Cake, 276
   Oolong Pineapple Cake, 263-64, *265*
   Pandan Sponge Cake, 276, *282*
   Sponge Cake Pieces, 276-77, *282*, *283*
   Strawberry Sponge Cake, 276
   Vanilla Bean Sponge Cake, *283*
Calabrian Sundaes, *204*, 204-5
caramel, 82-83
   Alfajores, 92, *93*
   Caramelized Honey Hojicha, *86*, 86-87
   Caramelized Milk Chocolate & Plantain Brittle, 75, *76*, 77
   Caramel Nougat Crème, 293
   Oatmeal & Scotch Honey Caramel, *214*, 214-15
   Pretzel & Rúgbrauð, 88-89, *89*
   Real Dulce De Leche, *90*, 90-91
   Salty Gula Melaka Caramel, *84*, 84-85
carboxymethyl cellulose (CMC), 24, 33
cardamom (kardemumma), 183
carrageenan, 25
casein, 20
cashews
   Brown Butter Halva, *124*, 124-25
   Crispy Cashew Dacquoise, *283*
cellulose gum, 24
cheese flavors, 152-53
   Burrata & Crema Di Pistacchio, *162*, 162-63

Kadaifi Crisp, 158
Knafeh, 157–58
Koldskål, 164, *165*
Labneh & Pomegranate Rose Jam, *154*, 155–56
Tea-Ramisu, *159*, 160–61
cherry blossom (sakura), 185
Chè Thái, 102, *103*, 104
Chicha Morada, *132*, 132–33
chiffon cake, 276–77
China, ancient, 15
chocolate, 30, *31*, 68–69
Abuelita Malted Crunch, 72, *73*, 74, 272
Caramelized Milk Chocolate & Plantain Brittle, 75, *76*, 77
Chocolate Freckles/Stracciatella, 279
Chocolate Sponge Cake, 276, *283*
Dark Chocolate Freckles, *282*
Earl Grey Milk Chocolate, 80, *81*
Namelaka Chocolate, *70*, 70–71
Namelaka Cubes, 278
Pa Amb Xocolata, *150*, 150–51
Passion Fruit Cacao, *100*, 101
Ruby Chocolate, *78*, 78–79
Ruby Chocolate Freckles, *282*
White Chocolate Freckles, *283*
chocolate freckling, 43, *43*
churning
basics of, *42*, 42–43, *43*
chocolate freckling, 43, *43*
mix-ins and, 43–44, *44*
citron honey tea, 96
citrus
Basil Lime with Strawberry, *196*, 196–97
Calabrian Sundaes, *204*, 204–5
Citrus Jellies, 280
Coconut Lime & Vietnamese Herbs, *200*, 200–201
Kalamansi Mignonette Sorbet, *110*, 110–11
Yuzu Creamsicle, *96*, 96–97
Yuzu Creamsicle Fluff, 293
Classic Halo Halo Ice Cream, 233
classics. *See* reinvented classics
CMC. *See* carboxymethyl cellulose
cocoa powder, 30, *31*
coconut
Coconut & Corn, *128*, 128–29
coconut cream, *28*, 29, 169
Coconut Jellies, 280
Coconut Lime & Vietnamese Herbs, *200*, 200–201
Coconut Pandan Waffle Cones, 291
Latik, 237
coconut oil, refined, 30, *31*, 279
coffee
Coffee or Tea Jellies, 280
Creole Coffee & Donuts, 144–45, *145*

Cold Stone Creamery, 8, 10, 171
Condensed Milk Marshmallow Crème, 293
cones. *See* waffle cones
cookies
Almond Cookies & Lychee Cream, *250*, 250–51
Cookie Crust, 288
Cook's Illustrated (magazine), 7
corn flavors, 126–27
Chicha Morada, *132*, 132–33
Coconut & Corn, *128*, 128–29
Corn Jam, 128
Corn Waffle Cones, 291
Elote Ice Cream Bars, 136, *137*, 138–39
Honey-Butter Corn Dalgona, 130–31, *131*
Thai Candy Corn, *134*, 134–35
coumarin, 185
cream
Almond Cookies & Lychee Cream, *250*, 250–51
coconut cream, *28*, 29, 169
whipping cream, 29
creamy mouthfeel, 23, 33
Creole Coffee & Donuts, 144–45, *145*
Crispy Cashew Dacquoise, *283*
Crispy Nut Dacquoise, 273
crunch
Abuelita Malted Crunch, 72, *73*, 74, 272
Malted Crunch, 272, *282*, *283*
Sakura Crunch, 185–86, *187*
Ube Malted Crunch, 225–26, *227*, 272, *283*
custards, 56–57
Custard Base, 50
Nanaimo Bars, 65–66, *67*
Pasteis De Nata, *58*, 58–59
Salted Egg Tart, *60*, 60–61
Salted Kaya Toast, 62, *63*, 64
cylindrical mixing vessel, tall, 36, *36*

D

Ddacquoise
Crispy Cashew Dacquoise, *283*
Crispy Nut Dacquoise, 273
daifuku, *174*, 175
Dalandan Jellies, 280
Dark Chocolate Freckles, *282*
DE. *See* dextrose equivalence
degraded carrageenan, 25
De Riso, Salvatore, 143
dextrose equivalence (DE), 21
disaccharides, 21
dish, small baking, 37, *37*
donuts
Creole Coffee & Donuts, 144–45, *145*
dried parmesan powder, 139

dry ice, 262
duck eggs
Salted Egg Tart, *60*, 60–61
dulce de leche
Real Dulce De Leche, *90*, 90–91

E

Earl Grey Milk Chocolate, 80, *81*
"economy" ice cream, 19
Ecuador, 245
eggs
Salted Egg Tart, *60*, 60–61
whites, *28*, 29
yolks, 24, *28*, 29
elderflower
Blueberry Elderflower, 183–84
electric spice grinder, 38, *38*
Elote Ice Cream Bars, 136, *137*, 138–39
emulsifiers, 30, *31*, 33
egg yolks, 24, *28*, 29
lecithin, 24, 32, *32*
equipment. *See* tools and equipment
Eurocentric dessert flavors, 8

F

faloodeh, 15
fat, 20
butterfat, 19, 23
fig leaf, 194
Fig Leaf & Pistachio, 202–3, *203*
Filipino-American flavors, 220–21
Brown Butter Sans Rival, *238*, 238–39
Halo Halo, *231*, 231–33
Lolo's Philippine Mango (Mangga), 240–41, *241*
Pandan Tres Leches, *222*, 223–24
Sapin Sapin, *234*, 235–37
Tita's Fruit Salad Pies, *228*, 228–30, *229*
Ube Malted Crunch, 225–26, *227*, 272, *283*
fine-mesh sieve, 37, *37*
fior di latte, 163
Fior di Sicilia, 209
floats
Pearl Diver Float, *216*, 217
flowers, 180–81
Blueberry Elderflower, 183–84
Jasmine Milk Tea with Boba, *266*, 266–67
Jasmine Tea Jellies, *283*
Labneh & Pomegranate Rose Jam, *154*, 155–56
Orange Flower Baklava, 192, *193*
Rose & Berry Stracciatella, *190*, 190–91
Sakura Crunch, 185–86, *187*
Violette Marshmallow, *188*, 188–89

flower viewing. *See hanami*
Food & Wine (magazine), 7
freckle. *See* stracciatella
freckling, chocolate, 43, *43*
French ice cream. *See* custards
fruit, 94–95
    Almond Cookies & Lychee Cream, *250*, 250–51
    Basil Lime with Strawberry, *196*, 196–97
    Blueberry Elderflower, 183–84
    Chè Thái, 102, *103*, 104
    Coconut Lime & Vietnamese Herbs, *200*, 200–201
    Green Mango Sorbet, 108, *109*
    Jellies, 280–81
    Kalamansi Mignonette Sorbet, *110*, 110–11
    Kinako & Kyoho Grape Jelly, 118, *119*, 120
    Lilikoi Li Hing Pineapple, 105, *106*, 107
    Lolo's Philippine Mango (Mangga), 240–41, *241*
    Lychee or Rambutan Jellies, 281
    Passion Fruit Cacao, *100*, 101
    Rose & Berry Stracciatella, *190*, 190–91
    Sapin Sapin, *234*, 235–37
    Strawberriest Ice Cream, 98–99, *99*
    Tita's Fruit Salad Pies, *228*, 228–30, *229*
    Tropical Fruit Halo Halo Ice Cream, 233
    Yuzu Creamsicle, *96*, 96–97

G

Gable, Clark, 211
Game of Thrones (TV series), 202, 214
gelato
    butterfat for, 19
    ice cream versus, 23
    overrun for, 23
    PAC for, 21
    temperature for, 23
George, Tyler, 90
glass measuring cup, 38, *38*
glucose powder, 28, 29, *31*
glutinous rice flour, 30
grandmother, of author, 12–13
grape
    Kinako & Kyoho Grape Jelly, 118, *119*, 120
Greece, 155
Greek yogurt, 155
Green Mango Sorbet, 108, *109*
guar gum, 24
Guava Jellies, 281
gula melaka
    Salty Gula Melaka Caramel, *84*, 84–85

H

Häagen-Dazs, 19
Hải Vân Pass, 247
Halo Halo, *231*, 231–33
hanami (flower viewing), 185
hand (immersion) blender, 36, *36*
hazelnuts
    Brown Butter Hazelnut Cake, *282*
    Brown Butter Hazelnut Waffle Cones, 291
heatproof spatula, 35, *35*
herbs. *See* plants, herbs, and botanicals
history, of ice cream, 15
hojicha
    Burnt Honey Hojicha, 87
    Caramelized Honey Hojicha, *86*, 86–87
    Hojicha Ice Cream Base, 255
homogenization, 19–20
honey
    Burnt Honey Hojicha, 87
    Caramelized Honey Hojicha, *86*, 86–87
    citron honey tea, 96
    Fig Leaf & Pistachio, 202–3, *203*
    Honey-Butter Corn Dalgona, 130–31, *131*
    Honeycomb Candy, *282*, 287
    Oatmeal & Scotch Honey Caramel, *214*, 214–15
hydrocolloids
    carrageenan, 25
    cellulose gum, 24
    guar gum, 24
    tara gum, 24, 30, *31*

I

ice bath, 39, *39*
Ice Cream "Boba," *283*, 284–85
ice cream maker, 34, *35*
ice cream spade, 38, *38*
Iceland, 88
immersion (hand) blender, 36, *36*
Indian black salt (kala namak), 50
Indian cooking, 24
ingredients
    agar-agar, 30, *31*
    chocolate, 30, *31*
    cocoa powder, 30
    coconut cream, 28, 29
    cream, 28, 29
    egg whites, 28, 29
    egg yolks, 28, 29
    glucose powder, 28, 29
    glutinous rice flour, 30, *31*
    milk, 28, 29
    nonfat dry milk powder, 28, 29
    nonfat yogurt powder, 28, 29
    refined coconut oil, 30, *31*

    stabilizers, 30, 33
    sugar, 28, 29
    sweetened condensed milk, 28, 29
Injeolmi, *178*, 179
instant-read thermometer, 35, *35*
inulin, 32, *32*, 96, 105, 108
iota carrageenan, 25
Italy, 19

J

jackfruit
    Chè Thái, 102, *103*, 104
    Jackfruit Jellies, 281
    Sapin Sapin, *234*, 235–37
James Beard Foundation, 9
jams
    Corn Jam, 128
    Labneh & Pomegranate Rose Jam, *154*, 155–56
    Mango Jam, 170
    Pineapple Jam, 264
Japan, 118, 185
Japanese Neapolitan, 252, *253*, 254–55
Jasmine Milk Tea with Boba, *266*, 266–67
Jasmine Tea Jellies, *283*
jellies
    Almond Jellies, 280, *283*
    Berry Jellies, *282*
    Citrus Jellies, 280
    Coconut Jellies, 280
    Coffee or Tea Jellies, 280
    Dalandan Jellies, 280
    Guava Jellies, 281
    Jackfruit Jellies, 281
    Jasmine Tea Jellies, *283*
    Jellies, 280–81
    Kinako & Kyoho Grape Jelly, 118, *119*, 120
    Lychee or Rambutan Jellies, 281
    Mango Jellies, 281
    Pandan Jellies, 281
    Pandan Jelly "Noodles," *282*
    Passion Fruit Jellies, 281, *283*
    Peach Jellies, 281, *282*
    Strawberry or Raspberry Jellies, 281
Jin Xuan oolong, 263

K

Kadaifi Crisp, 158
Kalamansi Mignonette Sorbet, *110*, 110–11
kala namak (Indian black salt), 50
kappa carrageenan, 25
kardemumma (cardamom), 183
Kinako & Kyoho Grape Jelly, 118, *119*, 120
kitchen scale, precision, 34–35, *35*
Klondike Bar, 65

Knafeh, 157–58
Koldskål, 164, *165*

L

Labneh & Pomegranate Rose Jam, *154*, 155–56
lactose, 20
lambda carrageenan, 25
large-scale mix-ins, 44, *44*
Latik, 237
Latino cuisine, 223
Latitude 29 (New Orleans), 217
lecithin, 24, 32, *32*
lemon granita
    Calabrian Sundaes, *204*, 204–5
lengua de gato, 228
Lilikoi Li Hing Pineapple, 105, *106*, 107
lime
    Basil Lime with Strawberry, *196*, 196–97
    Coconut Lime & Vietnamese Herbs, *200*, 200–201
Little Saigon, 102
Llera, Maynard, 111
loaf pan, metal, 36, *36*
Lopez-Alt, J. Kenji, 87
Los Angeles, California, 176, 225
    "artisanal" ice cream brands in, 8
    butterfat preference in, 19
    Kuya Lord in, 111
    Latino cuisine in, 223
    Little Saigon in, 102
    multicultural landscape of, 130
    Wanderlust Creamery locations in, 10
lychee
    Almond Cookies & Lychee Cream, *250*, 250–51
    Lychee or Rambutan Jellies, 281

M

Maciel's Plant-Based Butcher Shop, macapuno, 233
Magic Shell, 279
Magnolia, 13–14, *14*
mahleb, 115
Malted Crunch, 272, *282*, *283*. See also Abuelita Malted Crunch; Ube Malted Crunch
Mamet pit, 115
mango
    Green Mango Sorbet, 108, *109*
    Lolo's Philippine Mango (Mangga), 240–41, *241*
    "Mango Bango," 14
    Mango Jam, 170
    Mango Jellies, 281
    Sticky Rice & Mango, *168*, 169–70

marshmallow
    Condensed Milk Marshmallow Crème, 293
    flavor extract, 146
    Marshmallow Crème, 292–93
    Violette Marshmallow, *188*, 188–89
Mascarpone Base, 51, 257
matcha
    Matcha Ice Cream Base, 254
    Matcha Namelaka, *282*
    Matcha Sponge Cake, 276
    Matcha Stracciatella, 279
    Mochi dusted in matcha, *283*
measuring cup, glass, 38, *38*
meltdown, 18
meringue base, 146–47
metal loaf pan, 36, *36*
Mexico, 19
Middle East, 15
milk
    nonfat dry milk powder, 20, *28*, 29
    Sticky Rice Milk, 53
    sweetened condensed milk, *28*, 29
milk chocolate
    Caramelized Milk Chocolate & Plantain Brittle, 75, *76*, 77
    Condensed Milk Marshmallow Crème, 293
    Earl Grey Milk Chocolate, 80, *81*
    Milk Chocolate Namelaka, *282*
milk solids not fat (MSNF), 20, 25
Minori, 143
mint
    Palo Santo Mint Chip, *244*, 245–46
mixer, stand, 37, *37*
mixing vessel, tall cylindrical, 36, *36*
mix-ins, 25
    Crispy Nut Dacquoise, 273
    Halo Halo, 233
    large-scale, 44, *44*
    small-scale, 44
    when to add, 43
mochi
    dusted in kinako, *282*
    dusted in matcha, *283*
    flavored with ube, *282*
    Mochi Pieces, 286
monosaccharides, 21
Monroe, Marilyn, 211
Moors, 15, 92
mouthfeel
    carrageenan and, 25
    creamy, 23, 33
    inulin and, 96, 105, 108, 132
MSNF. See milk solids not fat

N

Namelaka Chocolate, *70*, 70–71
Namelaka Cubes, 278
Nanaimo Bars, 65–66, *67*

National Ice Cream Day, 10
Naxos, Greece, 155
Nesselrode Bula, 211–12, *213*
Nestlé, 12
New Orleans
    Café Du Monde, 144
    Latitude 29, 217
nieve de garrafa, 198
Ninja Creami, 34
nondairy stabilizer, 32, *32*, 33
nonfat dry milk powder, 20, *28*, 29
nonfat yogurt powder, *28*, 29
nonnegotiable tools and equipment
    heatproof spatula, 35, *35*
    ice cream maker, 34, *35*
    instant-read thermometer, 35, *35*
    precision kitchen scale, 34–35, *35*
    small-ish saucepan, 35, *35*
    whisk, 35, *35*
Nopal Sorbet, 198–99, *199*
North Africa, 15
"nostalgic" flavors, 8
nougat
    Caramel Nougat Crème, 293
    Nougat De Montélimar, 121–22, *123*
    Soft Nougat Crème, 293
noyaux, 185
    Noyaux & Pink Pralines, *114*, 115–17
nuts, 112–13
    Almond Cookies & Lychee Cream, *250*, 250–51
    Almond Jellies, 280, *283*
    Almond Shortbread, 275, *283*
    Brown Butter Halva, *124*, 124–25
    Brown Butter Hazelnut Cake, *282*
    Brown Butter Hazelnut Waffle Cones, 291
    Burrata & Crema Di Pistacchio, *162*, 162–63
    Crispy Nut Dacquoise, 273
    Fig Leaf & Pistachio, 202–3, *203*
    Kinako & Kyoho Grape Jelly, 118, *119*, 120
    Nougat De Montélimar, 121–22, *123*
    Noyaux & Pink Pralines, *114*, 115–17

O

Oatmeal & Scotch Honey Caramel, *214*, 214–15
oil, refined coconut, 30, *31*
Okinawan Mont Blanc, 148, *149*
Okinawan purple sweet potatoes (beni imo), 148
oligosaccharides, 21
Oolong Pineapple Cake, 263–64, *265*
Orange Flower Baklava, 192, *193*
orange flowers, 209
overrun, 22
    for gelato, 23

P

Pa Amb Xocolata, *150*, 150–51
PAC. *See* potere anti-congelante
Pakistani cooking, 24
Palo Santo Mint Chip, *244*, 245–46
Pandan Jellies, 281
Pandan Jelly "Noodles," *282*
Pandan Sponge Cake, 276, *282*
Pandan Tres Leches, *222*, 223–24
pans
    metal loaf, 36, *36*
    sheet, 37, *37*
Passion Fruit Cacao, *100*, 101
Passion Fruit Jellies, 281, *283*
Passion Fruit Ripple, 147
passions, 7
Pasteis De Nata, *58*, 58–59
Peach Jellies, 281, *282*
pear
    Amalfi Pear Torte, 143
Pearl Diver Float, *216*, 217
PepsiCo., 12
Perez, Alec and Celeste, 9
Persia, 15
Peru, 245
pies
    Tita's Fruit Salad Pies, *228*, 228–30,
      229
pineapple
    Lilikoi Li Hing Pineapple, 105, *106*, 107
    Oolong Pineapple Cake, 263–64,
      265
    Pineapple Jam, 264
pinipig, 231
Pink Neapolitan, *256*, 257
Pink Pralines, 117
pistachio, 112–13
    Burrata & Crema Di Pistacchio, *162*,
      162–63
    Fig Leaf & Pistachio, 202–3, *203*
pixtle, 115
plantains
    Caramelized Milk Chocolate &
      Plantain Brittle, 75, *76*, 77
plants, herbs, and botanicals, 194–95
    Basil Lime with Strawberry, *196*,
      196–97
    Calabrian Sundaes, *204*, 204–5
    Coconut Lime & Vietnamese Herbs,
      200, 200–201
    Fig Leaf & Pistachio, 202–3, *203*
    Nopal Sorbet, 198–99, *199*
plum powder, salted dried, 105
POD. *See* potere dolcificante
pomegranate
    Labneh & Pomegranate Rose Jam,
      154, 155–56
potere anti-congelante (PAC), 21, 25
potere dolcificante (POD), 21
powders
    cocoa, 30, *31*

dried parmesan, 139
glucose, *28*, 29, *31*
nonfat dry milk, 20, *28*, 29
nonfat yogurt, *28*, 29
salted dried plum, 105
"Toasted" Flavor Powder, 289
pralines
    Noyaux & Pink Pralines, *114*, 115–17
    Pink Pralines, 117
precision kitchen scale, 34–35, *35*
"premium" ice cream, 19
Pretzel & Rúgbrauð, 88–89, *89*
protein, 20
prunes
    Royal Prune Armagnac, *218*, 218–19

Q

QQ, 271, 284

R

rambutan
    Lychee or Rambutan Jellies, 281
Ramune Sherbet, *260*, 261–62
raspberry
    Strawberry or Raspberry Jellies, 281
    Strawberry/Raspberry Stracciatella,
      279
Real Dulce De Leche, *90*, 90–91
"Red Rubies," 281
refined coconut oil, 30, *31*, 279
reinvented classics, 242–43
    Almond Cookies & Lychee Cream,
      250, 250–51
    Japanese Neapolitan, 252, *253*,
      254–55
    Palo Santo Mint Chip, *244*, 245–46
    Pink Neapolitan, *256*, 257
    Vietnamese Rocky Road, 247, *248*,
      248
relative sweetness, 21
rice, 167–68
    Biko, 171–72, *173*
    glutinous rice flour, 30, *31*
    Injeolmi, *178*, 179
    Rice Cream Base, 52–53
    Risalamande, 176, *177*
    Sticky Rice & Mango, *168*, 169–70
    Sticky Rice Milk, 53
    Strawberry Daifuku, *174*, 175
Risalamande, 176, *177*
rose
    Labneh & Pomegranate Rose Jam,
      154, 155–56
    Rose & Berry Stracciatella, *190*,
      190–91
Royal Prune Armagnac, *218*, 218–19
Ruby Chocolate, *78*, 78–79
Ruby Chocolate Freckles, *282*
rúgbrauð, 88–89, *89*

S

saccharides, 21
Sakura Crunch, 185–86, *187*
salted dried plum powder, 105
Salted Egg Tart, *60*, 60–61
Salted Kaya Toast, 62, *63*, 64
Salty Gula Melaka Caramel, *84*, 84–85
San Miguel, 12–13
saucepan, small-ish, 35, *35*
sauces. *See* toppings, sauces, & special
    ingredients
scale, precision, 34–35, *35*
Serious Eats (website), 87
sheet pans, 37, *37*
sherbet
    Ramune Sherbet, *260*, 261–62
shortbread
    Almond Shortbread, 275, *283*
Sicilian Negroni, *208*, 209–10
sieve, fine-mesh, 37, *37*
sliced ice creams, 45
small baking dish, 37, *37*
small-ish saucepan, 35, *35*
small-scale mix-ins, 44
Smorgasburg LA, 10
"Snow of Orange Flowers," 180
Soft Nougat Crème, 293
sorbet
    Coconut Lime & Vietnamese Herbs,
      200, 200–201
    Green Mango Sorbet, 108, *109*
    Kalamansi Mignonette Sorbet, *110*,
      110–11
    Nopal Sorbet, 198–99, *199*
sorbet stabilizer, 32, *32*, 33
spade, ice cream, 38, *38*
Spain, 15, 92
spatula, heatproof, 35, *35*
special ingredients. *See* toppings,
    sauces, & special ingredients
spice grinder, electric, 38, *38*
sponge cake
    Chocolate Sponge Cake, 276, *283*
    Matcha Sponge Cake, 276
    Pandan Sponge Cake, 276, *282*
    Sponge Cake Pieces, 276–77, *282*,
      283
    Strawberry Sponge Cake, 276
    Vanilla Bean Sponge Cake, *283*
stabilizers, 23
    emulsifiers, 24, 30, *31*, 32, 32–33
    hydrocolloids, 24–25
    nondairy stabilizer, 32, *32*, 33
    sorbet stabilizer, 32, *32*, 33
stand mixer, 37, *37*
Sticky Rice & Mango, *168*, 169–70
Sticky Rice Milk, 53
stracciatella (freckle), 25
    Chocolate Freckles/Stracciatella,
      279
    Dark Chocolate Freckles, *282*

Rose & Berry Stracciatella, *190*,
190–91
Ruby Chocolate Freckles, *282*
strawberry
Basil Lime with Strawberry, *196*,
196–97
Strawberriest Ice Cream, 98–99, *99*
Strawberry Daifuku, *174*, 175
Strawberry or Raspberry Jellies, 281
Strawberry/Raspberry Stracciatella,
279
Strawberry Sponge Cake, 276
structure elements
air, 21–22
fat, 19–20
protein, 20
sugar, 20–21
water, 18–19
sucrose, 21
sugar, 20–21, *28*, *29*
sundaes
Calabrian Sundaes, *204*, 204–5
"super premium" ice cream, 19
Sweden, 183
sweetened condensed milk, *28*, *29*
sweet rice flour. *See* glutinous rice flour

T

Taiwan, 263
tall cylindrical mixing vessel, 36, *36*
tapioca, 284
tara gum, 24, 30, *31*
taste, overrun affecting, 22
tea
citron honey, 96
Coffee or Tea Jellies, 280
Earl Grey Milk Chocolate, 80, *81*
Jasmine Milk Tea with Boba, *266*,
266–67
Jasmine Tea Jellies, *283*
Oolong Pineapple Cake, 263–64,
265
Tea-Ramisu, *159*, 160–61
Thai Tea Marshmallow Crème, 293
techniques
for base, *39*, 39–44, *40*, *41*, *42*,
43, *44*
blast freezing, 45, *45*
for sliced ice creams, 45
tempering, 45
tejate, 115
temperature, for gelato, 23
tempering, 25, 45
Thai Candy Corn, *134*, 134–35
Thai Tea Marshmallow Crème, 293
thermometer, instant-read, 35, *35*
thermometer gun, 38, *38*
Thrifty, 19, 72
Tita's Fruit Salad Pies, *228*, 228–30,
229

toast
Salted Kaya Toast, 62, *63*, 64
"Toasted" Flavor Powder, 289
tools and equipment
nonnegotiables, *34*, 34–35, *35*
other, *36*, 36–38, *37*, *38*
toppings, sauces, & special ingredients,
270–71
Almond Shortbread, 275, *283*
Brown Butter Nut Cake, 274
Chocolate Freckles/Stracciatella,
279
Cookie Crust, 288
Crispy Nut Dacquoise, 273
Honeycomb Candy, *282*, 287
Ice Cream "Boba," *283*, 284–85
Jellies, 280–81
Malted Crunch, 272, *282*, *283*
Marshmallow Crème, 292–93
Mochi Pieces, 286
Namelaka Cubes, 278
Sponge Cake Pieces, 276–77
"Toasted" Flavor Powder, 289
Wanderlust Waffle Cones, 290, *290*
torte
Amalfi Pear Torte, 143
trehalose, 284
tropical fruit
Almond Cookies & Lychee Cream,
250, 250–51
Green Mango Sorbet, 108, *109*
Lilikoi Li Hing Pineapple, 105, *106*,
107
Lolo's Philippine Mango (Mangga),
240–41, *241*
"Mango Bango," 14
Mango Jam, 170
Mango Jellies, 281
Oolong Pineapple Cake, 263–64,
265
Passion Fruit Cacao, *100*, 101
Passion Fruit Jellies, 281, *283*
Passion Fruit Ripple, 147
Pineapple Jam, 264
Sticky Rice & Mango, *168*, 169–70
Tropical Fruit Halo Halo Ice Cream,
233

U

ube
mochi flavored with ube, *282*
Ube Malted Crunch, 225–26, *227*,
272, *283*
Ube Waffle Cones, 291
UHT (ultra-high temperature) cream,
29, 169
Uruguay, 92

V

Vanilla Bean Sponge Cake, *283*
variegate, 25
Vegan Base, 54, *55*
Vietnamese Rocky Road, 247, 248, *248*
Violet Marshmallow Crème, 293
Violette Marshmallow, *188*, 188–89

W

waffle cones
Black Sesame Waffle Cones, 291
Brown Butter Hazelnut Waffle Cones,
291
Coconut Pandan Waffle Cones, 291
Corn Waffle Cones, 291
Ube Waffle Cones, 291
Wanderlust Waffle Cones, *290*,
290–91
Wanderlust Creamery, 87, 101, 112, 129,
144. *See also specific topics*
bases for, 47, 51–54
blast freezer used at, 18
ingredients used at, 30
Magnolia and, 13–14, *14*
mission of, 15
story of, 9–10
tools and equipment used at, 36
Wanderlust Waffle Cones, *290*, 290–91
water, 18–19
whey, 20
wheying-off, 25
whipping cream, 29
whisk, 35, *35*
White Chocolate Freckles, *283*
White Rabbit, 268–69
"World's Finest" chocolate, 12
World War II, 229
Wright, Wil, 211

Y

yogurt. *See also* cheese flavors
Greek, 155
nonfat yogurt powder, *28*, *29*
Yogurt Marshmallow Crème, 293
Yuzu Creamsicle, *96*, 96–97
Yuzu Creamsicle Fluff, 293